The Other Voice in
Early Modern Europe:
The Toronto Series

SERIES EDITORS Margaret L. King *and* Albert Rabil, Jr.
SERIES EDITOR, ENGLISH TEXTS Elizabeth H. Hageman

Previous Publications in the Series

Enchanted Eloquence: Fairy Tales by Seventeenth-Century French Women Writers
Edited and translated by Lewis C. Seifert and Domna C. Stanton
2010

Leibniz and the Two Sophies: The Philosophical Correspondence
Edited and translated by Lloyd Strickland
2011

In Dialogue with the Other Voice in Sixteenth-Century Italy: Literary and Social Contexts for Women's Writing
Edited by Julie D. Campbell and Maria Galli Stampino
2011

Sister Giustina Niccolini
The Chronicle of Le Murate
Edited and translated by Saundra Weddle
2011

Liubov Krichevskaya
No Good without Reward: Selected Writings: A Bilingual Edition
Edited and translated by Brian James Baer
2011

Elizabeth Cooke Hoby Russell
The Writings of an English Sappho
Edited by Patricia Phillippy
With translations by Jaime Goodrich
2011

T0244219

EXHORTATIONS TO WOMEN
AND TO OTHERS IF THEY PLEASE

The Other Voice in Early Modern Europe:
The Toronto Series, 15

The Other Voice in
Early Modern Europe:
The Toronto Series

SERIES EDITORS Margaret L. King *and* Albert Rabil, Jr.
SERIES EDITOR, ENGLISH TEXTS Elizabeth H. Hageman

Previous Publications in the Series

MADRE MARÍA ROSA
Journey of Five Capuchin Nuns
Edited and translated by Sarah E.
Owens
2009

GIOVAN BATTISTA ANDREINI
Love in the Mirror: A Bilingual Edition
Edited and translated by Jon R. Snyder
2009

RAYMOND DE SABANAC AND SIMONE
ZANACCHI
Two Women of the Great Schism: The
Revelations *of Constance de Rabastens
by Raymond de Sabanac and* Life of
the Blessed Ursulina of Parma *by
Simone Zanacchi*
Edited and translated by Renate
Blumenfeld-Kosinski and Bruce L.
Venarde
2010

OLIVA SABUCO DE NANTES BARRERA
The True Medicine
Edited and translated by Gianna
Pomata
2010

LOUISE-GENEVIÈVE GILLOT DE
SAINCTONGE
Dramatizing Dido, Circe, and Griselda
Edited and translated by Janet Levarie
Smarr
2010

PERNETTE DU GUILLET
Complete Poems: A Bilingual Edition
Edited by Karen Simroth James
Translated by Marta Rijn Finch
2010

ANTONIA PULCI
*Saints' Lives and Bible Stories for the
Stage: A Bilingual Edition*
Edited by Elissa B. Weaver
Translated by James Wyatt Cook
2010

VALERIA MIANI
*Celinda, A Tragedy: A Bilingual
Edition*
Edited by Valeria Finucci
Translated by Julia Kisacky
Annotated by Valeria Finucci and
Julia Kisacky
2010

Exhortations to Women
and to Others if They Please

LUCREZIA MARINELLA

Edited and translated by

LAURA BENEDETTI

ITER

Iter Inc.
Centre for Reformation and Renaissance Studies
Toronto
2012

Iter: Gateway to the Middle Ages and Renaissance
Tel: 416/978–7074   Email: iter@utoronto.ca
Fax: 416/978–1668   Web: www.itergateway.org

Centre for Reformation and Renaissance Studies
Victoria University in the University of Toronto
Tel: 416/585–4465   Email: crrs.publications@utoronto.ca
Fax: 416/585–4430   Web: www.crrs.ca

© 2012 Iter Inc. & Centre for Reformation and Renaissance Studies
All rights reserved.
Printed in Canada.

Iter and the Centre for Reformation and Renaissance Studies gratefully acknowledge the generous support of James E. Rabil, in memory of Scottie W. Rabil, toward the publication of this book.

Library and Archives Canada Cataloguing in Publication

Marinella, Lucrezia, 1571–1653
Exhortations to women and to others if they please / Lucrezia Marinella ; edited and translated by Laura Benedetti.
(The other voice in early modern Europe series ; 15)
Co-published by: Centre for Reformation and Renaissance Studies.
Translation of: Essortationi alle donne et a gli altri, se a loro saranno a grado.
Includes bibliographical references.
Also issued in electronic format.
ISBN 978-0-7727-2114-3

1. Home economics—Italy—History—17th century. I. Benedetti, Laura, 1962– II. Victoria University (Toronto, Ont.). Centre for Reformation and Renaissance Studies III. Iter Inc. IV. Title. V. Series: Other voice in early modern Europe. Toronto series ; 15.

PQ4627.M84E8713 2012
854'.5   C2012-900565-7

Cover illustration:
Portrait of an Old Woman by Rembrandt Harmensz. van Rijn (1606–69) / Pushkin Museum, Moscow, Russia / The Bridgeman Art Library 50143.

Cover design:
Maureen Morin, Information Technology Services, University of Toronto Libraries.

Typesetting and production:
Iter Inc.

Contents

Acknowledgments   xi

Introduction   1

     The Other Voice: A Rediscovery and a Revision   1

     Marinella's Life and Works   2

     Esortazioni   17

Note on the Translation   34

Lucrezia Marinella: *Exhortations to Women and to Others if They Please*   39

To the Readers   41

1.   This exhortation will show that seclusion suits superior beings such as God, princes, and women. Nature and the First Cause prescribed seclusion to women more than to men.   43

2.   From this advice you will learn that it is laudable to attend to one's activities and tasks and that the study of literature is a useless vanity of little profit.   54

3.   We exhort women to realize how noble, useful, and appropriate womanly arts are. Empresses, queens, and goddesses have practiced them, and therefore I believe no one should be ashamed to be seen weaving.   80

4.   We exhort those who desire praise to be cautious when speaking, unless their arguments are to provide something good, useful, or worthy to the less fortunate.   99

5.   The origin of ornaments and luxury, and how they became increasingly important, is discussed. We exhort women to use them with modesty and moderation.   110

6.   Women's prudence.   120

7. We exhort husband and wife to live in harmony. This brings honor and prosperity to the household, praise to the husband and wife, glory and satisfaction to their children, and universal happiness.   126

8. We exhort parents to raise and educate their children to excellent habits and intellectual disciplines, so that they may bring glory and praise to themselves, their house, and the fatherland: this is what happiness is.   149

9. Exhortation to women so that they may know that there is no reason to boast or be proud of beauty, which is a fragile and fleeting thing. Rather than a divine ray, as some have gathered, beauty is ephemeral and mortal.   196

Bibliography   205

Index   217

Acknowledgments

Baffling, thought-provoking, at times even annoying, Lucrezia Marinella's last volume has accompanied me for a number years. Approaching the shore in Ariosto-like fashion, I feel truly grateful to those who have shared the joys and eased the pain of the journey. Enrico Musacchio accompanied me in my first visits to the "Bibliothèque Mazarine" in Paris, while my Venetian friends Franco Fido and Daria Perocco assisted me as I retraced Marinella's steps in their hometown. Back in Washington, D.C., my valiant research assistant Jacopo Meneguzzo helped with the transcription of the text and encouraged my first attempts to make sense of Marinella's advice, while Emily Langer read a first version of the translation. The journey was enlightened by correspondence with Maria Galli Stampino, Marco Arnaudo, Virginia Cox, Elissa Weaver, and Letizia Panizza. Classicists Josiah Osgood and Holt Parker, as well as L'Aquila-based Benedetta Colella and Luisa Nardecchia, came to the rescue when Marinella's cryptic Latin references bewildered me. Al Rabil was a constant source of support and common sense, while a Senior Faculty Research Fellowship from Georgetown University provided much-needed time to chart the itinerary.

A chi nel mar per tanta via m'ha scorto, my travelling companions Brad and Martina, this work is dedicated.

xi

Introduction

THE OTHER VOICE: A REDISCOVERY AND A REVISION

The publication of a portion of *Le Nobiltà et Eccellenze delle Donne* (*The Nobility and Excellence of Women*) in 1979 rescued Lucrezia Marinella from oblivion.[1] The pages in which the author defended women's virtues against detractors, counterattacked by underscoring men's flaws, and advocated equal access to education, struck late twentieth-century readers for their boldness and erudition.

The contemporary rediscovery of the works of Moderata Fonte and Arcangela Tarabotti drew additional attention to a traditionally neglected period in the history of Italian women's writings. While Carlo Dionisotti deemed 1560 the *terminus ante quem* for their production, the years between the end of the sixteenth century and the middle of the seventeenth suddenly revealed an unsuspected ferment of intellectual activity.[2] And while women's literary output in the mid-sixteenth century had been largely confined to lyrical poetry, Marinella, Fonte, and Tarabotti offered a refreshing variety of voices and genres.

Anyone interested in the history of Italian women's writing owes gratitude to Dionisotti, who cleverly surveyed the field at a time when interest in the subject was virtually non-existent. The need to revise his outline, however, is a natural and healthy consequence of the progress the discipline has made in the past thirty years. Virginia Cox has recently argued that Dionisotti's sketch, however influential, is "notably flawed." Departing from the traditional view of the mid-sixteenth century as the heyday of women writers, Cox stresses the continuity in women's literary production from the end of the fifteenth century through to the early decades of the seventeenth, effectively

1. Ginevra Conti Odorisio prompted the rediscovery with the publication of excerpts of *Le nobiltà* in her volume *Donna e società nel Seicento* (Roma: Bulzoni, 1979).

2. In a much-quoted passage, Dionisotti claimed that women 'fanno gruppo', that is, constitute a quantitatively significant presence, only in the literature of the mid-1500s. See Carlo Dionisotti, *Geografia e storia della letteratura italiana* (Torino: Einaudi, 1967), 191–92.

1

providing a much-needed new timeline.[3] Indeed, the triad of Fonte, Tarabotti, and Marinella alone points to the need to direct attention beyond the mid-sixteenth century and the lyric tradition.[4]

Compared with her contemporaries Fonte and Tarabotti, Marinella presents a more complex and elusive profile, despite the wealth of historical documents unearthed by Susan Haskins.[5] It is now clear that *Le nobiltà*, which has earned the author the attention of modern scholars, can hardly be considered representative of a literary career in which it constitutes, on the contrary, an anomaly. The bulk of Marinella's works is in fact hagiographical and fits well within the Counter-Reformation goal of promoting devotion through literature. Her forays into other genres, however, demonstrate both her ambition and her desire not to be confined to one category. Indeed, it is the sheer range of her production, rather than her achievements in any single genre, that deserves recognition. Marinella is the only early modern Italian woman writer to move so freely among different genres, leaving behind a number of hagiographical works, a psychomachy, a philosophical tract, a pastoral novel, and an epic poem. Her last work, *Essortationi alle donne et a gli altri, se a loro saranno a grado* (*Exhortations to Women and to Others if They Please*, hereafter *Esortazioni*), which she published at the remarkable age of 74, allows critics to add yet another genre to this formidable list: the book of advice.

MARINELLA'S LIFE AND WORKS

Like many early modern Italian women writers, including Fonte and Tarabotti, Marinella lived in Venice. Customs regarding women's education and participation in public life were no more enlightened in

3. Virginia Cox, *Women's Writing in Italy, 1400–1650* (Baltimore: Johns Hopkins University Press, 2008), xx–xxi.

4. See for instance Laura Benedetti, "Saintes et guerrières: l'héroïsme féminin dans l'œuvre de Lucrezia Marinella," in *Les Femmes et l'Ecriture. L'Amour Profane et l'Amour Sacré*, ed. Claude Cazalé Bérard (Paris: Presses Universitaires de Paris X, 2005), 98.

5. Susan Haskins "Vexatious Litigant, or the Case of Lucrezia Marinella? New Documents Concerning Her Life (Part I)," *Nouvelles de la République des Lettres* 1 (2006), 80–128, and "Vexatious Litigant, or the Case of Lucrezia Marinella? (Part II)," *Nouvelles de la République des Lettres* 1–2 (2007), 203–30.

Venice than in other Italian cities.[6] In his introduction to Moderata Fonte's *Il merito delle donne (The Worth of Women)*, Giovanni Niccolò Doglioni denounces "the false notion, so widespread in our city today, that women should excel in nothing but the running of the household,"[7] while Arcangela Tarabotti decried the custom of forbidding women from attending university lectures.[8] Yet the fact that some remarkable women of letters were able to emerge in this atmosphere suggests that this most learned of cities offered something of consequence even to its secluded female population. In the 1400s, Venice was home to Cassandra Fedele, who at age twenty-two was able to write in Latin the ornate *Oratio pro Bertucio Lamberto*; the 1500s witnessed the emergence of lyrical poets such as Gaspara Stampa and Veronica Franco; finally the 1600s produced the personalities of Marinella, Fonte, and Tarabotti, as well as that of the erudite Jewish poet Sarra Copia Sulam.[9] Exactly twenty-five years after Marinella's death, yet another Venetian, Elena Lucrezia Cornaro Piscopia, became the first woman in the world to be granted a university degree.[10] Clearly, even women benefitted from the learned atmosphere of the Queen of the Adriatic, where in the mid-sixteenth century more books were produced and

6. For a comparison between women in Italy and women in other European countries see Ruth Kelso, *Doctrine for the Lady of the Renaissance* (Urbana: University of Illinois Press, 1956), 51. For the seclusion of women in Florence see the reaction of French traveler Grangier de Liverdes, quoted by Judith C. Brown, "A Woman's Place Was in the Home: Women's Work in Renaissance Tuscany," in *Rewriting the Renaissance: The Discourses of Sexual Difference in Early Modern Europe*, eds. Margaret W. Ferguson, Maureen Quilligan, and Nancy J. Vickers (Chicago: University of Chicago Press, 1986), 215.

7. Moderata Fonte, *The Worth of Women: Wherein is Clearly Revealed Their Nobility and Their Superiority to Men*, trans. Virginia Cox (Chicago: University of Chicago Press, 1997), 39.

8. Arcangela Tarabotti, *La semplicità ingannata*, ed. Simona Bortot (Padova: Il Poligrafo, 2007), 292.

9. See Umberto Fortis, *Sara Copio Sullam, poetessa nel ghetto di Venezia del '600* (Torino: Zamorani, 2003), and Sarra Copia Sulam, *Jewish Poet and Intellectual in Seventeenth-Century Venice*, ed. and trans. Don Harrán. The Other Voice in Early Modern Europe (Chicago: University of Chicago Press, 2009).

10. See Francesco Ludovico Maschietto, *Elena Lucrezia Cornaro Piscopia (1646–1684): The First Woman in the World to Earn a University Degree*, ed. Catherine Marshall, trans. Jan Vairo and William Crochetiere (Philadelphia: Saint Joseph's University Press, 2007).

sold than in any other European center and where less expensive titles were affordable even for the average manual worker.[11]

In examining the education imparted to young Renaissance women, Margaret King observes that its difference from the one received by men lay not as much in content as in outcome. While historical evidence suggests that educators did scrutinize with greater caution the materials to be used in women's intellectual development, what made the position of the woman of letters particularly precarious was that her humanist training and knowledge had no professional application and could even hinder her pursuit of the main occupations available to her, those of wife and mother:

> Far from conferring upon women a new equality with men, a humanist education may well have created for women new and agonizing problems: for it opened up vistas of intellectual freedom among those whose sex confined them to traditional social roles in which intellectual attainment was unnecessary and, indeed, unwanted.[12]

King identifies two main patterns among women educated in the humanities, which are exemplified by the destinies of Isotta and Ginevra Nogarola. Pupils of Guarino Veronese, the two sisters earned enthusiastic praise in their youth but took different paths in adulthood. Isotta (1418–1466) "constructed within her mother's house an austere and book-lined cell where in near solitude she combined religious devotions with the study of sacred letters."[13] Ginevra (c. 1417–1461/8) married a Brescian nobleman and ceased all intellectual activity. King discusses other humanist women who also fall into one of these two categories: they either remained unwed or took religious vows and

11. For data on book publication and distribution in Renaissance Venice see Paul F. Grendler, *The Roman Inquisition and the Venetian Press, 1540–1605* (Princeton, N.J.: Princeton University Press, 1977), 3 and 14.

12. Margaret L. King, "Thwarted Ambitions: Six Learned Women of the Italian Renaissance," in *Humanism, Venice, and Women: Essays on the Italian Renaissance* (Burlington, Vt.: Ashgate, 2005), 282.

13. Ibid., 286.

continued to pursue some form of learning, like Costanza Barbaro and Cecilia Gonzaga, or they married and abandoned their scholarly pursuits, like Cataruzza Caldiera and Cassandra Fedele, although Fedele managed to return to her studies after her husband's death.[14]

The pattern King identifies lasted well beyond the 1600s. A university degree and the title of "magistra and doctrix" did not spare Elena Lucrezia Cornaro Piscopia from facing the same dilemma that had haunted her humanist predecessors. For one, both her social status and her gender prevented her from being a "magistra" in the full sense of the word. Barred from teaching and therefore from serving as a model for future generations, she was destined to have her accomplishments die with her.[15] Although she lived two centuries after the Nogarola sisters, her choices were no less stark, and she followed in Isotta's footsteps. A Benedectine oblate, Cornaro Piscopia "learned how to conduct her life with her family as if she were in a monastery," leaving the house only to visit the Abbey of San Giorgio Maggiore.[16]

This brief overview of the possibilities available to women in early modern Italy highlights Lucrezia Marinella's singularity. Unlike her humanist predecessors, she escaped the limitations of female adulthood. She was neither a courtesan nor a member of a religious order, yet she continued to write for most of her remarkably long life. Marriage slowed her down, but did not stop her.[17] She did not fall into the "either/or" pattern that has influenced women's creativity well

14. Another possibility, which King does not take into consideration in her study, is that of the so-called "cortigiana onesta," a sort of high-end prostitute who combined physical attractiveness with refined conversation and some poetic and musical ability. Veronica Franco is the most famous example in this category which, however, fell out of favor in the more austere times of the Counter-Reformation. See Margaret F. Rosenthal, *The Honest Courtesan: Veronica Franco Citizen and Writer in Sixteenth-Century Venice* (Chicago: University of Chicago Press, 1992).

15. Indeed, Cornaro Piscopia's achievements convinced the Reformers of the University of Padua to issue a document that explicitly prohibited granting degrees to women. It would take more than fifty years for the University of Bologna to crown Laura Bassi, its first female graduate (1732), and almost exactly a century for Pavia to do the same for Maria Amoretti (1777). See Maschietto, *Elena Lucrezia Cornaro Piscopia*, 83.

16. Maschietto, *Elena Lucrezia Cornaro Piscopia*, 109.

17. Marinella was also lucky enough to escape the fate that befell Moderata Fonte and many other early modern women, who died during or soon after delivery. On the risks associated

beyond the seventeenth century.[18] The circumstances that enabled her to achieve this significant feat deserve further scrutiny.

Giovanni Marinello, Lucrezia's father, is a fascinating figure, a man of science and letters whose publications included a tract on rhetoric (*La copia delle parole* [*The Abundance of Words*, 1562]), a manual on cosmetics (*Gli ornamenti delle donne* [*Women's Ornaments*, 1562]), and a treatise on gynecology (*Le medicine partenenti alle infermità delle donne* [*Medicines Pertaining to Women's Illnesses*, 1563]).[19] In the introduction to this last volume, Marinello defends his project against possible objections. He justifies writing a medical treatise in the vernacular by pointing to natural philosophers such as Hippocrates, Galen, and Avicenna who also wrote in their own language. And in response to those who deride him for wanting to serve women, the author explains that his work addresses those who can most benefit from it.[20] Marinello introduces *Gli ornamenti delle donne* in similar terms, claiming to be the first to deal with this topic in the vernacular and rejoicing "in being born in an age which has women more noble in lineage and virtue than any who ever lived in the past: These women, I am most confident, will gladly read this work, the fruit of sweet labors I bore because of them."[21]

Marinello's preference for a female audience—which, he claims, had also enjoyed his vernacular treatise on rhetoric, *La co-*

with childbirth see Margaret L. King, "La donna del Rinascimento," in Eugenio Garin, ed. *L'uomo del Rinascimento* (Bari: Laterza,1988), 276.

18. For the persistance of the "either/or" model see Susan Rubin Suleiman, "Writing and Motherhood," in *The (M)other Tongue. Essays in Feminist Psychoanalytic Interpretation*, ed. Shirley Nelson Garner et al. (Ithaca, N.Y.: Cornell University Press, 1985), 360.

19. See Girolamo Tiraboschi, *Biblioteca modenese o notizie della vita e delle opere degli scrittori nati degli stati del serenissimo signor duca di Modena* (Modena: Società Tipografica, 1783), Vol. III, 159–60. Excerpts from *Le medicine partenenti alle infermità delle donne* have been published in *Medicina per le donne nel Cinquecento. Testi di Giovanni Marinello e di Girolamo Mercurio*, ed. Maria Luisa Altieri Biagi et al. (Torino: UTET, 1992).

20. *Medicina per le donne nel Cinquecento*, 46-7.

21. "E molto più mi debbo gloriare di esser nato in una età, la quale ha le più illustri donne per sangue, et per virtù, che forse nel preterito siano state: le quali vivo io certissimo, che volentieri leggeranno questi dolci affanni a lor cagione sostenuti." (Giovanni Marinello, *Gli ornamenti delle donne tratti dalle scritture d'una reina greca* [Venice: Francesco de' Franceschi, 1562], vii). Here and elsewhere, translations are mine unless otherwise noted.

pia delle parole—and self-imposed role as a popularizer support the hypothesis that he played a formative role in Lucrezia's education, in spite of the fact that nowhere does she provide details about his influence. The family environment was certainly learned and presumably stimulating. Curzio, one of Lucrezia's brothers, followed in his father's footsteps and became a physician and a writer.[22] Lucrezia mentions both Giovanni and Curzio in her dedication of *Le nobiltà* to Lucio Scarano, a physician himself. Little is known of another brother, Antonio, a Servite monk at the monastery of S. Giacomo della Giudecca under the name "Fra Angelico," and of a sister, Diamantina, who married in 1594.[23] Lucrezia writes of them in affectionate if generic terms, without mentioning their relationship, at the end of *Vita del serafico et glorioso S. Francesco* (*Life of the Seraphic and Glorious St. Francis*). She describes Fra Angelico as a man who left the turbulent world to follow Saint Francis and Diamantina as a model of beauty, chastity, and goodness who showed mature judgment at a young age.[24] The information available on Lucrezia's father and siblings only underscores the mystery surrounding her mother, who is never mentioned and whose very name has not survived.

The origins of the family are not completely clear. In a letter that accompanies *Vita di Maria Vergine, imperatrice dell'universo* (*Life of the Virgin Mary, Empress of the Universe*) Lucrezia presents herself—somewhat instrumentally—as a servant and subject ("serva e suddita") of the duchess of Modena, on the basis of her father's birth in that city.[25] Other sources, however, point to a possible Southern origin. Giuseppe Tassini reports in fact that the Marinelli came from Naples,[26] while a list of Renaissance medical doctors suggests instead that Giovanni was originally from Mola, near Bari.[27]

The entry concerning Marinella in the Register of the Dead in the Venetian Parish of Saint Pantaleone indicates that she died in 1653

---

22. See Tiraboschi, *Biblioteca modenese*, 157–58.

23. Haskins, "Vexatious Litigant," 2006, 92.

24. Marinella, *Vita del serafico et glorioso S. Francesco* III, 57–58.

25. See Tiraboschi, *Biblioteca modenese*, 161.

26. Archivio Storico Veneto, Miscellanea Codici I, Tassini, Busta 13, p. 1285.

27. Juliana Hill Cotton, *Name-List from a Medical Register of the Italian Renaissance* [Oxford: [s.n.], 1976], 78. I thank Daria Perocco for bringing this work to my attention.

at the age of 82. On this basis, it is often assumed that she was born in 1571. This assumption, however, contradicts Marinella's presentation of herself as a young woman in the dedication of the *Vita di Maria Vergine* (1602). Since it would have been odd at the time for a thirty-one-year-old woman to refer to herself as "young," her date of birth may be somewhat closer to the end of the sixteenth century, although it is also possible that Marinella was intentionally trying to create a younger authorial persona.[28] It is likely, however, that Lucrezia was the youngest in her family and lived for some time—presumably after her father's death and before her marriage—with her brother Curzio in Campiello dei Squelini, as reported in the census of 1591.[29]

Marinella entered the literary scene in 1595 with the publication of *La colomba sacra* (*The Sacred Dove*). Dedicated to Margherita Gonzaga, duchess of Ferrara, this poem combines hagiography and the epic. While the title exploits the allegorical symbolism surrounding the name of the protagonist, Saint Colomba of Sens, the subtitle of "poema eroico" and the use of *ottava rima* are indicative of Marinella's fascination for the epic tradition.

This choice of topic seems curious for a writer who would later devote volumes to the celebration of much more famous religious figures such as Saint Catherine, Saint Francis, and the Virgin Mary. It is tempting to read Marinella's cautious first attempt at hagiography as an effort to follow the precepts Torquato Tasso outlined in *Discorsi dell'arte poetica*: while the subject matter for a heroic poem must derive from sacred history, it should be neither related to a dogma nor too recent. These conditions are essential to preserving what Tasso calls "la licenza del fingere," that is, the poet's prerogative to create characters and situations.[30] A recent event may also have influenced Marinella's choice. In 1581, the bishop of Rimini had brought back relics of Saint Colomba from the cathedral of Sens to his archdiocese, thus reinvigorating her cult.[31]

---

28. Giovanni Papa's portrait of the writer adds to the confusion by indicating that Marinella was twenty-two, rather than thirty, in 1601. See Haskins, "Vexatious Litigant," 2006, 83.

29. Haskins, "Vexatious Litigant," 2006, 92.

30. Torquato Tasso, *Discorsi dell'arte poetica*, in *Discorsi dell'arte poetica e del poema eroico*, ed. Luigi Poma (Bari: Laterza, 1964), 4–10.

31. See Guy Chastel, *Sainte Colombe de Sens* (Paris: Gigord, 1939), 200n1.

A victim of Aurelian's alleged persecution of Christians, Saint Colomba lived in the third century and was killed in Sens.[32] While most of Marinella's account follows the events as presented in a manuscript devoted to Saint Colomba's martyrdom,[33] one significant departure suggests another, more probable source. In *La colomba sacra,* the story takes place not in Sens, but in Scenoa, an imaginary Arab town on a tributary of the river Jordan (*La colomba sacra* I, 11). This surprising geographical transposition is found in the popular *Legendario delle Santissime Vergini,* which, first published in 1511, underwent several editions during the sixteenth century. The anonymous editor of the *Legendario* located the town of Saint Colomba's martyrdom in some generic region in the East ("nelle parti d'Oriente"), and italianized Senones—the Latin name of Sens—as Scenoua, which could in turn have become "Scenoa" in *La colomba sacra.* Marinella, seemingly intrigued by the possibility of merging Saint Colomba's story with Tasso's *Gerusalemme liberata,* infused the confrontation between Aurelian and Colomba with the same, subtle erotic tension that marked the encounter between Aladin and Sophronia in the second canto of the *Liberata.*[34]

Two years later, Marinella dedicated her second work to Cristina of Lorena, grand duchess of Tuscany. Once again, she chose a powerful woman as her addressee and neglected her ties to Venice. The *Vita del Serafico e Glorioso San Francesco, descritta in ottava rima, con un discorso del rivolgimento amoroso verso la Somma Bellezza* (*Life of the Seraphic and Glorious St. Francis, with a Discourse on the Loving Turn toward the Supreme Beauty*) is divided, as the title suggests, into two parts. The discourse that precedes the poetic account of St. Francis's life is remarkable for its vehement contempt for the body, described as a "ladro domestico [...] fracido cadavero [...] oscura tomba dell'anima" ("domestic thief [...], rotting corpse [...], dark grave for the soul") that those wishing to rise to the "infinita luce" ("infinite light") must despise and neglect. This paroxysmal aversion to all earthly at-

---

32. Modern historians are skeptical that such a persecution ever took place. See for instance Alaric Watson, *Aurelian and the Third Century* (London and New York: Routledge, 1999), 200.

33. The manuscript was published as an appendix to Chastel, *Sainte Colombe de Sens.*

34. For a more detailed analysis see Laura Benedetti, "Saintes et guerrières," 98–100.

tachment does not even spare one's family and children, mutable entities who serve as distractions from God, the "sommo sole" ("supreme sun").[35] Marinella also criticizes women's use of cosmetics , a striking departure from her father's recommendations on how women may improve their physical aspect. "I maintain that, although a woman may be beautiful," the elder Marinello wrote, "it is not inappropriate for her to try to improve her appearance, as nothing in this world is perfect."[36] Marinella's polemical stance would return in *Esortazioni*, which suggests a certain consistency of her views.[37] Another recurring feature of her career is her production of hagiographical works, both in prose and in rhyme. After *La colomba sacra and Vita del Serafico e glorioso San Francesco,* she wrote *Vita di Maria Vergine* (1602), *Vita di Santa Giustina* (Life of St. Justina, 1606), and *De' Gesti heroici, e della vita maravigliosa della Serafica Santa Caterina* (*The Heroic Deeds and Wonderful Life of the Seraphic Saint Catherine,* 1624).

The dedication of *Amore innamorato et impazzato* (*Cupid in Love and Driven Mad,* 1598) to Caterina Medici Gonzaga, duchess of Mantua, attests to Marinella's desire to strengthen her ties with the Gonzaga court. Recalling the favors and gifts already received ("titoli, e [...] magnificenza de' doni"), the author pledges all of her future works to the Gonzagas—a promise that she would not honor. Marinella introduces her poem, a psychomachy, with an explanation of its allegory: the protagonists Cupid, Iridio, and Ersilia respectively symbolize the struggle among the concupiscible, irascible, and rational parts of the soul, a battle that eventually ends with the triumph of rationality and faith.[38] In the poem's elaborate allegorical system, Venus, who asks Jupiter to forgive wayward Cupid, symbolizes the saint who intercedes with God on a sinner's behalf, while Cupid's cleansing

---

35. Marinella, *Vita del serafico et glorioso S. Francesco,* 7 and 10.

36. "Questo cotanto voglio dire, che, benché una donna sia bella; non le si disdica lo accrescere della sua bellezza: conciosia che niuna cosa sia al mondo perfetta" (Giovanni Marinello, *Gli ornamenti delle donne* vi).

37. In *Le nobiltà,* Marinella instead considers luxury a sign of women's superiority (26).

38. Plato discusses the tripartite structure of the soul in the *Republic* (see in particular 439e–441a).

in the fountain of Ardenna indicates the importance of the "redeeming waves of confessions, sacraments and penance."[39]

Nothing about Marinella's first steps into the literary world foreshadowed the ambitious treatise that she would publish in 1600 and that has earned her fame among modern readers: *Le nobiltà et eccellenze delle donne et i diffetti, e mancamenti degli huomini* (*The Nobility and Excellence of Women and the Defects and Flaws of Men*).[40] This work appears to be inspired in part by the author's desire to respond to Giuseppe Passi's *I donneschi difetti* (Women's Defects), a 1599 misogynist tract. In thirty-five chapters, Passi employed religious and classical sources to denounce women's alleged shortcomings.[41] In *Le nobiltà*, Marinella relied instead mainly on vernacular authorities to affirm women's superiority and denounce men's wrongdoings. The volume underwent two subsequent editions, in 1601 and 1621.[42] The former is particularly important and often considered, implicitly or explicitly, to be the reference edition.[43] In this version the first part, which is in praise of women, concludes with an additional four short chapters that reject the opinions of Ercole Tasso and Arrigo of Namur, Sperone Speroni, Torquato Tasso, and Giovanni Boccaccio. The audacity with which Marinella confronts such established authorities makes these chapters particularly impressive. She debunks Torquato Tasso's

39. "[...] l'onde salutifere delle confessioni, de' sacramenti, e delle penitenze." Marinella, *Amore innamorato et impazzato* (Venezia: Combi, 1618), 221.

40. Several scholars have discussed this work in recent times, including Adriana Chemello, "La donna, il modello, l'immaginario: Moderata Fonte e Lucrezia Marinella," in Marina Zancan, ed. *Nel cerchio della luna: figure di donna in alcuni testi del XVI secolo* (Venice: Marsilio, 1983), 95-170; Stephen Kolski, "Moderata Fonte, Lucrezia Marinella, Giuseppe Passi: an Early Seventeenth-Century Feminist Controversy," in *The Modern Language Review* 4 (2001), 972-89; Prudence Allen and Filippo Salvatore, "Lucrezia Marinella and Woman's Identity in Late Italian Renaissance," in *Renaissance and Reformation / Renaissance et Réforme* 4 (1992), 5-39: and Letizia Panizza, "Introduction to the Translation," in Lucrezia Marinella, *The Nobility and Excellence of Women and the Defects and Vices of Men*, trans. Anne Dunhill (Chicago: University of Chicago Press, 1999), 1-34.

41. Giuseppe Passi, *I donneschi difetti* (Venice: Somascho, 1599).

42. The 1601 and 1621 editions bear a slightly different title: *La nobiltà et l'eccellenza delle donne co' diffetti et mancamenti de gli huomini.*

43. Anne Dunhill's 1999 translation is based on the 1601 edition. *Nouvelles de la République des Lettres* 1–2 (2007) includes an anastatic reprint of the 1600 *editio princeps*.

distinction between "female virtue" (virtú femminile) and "womanly virtue" (virtú donnesca), and proceeds to claim equal rights for all women, regardless of social class or public role.[44] These are the most revolutionary passages Marinella would ever write. She also considerably expanded the part devoted to men's flaws, bringing it to thirty-five chapters—the same number in Passi's tract.

Marinella's attitude toward Aristotle is complex. The philosopher provides the foundation for her arguments—especially as far as the definitions of virtues and vices are concerned—but is also chastised as "tiranno et pauroso" ("a tyrant and a coward") and "huomo di poco ingegno" ("man of little wisdom").[45] She mockingly calls him "buon compagnone" ("good buddy") and "cattivello" ("mean little guy"),[46] a man whose judgment was ultimately obfuscated by negative personal experience. Plato, on the contrary, is celebrated as wise, a great man, and truly fair ("saggio", "grande huomo, in vero giustissimo")[47] for his support of women's participation in public life and access to education, especially in the fifth book of *Republic*.

Apart from customary references to the classics, Marinella's work displays a considerable degree of familiarity with the vernacular tradition, from Dante and Petrarca to Ariosto, Tansillo, Tasso and Fonte. She amasses quotes and examples, demonstrating her awareness of the tradition's preference for erudition over originality. As the first Italian woman to experiment in this genre Marinella needed to convince readers of her credentials, and she successfully accomplishes that goal.

The ambitious *Le nobiltà* constitutes a parenthesis in Marinella's outpouring of devotional literature, which resumed in 1602 with the publication of *La vita di Maria Vergine imperatrice dell'universo*. Forgetting her pledge to the Gonzagas, Marinella addressed this new work to the Venetian doge and Senate. *La vita* presents its subject in two formats, poetry and prose, and judging from the number of edi-

---

44. Marinella's answer to Tasso is discussed in Laura Benedetti, "Virtù femminile o virtù donnesca? Torquato Tasso, Lucrezia Marinella ed una polemica rinascimentale," ed. Gianni Venturi, *Torquato Tasso e la cultura estense* (Firenze: Olschki, 1999), 449–56.

45. Marinella, *La nobiltà* (1601 edition), 32.

46. Marinella, *La nobiltà* (1601 edition), 27 and 119.

47. Marinella, *La nobiltà* (1601 edition), 33 and 32.

tions (four in fifteen years, including the *princeps*), seems to have been Marinella's most successful work.[48] In her praise of Marinella as a "norma vera di virtú grande" ("true standard of great virtue"), Arcangela Tarabotti singles out *La vita* for being "descritta con sí alto stile, e con sí elegante e soave e dotta facondia, che genera sentimenti di stupore ne piú eminenti intelletti"[49] ("written in such high style, with such elegant, pleasing, and learned fluency that it excites amazement in the finest minds").[50] Rumors that questioned Marinella's authorship of *La vita di Maria Vergine* must therefore have been particularly painful and perhaps inspired her bitter comments in the later *Esortazioni*.[51]

In 1603 Marinella published her only collection of poems. *Rime sacre* consists mostly of sonnets and madrigals dealing with religious topics and figures, from the Ascension of the Virgin Mary to the life of Saint Nicholas of Tolentino. The few poems that concern the author are also spiritual in content: she repents for her sins, laments her lack of devotion, and expresses contempt for the world and its vain pursuits.

Marinella added yet another genre to her list in 1605 with the publication of the pastoral novel *Arcadia felice* (*Happy Arcadia*). The work, which deals with Emperor Diocletian's decision to abandon power and seek harmony among nature, seems at first glance to follow the model of Jacopo Sannazaro's *Arcadia* (1504), in which a disappointed poet leaves the city to find refuge in an idealized pastoral world. Marinella, however, departs significantly from that scheme: the prevalent use of prose, the scarce consideration of mythology, the significance of women, and the attention paid to history indicate her distance from the pastoral romance, as well as her proximity to the

---

48. For details on the editions of *Vita di Maria Vergine* see *Who is Mary? Three Early Modern Women on the Idea of the Virgin Mary*, ed. and trans. Susan Haskins (Chicago and London: University of Chicago Press, 2008), 120.

49. Tarabotti, *La semplicità ingannata*, 300-01.

50. Arcangela Tarabotti, *Paternal Tyranny*, ed. and trans. Letizia Panizza (Chicago and London: University of Chicago Press, 2004), 106.

51. The publisher Ciotti added a note dispelling these rumors in the introduction to *Arcadia felice* (2–3).

emerging genre of the baroque novel.[52] Marinella can more precisely be considered a precursor of this genre, as *Arcadia felice* predates by almost twenty years Giovan Francesco Biondi's *Eromena* (1624), which Martino Capucci considered the first Italian baroque novel.[53]

Marinella's artistic accomplishments in the years between 1595 and 1606 earned her acceptance in literary circles. She experimented in several genres, regularly revised her works for subsequent editions, received public praise from Boncio Leone—president of the Accademia Veneziana—and wrote the allegorical explanation and summary of each canto (*argomenti*) for the 1606 edition of Luigi Tansillo's *Lagrime di San Pietro* (Saint Peter's Tears).

This intense activity, however, would soon come to an abrupt stop. On March 17, 1607, Marinella married Girolamo Vacca, a doctor from Chioggia twelve years her senior, and plunged into eighteen years of silence during which—it seems reasonable to assume—she raised their two children, Antonio and Paulina. Little is known about this period of her life. She probably lived for some time in or near Padua,[54] but documents related to her daughter Paulina's marriage in 1628 suggest that by that time she had already moved back to the house in Campiello dei Squelini, where she lived apart from her husband.[55] Her financial condition was comfortable, especially after she became executor and usufructuary of her brother Curzio's will in 1624[56] and after her husband's death in 1629 allowed her to regain control of her dowry.[57] She took an active role in managing the family's finances, renting out houses and properties and delegating to her son Antonio only the most litigious aspects of these business transactions.[58]

In 1624 *De' Gesti heroici, e della vita maravigliosa della Serafica Santa Caterina da Siena* marked Marinella's literary comeback, followed, eleven years later, by *L'Enrico, ovvero Bisanzio acquistato*

52. Françoise Lavocat, "Introduzione," in Lucrezia Marinella, *Arcadia felice* (Firenze: Olschki, 1998), xxv–lx.

53. Martino Capucci, "Introduzione," in *Romanzieri del Seicento* (Torino: UTET, 1974), 13.

54. Susan Haskins, "Vexatious Litigant," (2007), 207.

55. Ibid., 213.

56. Ibid., 210.

57. Ibid., 216–19.

58. Ibid., 210-11.

(*Enrico, or Byzantium Conquered*). This lengthy work celebrates what is commonly referred to as the fourth crusade. Unique among the crusades in that the Christian army never had the occasion to confront the Muslims, the military expedition that culminated in the fall of Constantinople was nonetheless dear to Venetian pride. The city had indeed gained control of the islands of Cyprus and Crete, while its army had brought home priceless artifacts, including the four bronze horses that are still preserved in St. Mark's Basilica.[59] The 1577 cycle of commemorative paintings in the Ducal Palace attests to the patriotic fervor these events inspired more than three centuries later.[60] Marinella's choice of this topic might therefore be interpreted as her attempt to gain favor in her own town, after her earlier tributes to Modena and the Gonzagas. Praise for Venice indeed overflows, especially in Erina's historical overview and prophecy to Pietro Venier in Canto VII.

With the publication of *L'Enrico*, Marinella joined the select group of women who attempted to compose an epic poem,[61] the genre that could confer the most prestige upon a writer.[62] For Marinella, this was an occasion to take her long-standing admiration of and familiarity with Torquato Tasso to the next level, "getting a word in edgewise," as Deanna Shemek remarks of Laura Terracina's engagement with

59. On the fourth crusade see Thomas F. Madden, *Enrico Dandolo and the Rise of Venice* (Baltimore: Johns Hopkins University Press, 2003); John Godfrey, *1204, The Unholy Crusade* (New York: Oxford University Press, 1980); and Ernile Bradford, *The Great Betrayal: Constantinople 1204* (London: Hodder and Stoughton, 1967).

60. Wolfgang Wolters, *Storia e politica nei dipinti del Palazzo Ducale. Aspetti dell'autocelebrazione della Repubblica di Venezia nel Cinquecento* (Venice: Arsenale, 1987) 179–85.

61. Virginia Cox lists four other epic poems written by women in the years 1560–1635: Tullia d'Aragona's *Il Meschino overo il Guerrino* (1560), Moderata Fonte's *Floridoro* (1581), Margherita Sarrocchi's *La Scanderbeide* (1623), and Barbara Tagliamocchi degli Albizzi's *Ascanio errante* (1640). See Virginia Cox, "Women as Readers and Writers of Chivalric Literature," in *Sguardi sull'Italia. Miscellanea dedicata a Francesco Villari*, eds. Gino Bedani, Zygmunt Baranski, Anna Laura Lepschy, and Brian Richardson (Leeds: Society for Italian Studies, 1997), 134 and 141. On the boldness of Marinella's attempt see Maria Galli Stampino, "A Singular Venetian Epic Poem," in Maria Galli Stampino, ed. and trans., Lucrezia Marinella, *Enrico; or, Byzantium Conquered* (Chicago: University of Chicago Press, 2009), 4. On the originality of the author's approach to the epic tradition see Laura Lazzari, *Poesia epica e scrittura femminile nel Seicento: L'Enrico di Lucrezia Marinelli* (Leonforte [En]: Insula, 2010).

62. See Benedetto Croce, *Storia dell'età barocca in Italia* (Bari: Laterza, 1957), 287–88.

Ariosto's poem.[63] Marinella draws the precepts that inform *L'Enrico* from Aristotle's *Poetics*, but elaborates them in ways that show deference to Tasso's *Discorsi dell'arte poetica*:

> I resolved to tie other episodes and digressions to the main action in such a manner that one cannot easily remove a part without jumbling the whole.[64]

The poem indeed focuses squarely on the capture of Byzantium, and digressions are carefully controlled, even at the expense of internal coherence. Giacinto and Idilia, the only love story that is allowed to develop, is left inexplicably unresolved.[65]

Marinella's rewriting of Tasso's epic is apparent in her presentation of the main warrior woman, Claudia. Unlike Tasso's Clorinda, Claudia is given a clear genealogy. She indeed "descended, / noble offspring, from great Latin blood,"[66] while her deeds prove that "habit, not nature, instilled timidity in one sex, valor in the other,"[67] thus showcasing the core principles of *Le nobiltà*.[68]

Some passages in Marinella's poem seem inspired by a desire to provide alternative endings to corresponding episodes in Tasso's *Gerusalemme liberata*. Alfeo falls in love with Emilia, who kills him

63. Deanna Shemek, "Getting a Word in Edgewise: Laura Terracina's *Discorsi* on the *Orlando Furioso*," in *Ladies Errant: Wayward Women and Social Order in Early Modern Italy* (Durham, N.C.: Duke University Press, 1998), 126–57.

64. From Marinella's preface to *L'Enrico*: "Gli episodi ed altre digressioni pur, come piace allo stesso filosofo, ho procurato che sieno così unite colla principale azione, che non si potese facilmente levarne una parte senza confondere il tutto." Trans. Galli Stampino, 77-8.

65. Galli Stampino interprets this omission as a way for Marinella "to depict the promise of romantic love while implicitly recognizing its danger and the significance of the patriarchal order of society" ("A Singular Venetian Epic Poem," 57). See Lazzari, *Poesia epica*, 146-48 and 168.

66. "discese / dal gran sangue latin, progenie augusta" (Marinella, *L'Enrico* II.30). On the problematic genealogy of Tasso's heroines see Marilyn Migiel, *Gender and Genealogy in Tasso's Gerusalemme Liberata* (Lewiston, N.Y.: The Edwin Mellen Press, 1993).

67. "l'uso e non natura ha messo / timor ne l'un, valor ne l'altro sesso" (Marinella, *L'Enrico* II.30).

68. For an analysis of the similarities between *Le nobiltà* and *L'Enrico* see Lazzari, *Poesia epica*, 175-212.

immediately (VIII.93–94), as if she were hoping to avoid the tragic death met by Clorinda in Canto XII of the *Liberata*. Tasso prevents the two women warriors of his poem, Gildippe and Clorinda, from fighting each other (IX.71), explicitly reserving them for a "stronger enemy."[69] Marinella, on the other hand, pits Claudia against Meandra, and allows them to die at each other's hand, as if to imply that each is the other's best match.[70] These examples suggest that Marinella consciously attempted to reinterpret the epic tradition according to her own perspective.

This poem constituted a remarkable achievement, and its lukewarm reception[71] must have been rather upsetting for the author. *Esortazioni* may well reflect this disappointment.

ESORTAZIONI

Assuming that Marinella was born in 1571, by the time she published *Esortazioni* in 1645 she had reached the remarkable age of 74. She likely felt that her end was near. Indeed, she drafted her will that very year, leaving most of her belongings to her son Antonio and bequeathing to her daughter Paulina a silver cup as a sign of her love ("per segno de amore").[72] Marinella had every reason to be proud of her long life and its extraordinary output. However, the indifference with which her ambitious epic, *L'Enrico*, was received, and the disputed authorship of her *Vita di Maria Vergine* may have inspired instead a bleaker assessment. Looking around, Marinella may have felt like the

---

69. Tancredi kills Clorinda in *Liberata* XII.69, and Solimano kills Gildippe in *Liberata* XX.100.

70. Marinella, *L'Enrico* XXIV.48.

71. Discussing the scarce resonance of Marinella's poem in the context of the fading interest in women's literature in 17th-century Italy, Cox writes: "It is notable that even a work like her long-prepared *Enrico*, from which she had proudly announced in 1623 that she awaited 'a long and supreme honor,' aroused nothing of the literary frisson that had accompanied the circulation of the only previous female-authored epic, Margherita Sarrocchi's *Scanderbeide*" (Cox, *Women's Writing in Italy*, 223).

72. *Archivio Storico Veneto*, Notarile Testamenti 1146, 220 (Gaspare Acerbi, Testamenti II). While the bulk of the testament is dated May 1, 1645, the document also includes an addition dated January 26, 1648, in which Marinella mentions her granddaughter, Angioletta, daughter of Paulina.

last remnant of a bygone era. The dwindling patronage for women writers and the dramatic change in social attitudes that cast suspicion on the poetic interaction between men and women were among the factors that led women writers to withdraw from the literary scene.[73]

These elements help to explain the disenchantment toward education and literature that figures so prominently in *Esortazioni*. Divided into nine chapters, the volume tackles a variety of topics that relate primarily to domestic economy, such as the qualities of a good wife and the ideal curriculum for children. Its most striking characteristic, however, is its departure from the ideas Marinella expressed in *Le nobiltà*.

Indeed, in the often-quoted first and second chapters of *Esortazioni*, Marinella surprisingly recants the bold statements of her youth. The work begins by endorsing seclusion as the only sure way for a woman to protect her reputation. Marinella exhorts women to heed this recommendation and realize their vulnerability when they leave the protection of their homes and become "like the targets archers use in their practice—pierced and ripped apart by everybody and from all sides."[74]

The remainder of this chapter extols the beauty of seclusion. Only rarely do deities show themselves in public, Marinella writes, and the same is true of rulers and people of high status. Women likewise should be wary of showing themselves to the outside world and should confine their activities to the home. This sets the stage for a strong recantation:

> Some people believe that women are secluded because men want to keep them locked up, that they might remain inexperienced in the affairs of the world and become inept and of little courage and worth. I myself

73. See Cox, *Women's Writing in Italy*, 177–227. Cox defines this phenomenon as "reconventualization:" "As the world of secular literature became less hospitable to 'respectable' women, one sees something like a return to the situation of the late medieval period, when women's writing was largely cloistered in context and was generally published (Farnese, Alberghetti) only following the author's death" (213).

74. "[…] come que' segni che servono a sagittari, li quali sono percorsi e lacerati da ognuno e da ogni parte" (Marinella, *Esortazioni* 2).

made such a claim in my book *The Nobility and Excellence of Women*. After considering this issue with more mature judgment, however, I now conclude that women's condition has not been devised or brought about by resentful souls, but rather derives from natural and divine providence and will. We can easily prove this to be true. Were women's seclusion the result of violence, it would not have lasted for so many centuries and millennia. Violent practices do not last long.[75]

Marinella dissociates herself from those celebrators of women's virtue who attribute the differences between the sexes to social customs. Invoking her "mature judgment," she positions herself in unqualified agreement with those who interpret women's millenary oppression as proof of their inferiority. The abjuration could not be more total.

Her recantation complete, Marinella goes on to detail the providential plan that has prescribed seclusion for women. She chooses two Aristotelian concepts as the cornerstones of her argument. The first is drawn from the *Politics* and stresses the importance of households to the welfare of the city.[76] The second is the famous passage from the spurious *Economics* which establishes different prerogatives and domains for men and women: men, stronger and more resilient, work outside the home to ensure its welfare; women, more delicate, work inside the home to preserve the wealth the men have acquired.[77] Although Marinella declares these two spheres of action equally dignified, this rigid dichotomy nevertheless relegates women's activity to narrow confines. Once again, this reasoning contradicts that of the

---

75. "Credono alcuni che cagione siano di questa retiratezza gli huomini per tenerle senza esperienza delle cose del mondo rinchiuse, acciochè inesperte, di poco ardire, e poco valore riescano. Questo anchor io dissi nel mio libro intitolato *La nobiltà et eccellenza delle donne*. Ma ora più maturamente considerando, mi sono avveduta non essere invenzione nè azione di animo appassionato, ma volere e providenza della natura e di Dio, e possiamo conoscere questa verità facilmente. Se questa fosse stata violenza, non si sarebbe conservata per tanti secoli e migliaia di anni. Le cose violenti lungamente non durano." Ibid., 12.

76. Aristotle, *Politics*, I.i.7 (1252b16).

77. Aristotle, *Economics*, I.iii (1344a1).

young Lucrezia who, almost half a century earlier, exuberantly cited examples of other European countries to prove that women's subjection derived from custom rather than from nature.[78]

The second exhortation reaffirms these principles and then discusses the plight of the educated woman. The erudite references that crowd the margins of Marinella's pages become less prominent in this section, which suggests that she is drawing, rather uncharacteristically, from her own experience and observations rather than from her readings. The life of a *litterata*, as described in these pages, is a series of painful disappointments. Her mother and sisters blame her for not devoting her time to feminine chores, while her friends and neighbors praise her in public only to slander her in private. Any success she finds only intensifies the hostility, and the greater and supposedly enlightened community of lettered men offers no appreciation that might otherwise compensate for the animosity of her entourage. On the contrary, male writers dispense with a woman's work by either ignoring it or proclaiming condescendingly that it is not bad "for a woman." If forced to praise a book or a poem written by a woman, such scholars will be quick to suggest that its real author must be a man who graciously allowed a lady to put her signature on the frontispiece.

Here, Marinella briefly articulates an objection to her argument, conceding that knowledge may be a reward in itself, regardless of other people's approval.[79] She allows the objection to remain neither accepted nor rejected. Marinella repeats this pattern a few pages later. After reporting that some believe it is impossible for a woman to take care of her household and study at the same time, she states: "I say, on the contrary, that it is easy to attend to both, because ruling over your household is a pastime compared to the study of intellectual disciplines."[80] Yet, in both cases, she proceeds with her argument as if no objections had been raised: knowledge is not a reward in itself and women cannot attend to two different activities. Therefore, women should avoid literature and devote themselves entirely to their house-

78. Marinella, *La nobiltà* (1601 edition), 28–29.

79. Marinella, *Esortazioni*, 32.

80. "Io dirò chè cosa facile servire a questa e a quella; perché il governo del tuo albergo sarà come un passatempo paragonato allo studio delle scienze." Ibid., 43.

holds, confident that they will be honored and praised for their diligence in fulfilling their womanly duties. Loss of beauty is powerfully
added to the list of ills that befall the learned woman. The sleepless
nights spent in pursuit of knowledge and the bitterness at the world's
incomprehension leave women livid, thin, pale, and melancholy,
much like the Harpies Ariosto describes in *Orlando furioso* XXXIII.

After relegating the exercise of women's skills to such a narrow domain, Marinella devotes her third exhortation to the praise of
the womanly art of weaving. She celebrates Minerva, the goddess of
knowledge, for her invention of the spindle and for serving as proof
that spinning suits goddesses and queens as well as common women.
As usual, Marinella uses a wealth of examples to support her point,
carefully selecting those that reinforce the strict division of labor she
established in the first exhortation. Praising the only arts she considers
appropriate for women, Marinella occasionally abandons her learned
references to offer readers an enticing glimpse of everyday Venice:

> In my hometown, when the burning lion races across
> the sky blowing blazing breath from its nostrils and
> setting the surrounding air aflame, it is wonderful to
> see gracious and noble women in halls and on high
> balconies show their own pride and excellence. Their
> sleeves and smocks are adorned with priceless nee-
> dlework. Fine veils are enriched by an embroidery
> known as "air stitch" because it is made without be-
> ing attached to cloth. There you can admire leaves,
> branches, flowers, and fruit formed by industrious
> hands and equal to the most beautiful gardens in the
> Tyrrhenian Sea, desired by Achelous's daughters.[81]

81. "Bellissima cosa è nella mia patria il vedere, quando l'infocato Leone scorre per lo Cielo
soffiando dalle nari fiati di foco accendendo l'aria d'intorno, nelle sale, e sopra gli alti veroni
le gratiose, e nobili donne far di se stessa pomposa mostra, ornate le maniche, e li grembiuli
di fregi di lavoro di ago inestimabile, e li sottilissimi veli, arricchiti di lavoro, detto punto in
aria; perché è fatto senza essere attaccato a tela, in cui miri foglie, rami, fiori, e frutti pur da
industriouse mani formati, ch'ad invidiar non hanno alli piú belli giardini che sieno vagheg-
giati dal mar Tirreno dalle figliuole di Acheloo." Ibid., 97.

The fourth exhortation addresses the respective merits of silence and speech. Warning that words reveal a person's intimate nature and that "infinite is the damage that derives from the tongue,"[82] Marinella follows Xenocrates and counsels her readers to be attentive listeners and cautious speakers. She also praises eloquence, when circumstances require it. Although this exhortation deals with women only marginally, the effects of their seclusion only reinforce the prescription of silence:

> Paucity of words is attributed to women in particular, as they do not have much experience and therefore cannot talk about many things. Experience, like a wise master, schools man in his life, deeds, and speech. This is why Gorgias of Leontini, that great legislator, said that "silence bestows glory upon a woman but not upon a man." Seclusion brings little knowledge of human life, and therefore "silence bestows glory upon a woman."[83]

The fifth exhortation addresses women's ornaments and luxury, a topic that had inspired intense debate and extensive legislation in Venice. Over the years, authorities tried to legislate a variety of practices, from the wearing of high heel shoes ("planessas altiores") to the use of wigs ("capillos non suos").[84] Marinella bases her opposition to the ornaments of her contemporaries on aesthetic as well as moral criteria. She dislikes the latest garments, calling them unbecoming to the female body, and longs for the style of bygone days. She also criticizes the excessive display of jewelry and the use of cosmetics and wigs.

---

82. "Infiniti sono i danni che dalla lingua procedono." Ibid., 111.

83. "La parcità delle parole è particolarmente attribuito alla donna la quale, non essendo molto esperimentata, non potrà neanco di molte cose ragionare, perché l'esperienza, quasi dotto maestro, insegna la vita, l'opre, e li ragionamenti all'uomo. Considerando questo, Gorgia leontino, quel gran legislatore, disse *mulieri decus affert taciturnitas, non ita viro*, perché la retiratezza cagiona inscitia del vivere humano, e però *taciturnitas affert decus mulieri*." Ibid., 121-22.

84. Wilmen Di Renzo Vianello. *Proibito alle donne dalle leggi suntuarie a Venezia e in Romagna III sec. a.C.-XIX sec.* (Cesena: Comitato Consorti del Rotary Club, Anno Rotariano 1993–94), 27.

She spares only the infamous *pianelle*, Venetian shoes with platform heels as high as two feet that, she claims, increase women's gravitas by slowing them down. The *pianelle* also oblige men to look up at a woman, as if they were contemplating a divinity. Marinella's feelings aligned perfectly with the latest provisions of sumptuary law. In 1644, the officers responsible for this legislation (*Provveditori alle Pompe*) issued a new document. The *Provveditori* set strict limits on a variety of luxury items one could wear, including the number of strings in a pearl necklace and precious stones in a ring, and listed separate rules for men and prostitutes. However, they were remarkably lenient when it came to footwear. In this area, they simply mandated the use of ordinary leather and minimal decorations ("gli zoccoli di pelle ordinaria senz'intaglio, ricamo, o guarnitione").[85]

Marinella's stern opposition to luxury marks a significant divergence not only from her father's benevolent tolerance and from the opinions she herself had expressed in *Le nobiltà*,[86] but also from the attitude of Arcangela Tarabotti, who just the year before the publication of *Esortazioni* had penned the *Antisatira*, a defense of women against the criticism of Francesco Buoninsegni's *Satira menippea*.[87] This timing supports Virginia Cox's hypothesis that *Esortazioni* constitutes, among other things, Marinella's "sharp self-distancing from Arcangela Tarabotti, precisely in 1643–44 establishing herself as a published presence on the Venetian literary scene."[88] Indeed, Marinella's disapproval of luxury provided ammunition to Tarabotti's critics and in particular to Angelico Aprosio. Under the pseudonym of Scipio Glareano, he wrote *Lo scudo di Rinaldo, ovvero lo specchio del disinganno (Rinaldo's Shield, or the Mirror of Disenchantment)*, a response to Tarabotti's *Antisatira*. Introducing his work, Aprosio criticizes Tarabotti by quoting

---

85. In 1648, the *Sopraproveditori* and *Proveditori* had these prescriptions published to refresh the Venetians' memory ("per ravivar anco nella memoria d'ogn'uno l'osservanza delle leggi"), which seems to indicate a persisting love of luxury on the part of the citizens (*Proclama publicato d'ordine degl'Illustrissimi Signori Sopraproveditori, e Proveditori alle Pompe, in materia d'ogni sorte di pompe* [Venezia: Gio. Pietro Pinelli, 1648]).

86. See n36 and n37.

87. Francesco Buoninsegni and Suor Arcangela Tarabotti, *Satira e antisatira*, ed. Elissa Weaver (Roma: Salerno, 1998).

88. Cox, *Women's Writing in Italy*, 225.

a long passage from *Esortazioni* and citing its author as an example of a woman who attained fame thanks to her disregard for vanity.[89] The relationship, or lack thereof, between these two important Venetian women is intriguing. Tarabotti praises Marinella for *Vita di Maria Vergine*[90] yet never mentions *Le nobiltà*, a work that she, however, seems to know very well.[91] For her part Marinella, who contributed a sonnet to the voluminous introduction to Tarabotti's *Paradiso monacale* (*Monastic Paradise*, 1643) ignores Tarabotti in her writings, although her criticism of women "who, because of some noble and high virtue that does not suit them, desire their names to circulate in the city" could well be directed at the nun's relentless self-promotion, as suggested by Cox.[92] Some similarities between Marinella's *Esortazioni* and Tarabotti's *Antisatira*, such as the defense of the *pianelle*[93] and the criticism of men's use of wigs,[94] make their reciprocal indifference all the more puzzling.

The sixth exhortation explores yet another topic, women's prudence, which is introduced with a simple title ("Prudenza donnesca" [Women's Prudence]) rather than with an explicit recommendation as are the previous exhortations. Readers may recall that *Le*

---

89. "Chi impiega hore davanti allo specchio non ha tempo di arricchire la republica letteraria di tanti dottissimi volumi com'ella [Marinella] ha fatto, né d'impossessarsi delle dottrine platoniche e peripatetiche che la rendono degna di ammirazione appo coloro che la senton discorrere." ("Those who spend hours in front of the mirror do not have the time to enrich the republic of letters with many very learned volumes as Marinella has done, or to master the principles of Plato and Aristotle that make her worthy of the admiration of those who hear her talk.") (Angelico Aprosio [Scipio Glareano], *Lo scudo di Rinaldo, ovvero lo specchio del disinganno* [Venezia: Herz, 1646]).

90. Tarabotti, *La semplicità ingannata*, 300-01.

91. For Simona Bortot, Tarabotti's failure to mention *Le nobiltà* is due to her disappointment with the conservative stance Marinella adopted in *Esortazioni* ("Introduzione. La penna all'ombra delle grate," in Tarabotti, *La semplicità ingannata*, 132). Letizia Panizza suggests instead that the omission of *Le nobiltà* can be attributed to "reasons that have to do, probably, with the practice of naming main sources in a general, indirect way, if at all" (Tarabotti, *Paternal Tyranny*, 106, n44).

92. Cox, *Women's Writing in Italy*, 372-73, n252.

93. Both Marinella (*Essortationi* 138-41) and Tarabotti (*Antisatira* 79) find that the height of the *pianelle* suits women's excellence.

94. See Marinella, *Essortationi* 141, and Tarabotti, *Antisatira* 95.

nobiltà strove to prove how every virtue, from temperance to courage, shines in women. After reducing women to their domestic functions in *Esortazioni*, however, Marinella struggles to find in them any virtue at all. In this new context, even the idea that women may exercise prudence (defined, in Aristotelian terms, as practical wisdom regarding matters that are subject to change) requires an elaborate justification and a laborious rereading (or misreading) of Aristotle. The first step is to break the association between practical wisdom and experience. Having stated, in the previous exhortation, that women should be silent because they are inexperienced, Marinella must now reconcile women's lack of experience with their role as rulers of the household. Her strategy is twofold. She starts with the example of generals who, like Alexander, Hannibal, and Scipio, accomplished extraordinary feats at a young age when they were still inexperienced. This allows her to conclude that prudence derives not from experience but rather from good judgment, "a certain natural light [. . .] that shows women what to follow and what to flee."[95] She then proceeds to delineate what we might define as small-scale prudence, namely, prudence germane to the narrow sphere women occupy. Although women are not experienced in the world at large, they nevertheless have vast experience in matters concerning the household, and this is all they need to perform their duties. This type of practical wisdom differs from the type necessary to rule a state in scale rather than essence:

> A large household is similar to a small city, which comprises many different parts. If a city is to be ruled by a prudent prince, so, too, is a house to be governed by a prudent woman.[96]

Although Marinella bases her argument on the first book of Aristotle's *Politics*, her conclusions diverge from Aristotle's. In the *Poli-*

---

95. "[...] un certo lume naturale [...] che mostra a quelle ciò che seguire, ciò che fuggir bisogna." Marinella, *Esortazioni*, 154.

96. "Essendo la casa grande emula ad una picciola città la qual è constituita di tante e diverse parti, se la città è da esser retta da principe prudente cosí la casa dalla donna prudente." Ibid., 148–49.

tics, Aristotle mentions the analogy between the state and the household only to denounce it as faulty:

> Some people think that the qualifications of a statesman, king, householder, and master are the same [...] as if there were no difference between a great household and a small state [...] But all this is a mistake.[97]

Whether Marinella's inaccurate representation of Aristotle's thought is the product of flawed interpretation or creative appropriation is difficult to determine. In her discussion of Arcangela Tarabotti's sources, Letizia Panizza warns about the risks of attributing to a writer's mistaken reading or conscious manipulation what could be the result of years of heterodox intertextual practices.[98] Modern researchers, who rely on polished and philologically sound versions of classic authors, must reckon with the Renaissance proliferation of commentaries, paraphrases and summaries, along with the peculiar problems it poses. It is therefore difficult to determine in each case whether a writer's unconventional reading of a particular source should be attributed to approximation, conscious elaboration, or simply to the author's reliance upon the specific edition available to her. Marinella's *Esortazioni* poses a particular challenge in that it is essentially a bilingual book, wherein Latin passages are freely inserted and only occasionally translated for the "beloved women" who otherwise would be unable to understand them. The overall impression is that of a general depository of proverbs, maxims, and formulations of wisdom that belonged to the author's vocabulary and worldview. It is unfortunate that the titles of the "old and badly worn books"[99] left in the Marinelli household after Antonio's death are destined to remain unknown, given that one of the tasks researchers face is that of reconstructing the

---

97. Aristotle, *Politics* I,1 (1252a6–9). Trans. Benjamin Jowett in *The Complete Works of Aristotle*, ed. Jonathan Barnes 2 vols. (Princeton: Princeton University Press, 1984), 2.1986.

98. Letizia Panizza, "Reader Over Arcangela's Shoulders: Tarabotti at Work with Her Sources," in *Arcangela Tarabotti. A Literary Nun in Baroque Venice*, ed. Elissa Weaver (Ravenna: Longo, 2006), 107–9. See also Bortot, "Introduzione. La penna all'ombra delle grate," in Tarabotti, *La semplicità ingannata*, 127-31.

99. Haskins, "Vexatious Litigant," Part 1 (2006), 99.

channels through which women gained access to a knowledge from which they were officially excluded. In Marinella's case, we can tentatively place three books back on the shelves that time and neglect have emptied out. The first is the abovementioned *Legendario*, from which she drew information on Saint Colomba, the protagonist of her first poem; the second is Pierre Lagnier's compendium, which seems to have provided some of the maxims she quotes;[100] and the third, which is particularly relevant to *Esortazioni*, is Leonardo Bruni's translation of Aristotle's *Politics*, which matches Marinella's Latin quotes word by word. For the most part, however, reconstructing Marinella's dialogue with her sources is an ongoing challenge.

While most of the sixth exhortation expounds on the importance and dignity of women's practical wisdom, its conclusion explicitly distinguishes this newly defined virtue from the one described in *Nobiltà*:

> I am not claiming that women must be as prudent as Semiramis when she devised how a well-protected city could be conquered or many other things that I mentioned in my book *The Nobility and Excellence of Women*. We will be content if they be prudent in womanly tasks and manage their family and household in devoted and endearing ways.[101]

After exhorting women to be happy with their limited role and domestic concerns, Marinella dedicates the seventh exhortation to harmony between husbands and wives. Here, her main addressees are not women but men, who are invited to follow Hesiod's precepts and choose maidens so that they can shape their wives according to their desires. Marinella compares this ideal female companion to a blank

---

100. Pierre Lagnier, *Ex M.T. Cicerone insignium sententiarum [...] compendium* (Lyon: Jean de Tournes and Guillaume Gazeau, 1552).

101. "Io non dirò che habbia in sé la prudenza di Semiramis nel giudicare da qual parte battere si deve una città difficilissima da essere battuta, né di tante altre cose, che ho commemorate nel mio libro intitolato *La nobiltà et eccellenza delle donne*; perché appagate ci ritroveremo che prudenti sieno nelle operazioni donnesche e con seduli e cari modi reggano la famiglia e la propria abitazione." Marinella, *Esortazioni*, 155.

slate, a white cloth, and a young plant that an experienced gardener can bend however he pleases. It is striking to find in Marinella's work the same treatment of women as inert matter that inspired so much misogynistic writing. Having reduced women to nonentities incapable of initiative or thought, Marinella refocuses on the men, whose behavior almost automatically shapes their companions. Marriage, therefore, must be preceded by a close examination of one's soul. Not only is it impossible for a vicious man to find comfort in the company of a just woman, but a woman's personality will tend to change over time to become similar to her companion's.

Marinella's strategy for absolving women from moral responsibility may recall the one Isotta Nogarola employed in her dialogue with Ludovico Foscarini (*De pari aut impari Evae atque Adae peccato*).[102] Nogarola argued that because Eve was less intelligent and constant than Adam, she carried less of the blame for the original sin. Both Marinella and Nogarola sacrifice women's individual agency to affirm their moral innocence, although Marinella admits the possibility of exceptions, such as a virtuous wife reforming her dissolute husband.

At times, *Esortazioni* reads like a random collection of eclectic remarks. In other instances, however, Marinella tries to organize her observations into a coherent structure. This attempt is particularly apparent in the seventh exhortation, wherein she both recalls her previous arguments, such as her opposition to ornaments, and anticipates the volume's ending remarks on the fleeting nature of human beauty.

The opening of the eighth chapter likewise underscores the linear progression of her work. Having addressed women and married couples, Marinella now turns her attention to children's education. This chapter is the longest in the volume and also the most generic. The author disappears behind a compilation of precepts drawn primarily from Aristotle's *Politics*. We thus read that a mother's milk is an

---

102. A translation of the dialogue was published by Margaret L. King and Albert Rabil in *Her Immaculate Hand: Selected Works By and About the Women Humanists of Quattrocento Italy* (Binghamton, N.Y.: Medieval and Renaissance Texts and Studies, rev. ed., 1997), 57–69. It is also included in Isotta Nogarola, *Complete Writings: Letterbook, Dialogue on Adam and Eve, Orations*, trans. Margaret L. King and Diana Robin. The Other Voice in Early Modern Europe (Chicago: University of Chicago Press, 2004), 145–58.

infant's ideal source of nourishment; that babies should be exposed to the cold to increase their strength; that children under five should play only games that are in some way educational and should not be exposed to inappropriate speech—especially to servants' conversation. Following her superficial tribute to Christian precepts ("It is laudable and honorable for parents to educate their children in the Christian faith"),[103] Marinella outlines an Aristotelian curriculum based on reading and writing, gymnastics, drawing, and music. Of these subjects, music receives the most in-depth treatment, which is not surprising given that Marinella earned praise among her contemporaries for her musical talent.[104] Unfortunately, she closely follows Aristotle even when treating this subject. Her discussion of music's different modes and its importance as a form of relaxation repeats the *Politics* almost verbatim, supplementing it with examples drawn mainly from Plato.

Children are to read inspirational stories about great leaders, avoid tragedies and comedies, and exercise in reasonable ways, while mothers should shun scary narrations. In her discussion of human qualities, Marinella relies yet again on Aristotle, invoking his formulation of virtue as a happy medium between defect and excess. She emphasizes the fact that virtue can be acquired through practice and explores the four cardinal virtues of wisdom, courage, temperance, and justice. This exhortation ambitiously concludes by prescribing the virtues of the perfect prince.

Of all the chapters, the eighth is undoubtedly the most abstract. In her unquestioning reverence for her sources, Marinella fails to manifest what a twenty-first-century critic could call "gendered identity." It is striking that an obviously educated woman like Marinella does not feel the need to draw a curriculum for girls, unless we are to assume — somewhat optimistically—that she interprets Aristotle's curriculum as gender-blind. The plea for equal access to education, which constituted the core of *Le nobiltà*, is all but absent here,

103. "Sarà di laude et di honore alli genitori instituirli [i figli] nella cristiana verità." Marinella, *Esortazioni*, 212.

104. Both Cristoforo Bronzino in *Dialogo dela dignità e nobiltà delle donne* (1624) and F.S. Quadrio in *Della storia e della ragione d'ogni poesia* (1741) mention Marinella's musical talent (qtd. in Haskins, "Vexatious Litigant," 2006, 86).

suffocated under erudite references. It is as if, by becoming increasingly conversant in the literary and philosophical traditions of men, Marinella had grown progressively more distant from other women, and their exclusion from the world of learning no longer bothered her, as it had in her youth.

Esortazioni concludes with a final recantation. In *Le nobiltà*, Marinella, following Plato, proclaimed that beauty was divine and served as evidence of women's worth. In *Esortazioni*, however, Marinella, considering how beauty withers and fades away, draws the opposite conclusion and invites women to put all their hope and effort in their immortal souls.

"It flees; it is mortal, not divine!"[105] Marinella's lament over the mortality of beauty permeates her farewell to her public. A somber "cupio dissolvi," indicating her desperate awareness of the imminent end, resonates in these last pages. Death or perhaps lack of inspiration prevented her from adding a second part to her last work.

Esortazioni was Marinella's last chance to dazzle her audience with her display of erudition, dutifully highlighted by a wealth of references printed in the page margins. It is also a rather repetitive volume, which the author justifies in the name of pedagogical strategy.[106] The uneven tone (ranging from the familiar to the erudite), the imbalanced distribution of the material (the shortest exhortation runs just eight pages, the longest eighty), and the abovementioned unresolved contradictions suggest that the volume did not undergo a final authorial revision. Altogether, *Esortazioni* can safely be defined as a reactionary work, not only because of Marinella's endorsement of conservative views of women but also for her disregard for the contemporary literary scene. The only living author she mentions, Tommaso Stigliani, is cited only once. Her ideal interlocutors all belong to the past: Aristotle and Plato, Homer and Virgil, Petrarch, Ariosto, Tasso, and Guarini form a dead society of poets and philosophers that pro-

---

105. "Fugge, è cosa mortale, non divina!" (Marinella, *Esortazioni*, 294).

106. "Ritorneremo a ricordare le cose dette; perché il reiterare spesso le buone essortationi, sono cagioni che si imprimono nell'animo più efficacemente, come il Maleatore con molti colpi e spessi riduce a perfettione l'opera sua" (182) ("We will go back to what we have already said, as repetition is the best way to impress these good exhortations upon your soul. In a similar way, the blacksmith brings his work to perfection with many frequent blows.")

vides enlightenment and examples. Marinella's apparent withdrawal from contemporary society is accentuated by the volume's lack of the traditional introductory letters or sonnets in praise of the author. In contrast, the paratextual material included in Tarabotti's *Paradiso monacale* constituted one third of the volume.[107]

It is probably inevitable that *Esortazioni* will be remembered mainly as a recantation of *Le nobiltà* and interpreted as a symbolic "death knell of the Renaissance tradition of women's writing."[108] The passages in which Marinella, in the name of "more mature wisdom," bluntly rejects the views she upheld in her youthful tract are indeed striking. However, by writing a book of advice and thus adding yet another genre to the list of her publications, Marinella was effectively invalidating her own argument and placing herself in a double bind.[109] How could a woman argue convincingly against women's education without, at the same time, demonstrating her knowledge of established authorities and thereby providing an example of women's erudition and argumentative skills? But perhaps, instead of "women," we should speak here of "a woman:" this Lucrezia Marinella who positions herself in the wasteland of learned women, in plain sight of and yet removed from both the exclusive kingdom of masculine knowledge and the vast domain of female domesticity. While the text's wealth of philosophical and literary references designates men as its ideal addressees and interlocutors, the frequent, affectionate apostrophes to women underscore their rhetorical function. These implied female readers are called to witness the learned woman's stunning display of erudition without ever being encouraged to join her in her pursuits. Even as Marinella somewhat condescendingly explains and translates her references for her "beloved women," she insists on maintaining the very ignorance that forces them to depend on her mediation. The model is, once again, that of the Amazon, the woman who soars above her sex because of excep-

---

107. Beatrice Collina, "Women in the Gutenberg Galaxy," in *Arcangela Tarabotti*, ed. Weaver, 95.

108. Cox, *Women's Writing in Italy*, 204.

109. Cox speaks of *Esortazioni* as "something of a paradox, in that a work that contains the period's most despondent analysis of women's literary possibilities is also probably the most confident and wide-ranging female-authored secular didactic text of the age." Ibid., 224.

tional merit and circumstances but who, in so doing, severs her link with the community of women and harbors no illusion of serving as an example to them. The model is Marfisa who, in the most striking anticipation of twentieth-century feminism, claims full rights over herself ("Io sua non son, né d'altri son che mia"[110] ["I am not his nor anybody else's but mine"[111]]), but does not think those rights should extend to other women. The model is Clorinda who, in recommending her maidens and aged tutor to Argante, distances herself from them, marking womanhood and old age as two conditions that are intrinsically foreign to her: "di pietate / ben è degno *quel* sesso e *quella* etate"[112] ("their sex and his age deserve what pity you take"[113]).

In *Esortazioni*, Marinella implicitly presents herself as an Amazon, a phoenix, an exception to the rule, established by God and nature, that women should not waste their time in intellectual endeavors. Her vehemence is so great that one might suspect it is motivated by self-interest, as if the learned woman, proud of her uniqueness, used her formidable rhetorical arsenal to preserve her exceptional status, which would inevitably be compromised if scores of women joined her in the pursuit of knowledge. Marinella tries to preempt such an objection by reassuring the women in her imaginary audience:

> However, I would not want you to believe that I am trying to discourage you from pursuing literature because I am afraid of being surpassed by you. This would be the act of an envious soul, not that of a heart which truly loves you as I do.[114]

---

110. Ariosto, *Orlando furioso*, eds. Santorre Debenedetti and Cesare Segre (Bologna: Commissione per i testi di lingua, 1960) XXVI.79.

111. Ariosto, *Orlando furioso*, trans. Guido Waldman (Oxford and New York: Oxford University Press, 1974) XXVI.79.

112. Tasso, *Gerusalemme liberata*, ed. Fredi Chiappelli (Milano: Rusconi, 1982) XII.6 (emphasis mine).

113. Tasso, *Jerusalem Delivered* (*Gerusalemme liberata*), trans. Anthony M. Esolen (Baltimore: Johns Hopkins University Press, 2000), XII.6.

114. "Però io non vorrei che voi credeste, ch'io dubitando da voi essere superata, facessi questo uffizio di stogliervi dalle lettere, perché questo sarebbe atto di animo invidioso e non di cuore che veramente ami, come faccio io." Marinella, *Esortazioni*, 28.

Esortazioni is only one of a series of texts that discouraged women from applying themselves to literature. Their authors share the conviction that reading and writing endanger women's morals by exposing them to the variety of human experience. Even when arguing in favor of education, Juan Luis Vives warned his readers about the risks knowledge poses for women: "Learned women are suspect to many, as if the mental ability acquired by learning increased their natural wickedness."[115] More precisely, activities related to the acquisition and transmission of knowledge, such as writing, debating and especially publishing—which, as its etymology indicates, is suspiciously close to "going public"—entailed interacting with people outside the domestic sphere, along with its attendant dangers. In *Ragguagli di Parnaso* (*Reports from Parnassus*) Traiano Boccalini mocks the Accademia degli Intronati for allowing women poets such as Vittoria Colonna, Veronica Gambara, and Laura Terracina to join their ranks. The God Apollo decides to stop such a practice,

> For he had realized at last that women's true poetry consisted in their needle and spindle, and that the women's literary exercises with the *Virtuosi* was like the sporting and playing of dogs, which after a while ends in getting one on top of the other.[116]

Marinella approaches the issue differently. Nowhere does she claim that women cannot reach or surpass men in their studies, and she ignores the pernicious equation of erudition with licentiousness. What she offers, rather, is advice on how women might operate in a world that does not accept their learning: the world of seventeenth-

---

115. Juan Luis Vives, *The Education of a Christian Woman: A Sixteenth-Century Manual*, ed. and trans. Charles Fantazzi. The Other Voice in Early Modern Europe (Chicago: University of Chicago Press, 2000), 63.

116. "[…] percioché si era finalmente avveduto che la vera poetica delle donne era l'aco e il fuso, e gli esercizi letterari delle dame co' virtuosi somigliavano gli scherzi e i giuochi che tra loro fanno i cani, i quali dopo brieve tempo tutti forniscono alla fine in montarsi addosso l'un l'altro." (Traiano Boccalini, *Ragguagli di Parnaso e scritti minori*, ed. Luigi Firpo [Bari: Laterza, 1948], Vol. I, 66 [*ragguaglio* XXII]). Cfr. Cox, *Women's Writing in Italy*, 198.

century Italy, so different from the one that had welcomed *Le nobiltà* almost half a century earlier.

I am well aware that my reading of *Esortazioni* may seem hopelessly conservative. I therefore conclude by expressing my uneasiness with interpretations, such as the one Paola Malpezzi Price and Christine Ristaino propose, that require ideological leaps of faith. Citing the Roman Inquisition's influence on the publishing industry, these authors invoke Bakhtin, Girard, and Pirandello to conclude that Marinella's "entreaty to women to live a private life focusing on domestic tasks masks her true feelings, preserving the ritual in which she participates but pointing instead to its opposite."[117] Although *Esortazioni* is certainly a complex and sometimes contradictory work, one must be wary of reaching such confident conclusions about the author's "true feelings," especially when they are at odds with a more literal interpretation of the text. I disagree with the impulse to take Marinella's texts at face value when they proclaim principles appealing to twenty-first-century readers but to dismiss or creatively deconstruct them if they let us down. It seems to me that such ideological stance contributes little to our understanding of early modern women's writing. For this reason, I have adopted a cautious approach that I consider more respectful of Marinella's historical "otherness."

NOTE ON THE TRANSLATION

Esortazioni was published in Venice by Francesco Valvasense in 1645. The year before, the same publisher had released both Francesco Buoninsegni's *Satira* and its rebuttal, Arcangela Tarabotti's *Antisatira*.[118] Valvasense's penchant for controversial subjects may have played a role in his decision to publish Marinella's last work. Just three years after the publication of *Esortazioni*, in fact, Valvasense and his Bellunese colleague Giacomo Batti were defendants in a trial that exposed

---

117. Paola Malpezzi Price and Christine Ristaino, *Lucrezia Marinella and the 'Querelle des Femmes' in Seventeenth-Century Italy* (Madison, N.J.: Fairleigh Dickinson University Press, 2008), 155.

118. Francesco Buoninsegni's *Contro 'l lusso donnesco satira menippea* had originally been released in 1638, but was republished in 1644 together with Tarabotti's rebuttal (*Antisatira*). See Elissa Weaver, "Introduzione," 8.

the ruses publishers employed to escape censorship. Searches of their shops turned up books the church deemed objectionable, including works by Ferrante Pallavicino and Francesco Pona, both members of the Accademia degli Incogniti.[119] Matteo Leni, a witness in the trial, testified that the infamous 1647 booklet *Che le donne non siano della stessa specie degli uomini* (*Women Do Not Belong to the Species Mankind*) had not been printed in Lyon, as its frontispiece indicated, but rather in Venice, and by none other than Valvasense. In its original, anonymous Latin version (*Disputatio nova contra mulieres qua probatur eas homines non esse*), the pamphlet had circulated for almost half a century before being translated into Italian by a mysterious "Orazio Plata Romano" who, many believe, was a pseudonym of Giovan Francesco Loredan, founder of the Accademia degli Incogniti.[120] The claim that women did not belong to the human species prompted Arcangela Tarabotti's vehement reaction and the church's condemnation.[121] Surprisingly, Giovan Francesco Loredan was not summoned, in spite of his important role in the publishing industry of the time, his ties with Valvasense, and his possible identity as translator of *Disputatio nova*. The choice of Valvasense as the publisher for *Esortazioni* is therefore an interesting one, as it points to a possible link between Marinella, Tarabotti, and the Accademia degli Incogniti. Loredan was in fact instrumental in the publication of Tarabotti's *Paradiso monacale* (1643), whose rich introduction featured a sonnet by Marinella.

A small-format volume of 300 pages, *Esortazioni* seem to have survived in just three copies, housed at the Biblioteca Civica Aprosi-

119. On the Valvasense trial see Mario Infelise, "Book and Politics in Arcangela Tarabotti's Venice," in *Arcangela Tarabotti*, ed. Weaver, 57–72, and Monica Miato, "Gli stampatori veneziani e la censura", in *L'Accademia degli Incogniti di Giovan Francesco Loredan. Venezia (1630-1661)* (Firenze: Olschki, 1998), 121–66.

120. See Emilio Zanette, *Suor Arcangela. Monaca del Seicento veneziano* (Roma-Venezia: Istituto per la collaborazione culturale, 1960), 397-406. For the history of the debate see Letizia Panizza, "Introductory Essay," in Arcangela Tarabotti, *Che le donne siano della spezie degli uomini. Women Are No Less Rational Than Men* (London: Institute of Romance Studies, 1994).

121. Writing under the pseudonym of Galerana Barcitotti, Tarabotti in 1651 published *Che le donne siano della spezie degli uomini* (*Women Do Belong to the Species Mankind*). The same year, *Che le donne non siano della stessa specie degli uomini* was enlisted in the *Index Librorum Prohibitorum*.

ana in Ventimiglia, the Bibliothèque Mazarine in Paris, and the Biblioteca Antoniana in Padua.[122] One could speculate that the extreme rarity of the volume indicates its lack of resonance with the audience of the day or that, on the contrary, its reduced circulation prevented it from achieving greater fame.[123] In either case, the fact that two of the surviving copies of *Esortazioni* are housed at the Aprosiana and the Mazarine is in itself revealing and strengthens the hypothesis of a relationship between Marinella, Tarabotti, and the Incogniti.

The project that would lead to the establishment of the Bibliothèque Mazarine began in 1642, when Cardinal Mazarin assigned Gabriel Naudé the task of creating the first French public library. A graduate in medicine from the University of Padua and familiar with—though not particularly fond of—Loredan's works, Naudé searched all of Europe for books to include in the library and was logically drawn to Venice. Tarabotti spared no effort to promote her literary activity among French literary circles. She wrote to Naudé and to Cardinal Mazarin himself to recover the manuscript of *Tirannia paterna*, and corresponded with Anne de Gremonville, wife of the French ambassador to Venice, to try to secure a place for her publications at the Bibliothèque Mazarine.[124] She also met and exchanged letters with another adventurous scholar, Angelico Aprosio, though their relationship turned sour when Aprosio attacked Tarabotti's *Antisatira*.[125] An Augustinian friar and fervent bibliophile, Aprosio would later found

---

122. I am indebted to Lynn Westwater for locating the volume at the Biblioteca Antoniana, and to Elissa Weaver for lending me her copy. Françoise Lavocat mentions the existence of another copy at Biblioteca Nazionale in Rome in her introduction to *L'Arcadia felice* (XXIII, n85). In spite of multiple attempts, I was unable to find this copy.

123. Miato's list of books published by Valvasense does not include *Esortazioni*. See "Appendice I" in *L'Accademia degli Incogniti*, 171–234.

124. Arcangela Tarabotti, *Lettere familiari e di complimento*, ed. Meredith Kennedy Ray and Lynn Lara Westwater (Torino: Rosenberg & Sellier, 2005), 194-97 and 215-16. On the relationship between Tarabotti and Naudé see Stephanie Jed, "Arcangela Tarabotti and Gabriel Naudé. Libraries, Taxonomies and *Ragion di stato*," in Weaver, ed. *Arcangela Tarabotti*, 129-40.

125. Aprosio's first response to the *Antisatira* bore the title of *La maschera scoperta di Filofilo Misoponero* and contained a venomous personal attack against the nun. Tarabotti managed to prevent its publication, but not that of *Lo scudo di Rinaldo ovvero lo specchio del disinganno*, which was however much less acrimonious. See Zanette 235-68.

one of the first Italian public libraries, the Biblioteca Aprosiana, in his hometown of Ventimiglia.[126] Aprosio and Naudé met in 1645 in the convent of Santo Stefano in Venice, and there Aprosio showed the French visitor the books he had purchased.[127] Perhaps the two copies of *Esortazioni* that would soon travel to the Biblioteca Aprosiana and the Bibliothèque Mazarine were among them. Although the scant information available on Marinella's literary relations make it impossible to know if she also corresponded with Aprosio and Naudé, the fact that the two of the three surviving copies of *Esortazioni* are hosted precisely in those two libraries is certainly intriguing.

While the copies of *Esortazioni* at the Biblioteca Aprosiana and Biblioteca Antoniana present no editorial anomalies,[128] the one at the Bibliothèque Mazarine contains some errors of pagination.[129] This copy was housed in the seminary of Saint-Sulpice until the eighteenth century, as indicated by the seal on the frontispiece and by the fact that it is listed in the seminary's catalogue.[130] In 1645, the year *Esortazioni* was published, the library of the seminary had been enlarged thanks to Jacques Olivier's purchase of additional space in Rue du Vieux-Colombier.[131] With the confiscation of ecclesiastical property that took place during the French Revolution, however, the collection

126. On Angelico Aprosio, see Alberto Asor Rosa's entry in *Dizionario Biografico degli Italiani* (Roma: Treccani, 1961), Vol. 3, 650–53, and Quinto Marini, *Frati barocchi. Studi su A.G. Brignole Sale, G.A. De Marini, A. Aprosio, F.F. Frugoni, P. Segneri* (Modena: Mucchi, 2000).

127. Writing under the pseudonym of Cornelio Aspasio Antivigilmi, Aprosio himself reported the encounter in *Biblioteca Aprosiana* (Bologna: Manolessi, 1673), 245. See Zanette 307 and Miato, *L'Accademia degli Incogniti* 100–06.

128. I would like to thank Virginia Cox for her help locating the copy at the Aprosiana and Ruggero Marro of the Biblioteca Aprosiana for making it available to me.

129. Page 216 is repeated and numbered 217. A group of pages numbered 217–220 is inserted after page 294. They do not replicate previous pages with the same numbers in this volume but instead reproduce the corresponding pages in the Aprosiana copy. A second group of pages, numbered 237–240, appears both at its proper place and as an addition between pages 294 and 295.

130. *Bibliothecae seminarii Sancti Sulpitii catalogus triplex, materiarum ordine dispositus,* Bibliothèque Mazarine, Ms 4179–4184 (eighteenth century), 5 vols.

131. Alfred Franklin, "Les Anciennes Bibliothèques de Paris," in *Histoire Générale de Paris* (Paris: Imprimerie nationale, 1873), 3.33.

was moved to the Mazarine, while the seminary itself was demolished in the year 1800.[132]

Although the introductory letter to readers claims that *Esortazioni* are inspired by "historical, straightforward, and accurate reasoning,"[133] Marinella's prose features frequent metaphors, redundancy, and the long and convoluted sentences characteristic of her times. In the translation, I have tried to strike a balance between faithfulness to the original and the need to provide a readable text for the modern Anglophone public. Quotes from vernacular and Latin sources have been identified whenever possible, translated in the body of the text, and reproduced in the original language in the notes. In addition to these extensive passages, Marinella's prose includes many Latin expressions. I have translated these shorter sentences but left them in parentheses to convey to modern readers the original's bilingual flavor. I have omitted from the main body of the text the numerous glosses printed in the margins, which either repeat in Latin or point to possible sources of a concept found in the text; when relevant, I discuss these in the notes.

With the present, integral translation,[134] this extremely rare volume is made available to the public for the first time since the 1645 *editio princeps.*

---

132. I would like to thank the kind and knowledgeable staff at the Bibliothèque Mazarine, and in particular curators Jacqueline Labaste and Patrick Latour, for facilitating my research at the library.

133. Marinella, *Esortazioni*, 8.

134. The only omission is an index of the topics discussed.

Lucrezia Marinella:
Exhortations to Women and to Others if They Please

To the most illustrious and Excellent Don Gaspar de Teves y Guzman, Marquis of La Fuente, Lord of Lerena and Benazuza, *Commendator* of Colos, of the order of Saint James, *Alcalde Maggior Perpetuo*, *Scrivano Maggior* of the City of Seville, Gentleman of the Chamber of His Catholic Majesty, *Azemiliero Maggior* of His Counsel, Ambassador Extraordinary to the Princes of Italy and Germany, and to this Most Serene Republic of Venice, etc.[1]

Though lowly and hardly valuable, the mists arising from the earth are rarefied by the Sun's kindness and lifted to the air's supreme region. There—thanks to the Sun—they look noble and delightful with their appearance of light and brilliance.

Similarly, these exhortations of mine, although born of humble, lowly, and domestic origins, will earn some praise if favored by the Sun of Your Excellency's benevolence. The splendor of your infinite virtue and worth, which the world has acknowledged so many times, will penetrate the dense obscurity of my essays, making them bright and clear. Although they are obscure, I will not discourage Your Excellency from reading them, but rather beg you to grant me this favor. In keeping, as always, with your kind and gentle nature, I am sure that you will be favorable to me. Although my exhortations address domestic matters, you will find them adorned with many philosophical sayings from Aristotle, Plato, and others. You will also find maxims

---

1. I thank Alfonso Morales-Front and Goretti Gonzalez for discussing this impressive string of honorific titles, which must often have accompanied references to Gaspar de Teves y Guzman. The same list appears in fact in a pass issued to English writer John Evelyn, who mocks its "pompous form" (John Evelyn, *Diary*, ed. William Bray [Washington and London: M. Walter Dunne, 1901], 215). On Spain's ambitious ambassador to Venice, see R.A. Stradling, *Philip IV and the Government of Spain, 1621–1665* (Cambridge: Cambridge University Press, 2002), 113ff. Gaspar de Teves y Guzman (1608–1673) accepted his post in 1644, only one year before the publication of *Esortazioni*. It is therefore possible that Marinella had not met him personally, which would explain the emphatic yet generic phrasing of this dedication.

from Hesiod and Homer, full of the morality that is necessary for lead-ing a good life, which brings civil happiness.

I will not even attempt to demonstrate and praise the greatness of your most noble family or your deeds, which have brought profit and honor to citizens and people, as I know this is too great a burden for me to shoulder. Thus, I will remain silent in my admiration, while fame with its eternal voice rejoices and takes pride in making your actions known in every corner of the world.

Your Excellency will not disdain my small gift. The benevo-lence and goodness of your indomitable soul will excuse my lack of knowledge and my having the temerity to ennoble this little volume's rustic roughness with the honor of your name.

In conclusion, I humbly bow in all reverence, and I wish you the highest happiness.

Your most devout and humble servant,
Lucrezia Marinella

To the Readers

In these exhortations, Signora Lucrezia[2] did not imitate those writers who are always looking for new words and extravagant and deceiving expressions, altered and extended from their common meaning. These writers think that, by entertaining their readers' senses with words of little value, they will become the rulers of Parnassus.[3] Instead, Signora Lucrezia chose a historical, straightforward, and accurate reasoning. She did not want to attract her readers with only the appearance of knowledge and doctrine but rather with its substance. This administers to their minds the philosophical and moral evidence that brings goodness and honesty to our souls and lives.

Readers can rest assured of the knowledge these few exhortations contain by considering the perfection of the many volumes of verse and prose their author has published at different times, and particularly of her last works. The first, *Victories of Saint Francis*, is richly adorned with many Aristotelian, Platonic, and theological concepts and precepts. The other, a poem in twenty-seven cantos, addresses the glorious deeds of Enrico Dandolo at Constantinople, one of our Republic's greatest and most magnificent accomplishments. This poem, *Enrico, or Constantinople Conquered*,[4] contains all of poetry's military science, including ways to assemble, form, order, and rule armies, to build trenches, and to lead squadrons in battle, horrible fights, and assaults on citadels and ramparts. Duels are also skillfully described,

2. The use of the third person suggests that this address to the readers may have been written by a person other than the author—perhaps her publisher Valvasense.

3. Mount Parnassus in central Greece, the mythical home of the Muses, is often used as a metaphor for poetry. The criticism of those who believe they are "the rulers of Parnassus" could be directed at Traiano Boccalini, who in 1613 had published a book titled precisely *Ragguagli di Parnaso (Reports from Parnassus)*.

4. Published in 1597, *Vita del Serafico e Glorioso San Francesco* (here referred to as *Vittorie di San Francesco*) is a verse narration of the life of Saint Francis, preceded by an allegorical discourse on the human soul. It is curious however that this volume, published almost half a century before *Esortazioni*, should be referred to as one of Marinella's "last works." The heroic poem *Enrico, o Bisanzio acquistato* (referred to as *Enrico, o Costantinopoli acquistato*), published in 1635, focuses on Enrico Dandolo, the Venetian doge (1192–1205) who led the fourth crusade that culminated in the sack of Constantinople (1204).

as are sorties, stratagems to deceive the enemy, and many other un-foreseen events that occur in dangerous combat; indeed, a naval battle is so artfully described, the God of War could have done no better. Were military experts to examine this poem, they would but marvel and praise its art and learning.

Reader, if in this booklet you find expressions such as Dei-ties, Fate, Destiny, and Fatal Star, please keep in mind that the author meant only to indicate Second Causes, ministers, and servants of the Eternal Agent.[5] And while you read these moral and philosophical exhortations, she will prepare the second part.[6]

May God bring you happiness.

---

5. At the height of the Counter-Reformation, readers are advised to interpret all references to pagan entities metaphorically.

6. There is no evidence that this second part was ever written.

1. THIS EXHORTATION WILL SHOW THAT SECLUSION SUITS SUPERIOR BEINGS SUCH AS GOD, PRINCES, AND WOMEN. NATURE AND THE FIRST CAUSE PRESCRIBED SECLUSION TO WOMEN MORE THAN TO MEN.

Gorgias of Leontini, that most famous legislator, left us a maxim as worthy and precious as those left by the oracle of Apollo in Delos: a woman's reputation must not leave the walls of her home.[7] He considered a woman's reputation so fragile and valuable that were it to leave the home and become the object of men's conversation—which is always full of lies and cowardice—it would return offended and disparaged. This, I believe, was that great legislator's thought and opinion. The virtue and goodness that proceeds from the good deeds one performs at home must be kept within those walls as a just and decent thing. I cannot but praise the thoughts and words of such a great man, and condemn the ambition of some women who, because of some noble and high virtue that does not suit them, desire their names to circulate in the city and among men. They do not realize that, once they leave their homes, they are like the targets archers use in their practice—pierced and ripped apart by everybody and from all sides. Neither do they realize that, as I said earlier, their reputation is divine. Like the whiteness of a swan, it can be darkened by the slightest shadow.

---

7. Marinella may have found Gorgias's ideas on women in Plutarch's *Mulierum Virtutes* (*Bravery of Women*), which had been translated into Latin by Alamanno Rinuccini in 1485 and had enjoyed great success, particularly in Giovanni Tarcagnota's Italian translation, *Opuscoli morali* (Venezia: Comin da Trino, 1567). See Maria Luisa Doglio, ed. Torquato Tasso, *Discorso della virtù feminile e donnesca* (Palermo: Sellerio, 1997), 74. However, Gorgias's ideas are reported quite differently by Plutarch, who at the beginning of *Bravery of Women* states: "I do not hold the same opinion as Thucydides. For he declares that the best woman is she about whom there is the least talk among persons outside regarding either censure or commendation, feeling that the name of the good woman, like her person, ought to be shut up indoors and never go out. But to my mind Gorgias appears to display better taste in advising that not the form but the fame of a woman should be known to many." (Plutarch, *Moralia*, 242E–F, trans. Frank Cole Babbitt [Cambridge, MA.: Harvard University Press, 1968], 3.475).

The sun, however bright, can be dimmed by a small cloud. Therefore, it is good to flee all things that cause damage, particularly to one's honor. The remedy is seclusion. You will keep your reputation in the secrecy of your house. Seclusion is perhaps worthier than is commonly believed. All precious things flee the gaze of others, as it seems that in showing themselves they would lose value and worth. Nature hides gems, gold, silver, and other treasures in the depths of the earth because they are precious and coveted. All things of beauty flee people's sight because, if they manifested themselves, they would appear less important, and even vulgar. This is the reason the ancient wise men hid the beauty of their Gods in the rough guise of ugly monsters. In this way, their excellence would not be revealed to everyone. Only on occasion, when their rough cover was open, did people understand their wonderful and venerable nature. Tasso discusses this in the eighth canto of his *Goffredo*:

> When a rustic Silenus opened,
> The people of old saw wonders.[8]

From these lines, we realize that seclusion and secrecy are to be revered. Sacred matters, worthy of respect and praise were kept under the veil of silence, and the Gods remained hidden behind various images and mysterious guises. The Ancients wanted only priests and few others to understand the greatness of their Gods.

---

8. Torquato Tasso, *Gerusalemme liberata*, ed. Fredi Chiappelli (Milano: Rusconi, 1982) XVIII.30: "Tal ne l'aprir di un rustico Sileno / Maraviglie vedea l'antica etade." Here and elsewhere, translations are mine unless otherwise noted. A series of references to *Jerusalem Delivered*—also known at the time as *Goffredo*—attests to Marinella's long-standing familiarity with and admiration for Tasso's masterpiece. It is impossible to determine which of the many editions of the poem circulating at the time she used, except to note that it is *not* the second Bonnà edition published in 1581 that modern editors consider the most reliable and that in this particular instance reads: "Già ne l'aprir d'un rustico sileno / meraviglie vedea l'antica etade". It is also possible that Marinella relied on her memory, which would explain why she erroneously situates the passage in the eighth canto, rather than in the eighteenth. Here and elsewhere, I report Marinella's quotes from Tasso verbatim, while pointing out occasional major discrepancies between them and modern editions. Tasso is referring to the hollow statues of Silenus, which contained small golden statues of the gods beneath their ugly appearance. Alcibiades compares Socrates to a Silenus in Plato's *Symposium* 216e-217a.

To be known by common people degrades and humiliates the greatness of the divine majesty and honor. Marsilio Ficino writes:

> Here and often elsewhere it is forbidden to spread the
> deepest theological mysteries among common people,
> so that they not conceive false and vain opinions be-
> cause of their faulty judgment.[9]

This is the reason why excellent things should not be exposed to people's desire or judgment. For this reason, the Ancients hid their superhuman deities under marvelous guises, preserving them from the rough and paltry wisdom of the masses. Women must bask in the glory of seclusion because they are to be kept like something sacred and divine. We notice how emperors, kings, and great princes do not show themselves to people every day, thereby making their presence common. On the contrary, as they partake of the divine, they hide themselves and only rarely consent to being seen by others. Rarely does the king of Spain manifest himself, and the same is true of people of great dignity.

In my most noble city, Venice, a newly elected Serene Doge, having gathered new inner strength, rarely fulfills people's curiosity by showing himself. Seclusion brings majesty and honor to those destined by fortune or their own merit to achieve superiority and regal heights.

It seems that God and nature have assigned such seclusion to women more than to others. Women will keep their looks, beauty, and reputation in their solitary homes and exercise their peaceful occupations within the domestic walls. Please consider, my beloved ladies, the greatness of your dignity and how much honor and respect this seclusion brings to your virtue and status.

Let us also consider how God—the First Cause, the Eternal Agent, He who is excellent above all excellence, He who attracts and moves every perfection and beauty and who presides over divine

---

9. "Hic et saepe alibi vetat secretissima theologiae misteria inter profanos effundere propter iudicii defectum, ne falsas vanasque opiniones concipiant." See Marsilio Ficino, "Dionysii Areopagitae *De Mistica Theologia Translatio*," in *Opera Omnia* (Torino: Bottega d'Erasmo, 1959-60) II.1015–16.

beauty—refuses to be known by us, except in the effects of his clemency. His dignity cannot be comprehended by our lowliness, for it would thereby lose prestige (*evilesceret utique*). He therefore not only shields Himself from our sight behind many celestial spheres, but also resides in the laps of Cherubim, as far above the sky as the sky is far from hell, as the aforementioned poet says of God in the first canto of *Goffredo*:

> And as far as from the stars to the depths of hell,
> so far is He above the starry sphere.[10]

The virgins who, like sacred creatures, devote themselves to God in the solitude and secrecy of their monasteries, lead lives that are dear to Heaven and can never receive sufficient praise. When he wanted to exalt Sophronia, that same poet mentioned her seclusion. Of her many qualities, he says, she deserves the most praise for keeping her worth hidden:

> She hides her worth within the narrow cage
> Of a small house, so far the worthier.[11]

Later on, he praises her, saying that while Love allowed Olindo to see her, she led a secluded life, far from the sight of other people, protected by a thousand guards:

> Although a thousand sentinels are placed
> you lead his glances from haunts most chaste.[12]

The Vestal Virgins, who lived pure and chaste lives, loved secluded, enclosed, and remote places. They loved solitude because it

---

10. Tasso, *Gerusalemme liberata*, I.7: "E quant'è da le stelle al basso Inferno / Tant'è più in su da la stellata sfera." The English translation comes from Torquato Tasso, *Jerusalem Delivered* (*Gerusalemme liberata*), trans. Anthony M. Esolen (Baltimore, Md.: Johns Hopkins University Press, 2000), 18.

11. Tasso, *Gerusalemme liberata*, II.14: "Il suo pregio maggior che tra le mura / d'angusta casa asconde i suoi gran pregi." Trans. Esolen, 38.

12. Tasso, *Gerusalemme liberata*, II.15: "Tu per mille custodie entro i più casti / Verginei alberghi il guardo altrui portasti." Trans. Esolen, 39.

fostered virtue, contemplation, and wisdom. They were worshiped and honored as people who longed for the divine. Claudia, a Vestal Virgin who did not practice solitude and seclusion, was believed to be unchaste. For this reason, the magistrate condemned her to death. To prove her innocence, she carried water in a sieve before the judges. As Petrarch writes:

> Among the others was the vestal maid
> Who that she might be free of ill report
> Sped boldly to the Tiber, and from thence
> Brought water to her temple in a sieve.[13]

The Goddess Vesta was believed to be a virgin and a lover of solitude, as Virgil writes in the fourth book of the *Aeneid*:

> By the Lar of Assaracus, and by hoary Vesta's shrine.[14]

Notice that, here, Virgil uses the word "penetralia" to indicate secluded places, remote from the crowd. Praising Laura for her solitude, Petrarch says in a *canzone*:

> Within there could be seen a lofty throne
> of diamond squarely cut, without a fault,
> on which the lovely lady sat alone.[15]

---

13. Petrarch, *Trionfo della pudicizia*, 148–51: "Fra l'altre la vestal vergine pia, / Che baldanzosamente corse al Tibro, / E per purgarsi d'ogni fama ria / portò del fiume al tempio acqua col cribro." (Petrarca, *Opere. Canzoniere, Trionfi, Familiarum Rerum Libri con testo a fronte*, vol. I. [Firenze: Sansoni, 1990]). For the English translation see Petrarch, *The Triumphs*, trans. Ernest Hatch Wilkins (Chicago: University of Chicago Press, 1962), 45.

14. Virgil, *Aeneid*, trans. H. Rushton Fairclough (Cambridge, MA: Harvard University Press, 1999–2000) IX.259, p. 133: "Assaracique larem et canae penetralia Vestae." In this passage, Ascanius solemnly addresses Nisus by invoking the deities of his household (the Lar of Assaracus) and Vesta's shrine. Marinella is interested in Virgil's use of the word "penetralia."

15. Petrarca, *Canzoniere*, ed. Marco Santagata (Milano: Mondadori, 1996), 325.23–26. "D'un bel diamante quadro et mai non scemo / Vi si vedea nel mezzo un seggio altero, / Ove sola sedea la bella donna." The translation is from Petrarch, *The Canzoniere, or Rerum Vulgarium Fragmenta*, trans. Mark Musa (Bloomington: Indiana University Press, 1999), 449.

Oh, how pleasing solitude is! She was sitting alone, accompanied only by her thoughts. When you are sitting, your mind is resting and is not harassed by the senses. It can therefore retrieve the truth of the most secret things Nature hides in her womb. In this peace, your mind becomes perfect. This is why many men, indeed the most learned philosophers and inventors of the arts, embrace seclusion that they might contemplate the secret Essences and penetrate nature's hidden treasures. Nothing raises our minds to the heights of understanding more than withdrawing from common practices. Withdrawn into itself, our mind opens its eyes, which are as sharp as the lynx's in the darkness.

So, too, will you, valorous women, be able to fully understand what is useful and what is dangerous in your home's affairs by remaining within the domestic walls. As your mind is not perturbed by the confusion that always fills the world, with industrious ways you will find various ornaments to make your house shine and enrich it with new excellence. If you desire to be known for your wise womanly activity, you can rest assured that your fame will not be confined within narrow walls, but will spread in such a way that its brilliant light will shine throughout the entire universe. The fire that burns enclosed in a grand palace shows its splendor through an opening, and it appears more beautiful and noble when it emerges like a secret from its surrounding walls. Diamonds are no less precious in their native dwellings than when they are mined and artfully prepared to adorn royal crowns.

Some people believe that women are secluded because men want to keep them locked up, that they might remain inexperienced in the affairs of the world and become inept and of little courage and worth. I myself made such a claim in my book *The Nobility and Excellence of Women*. After considering this issue with more mature judgment, however, I now conclude that women's condition has not been devised or brought about by resentful souls, but rather derives from natural and divine providence and will. We can easily prove this to be true. Were women's seclusion the result of violence, it would not have lasted for so many centuries and millennia. Violent practices do not last long.[16] Some may object and claim that, according to historians,

16. In this remarkable passage, Marinella recalls the bellicose tract of her youth only to retract its proud pronouncements. In claiming that "violent practices do not last long,"

the Amazons were under their own rule for a long time.[17] To them I reply that compared with the time the Amazons spent with men, their independent rule did not last long. Indeed, what comes from Nature and God cannot be taken away.

Therefore, we maintain that women were kept within domestic walls not by men's evil desire to dominate them or by some other external force, but by God and Nature. With the same immense knowledge out of which He created everything, God, who built the universe with wisdom and providence, gave natural and different tasks to the male and the female. He knew that were they assigned the same tasks, they would not achieve a perfect life. In light of their different duties, He gave them different constitutions, making men the stronger and tougher of the two. Women also possess strength, but theirs is of a more modest and gentle kind, that they might be happy in ruling over everything in their houses and rest satisfied without complaint. Stronger and more resilient, men can withstand danger, travel, and other difficulties to gain all that is necessary for the home and family. Sweat would be wasted, fatigue and tribulation would be useless, and all profit would be lost had they been given equal strength and virility and were both keen to gain things, while neither attended to preserve what had been gained. Preservation is as praiseworthy as acquisition. Therefore God and nature, who never lack in what is necessary and never act uselessly, created one to be strong and able, and the other to be gentle and not as strong. This was done in light of the benefits these different tasks provide. While the woman takes care of the house, the man conducts commerce and deals outside of the house, that these different tasks might result in harmonious peace and civil happiness.

As I said, God gave courage and audacity to one of these creatures and beauty and grace to the other. As women are tender and delicate, it is not appropriate for them to travel, suffer, and exhaust themselves. The excessive suffering that travel entails does not agree

---

Marinella may have remembered the Latin phrase "nil violentum durabile" Boccaccio used to introduce Symiamira's demise in *De mulieribus claris* XCIX, 14.

17. Marinella could be referring to Strabo, who in *Geografia*, XI.5.1–4 describes the Amazons' habits and self-governing practices (Strabo, *Geography*, trans. Horace L. Jones [Cambridge, MA: Harvard University Press, 1928, rpt 1988], vol. 5, 233–39). Alfonso Bonaccioli had published an Italian translation of Strabo's work in Venice in 1562.

with their nature. This is why Virgil's Gallus tells Lycoris, who is leaving to follow Antonius to France:

> While you, far from your native soil—O that I could
> but disbelieve such a tale!—gaze, heartless one, on Al-
> pine snows and the frozen Rhine, apart from me, all
> alone. Ah, may the frosts not harm you! Ah, may the
> jagged ice not cut your tender feet![18]

This is what Gallus, in love and tearful, said for fear that suffering would make his beloved's beauty disappear. He did not think it appropriate for her delicate nature to remain in such a rough environment. He believed that, in her beauty and delicacy, she should preserve such treasure in the shade, tranquility, and peace of her home. Guarding the harvest is no less laudable than harvesting. The labor of accumulating wealth would be pointless if that wealth were not guarded and preserved. This is how households prosper, and households are part of the city. Many households form hamlets, which in turn form fortified villages and cities. Every city is made of households, as Aristotle says.[19]

Acquisition and preservation bring forth wealth, which produces liberal and magnificent deeds, such as the building of temples and palaces and the establishment of public places devoted to virtues, studies, and noble actions. Silver and gold are the foundation of nobility and wealth, and they allow for great and wonderful works.

Different tasks make for a happy union between man and woman, giving rise to famous and excellent households that, in turn, form cities and glorious and praiseworthy civil societies. This is why God and His minister Nature have established that women spontaneously—and not out of obligation—exercise their virtue at home. For

---

18. Virgil, *Eclogues*, X.46–49: "Tu procul a patria (nec sit mihi credere tantum) / Alpinas, a! dura, nives et frigora Rheni / me sine sola vides. a, te ne frigora laedant! / a, tibi ne teneras glacies secet aspera plantas!" Trans. H. Rushton Fairclough, rev. G. P. Goold (Cambridge, MA: Harvard University Press, 1999), 93.

19. Aristotle, *Politics*, I.i.7 (1252b16): "Omnis enim civitas ex domibus constat." Marinella always quotes Aristotle's *Politics* in Latin using the translation by Leonardo Bruni (*Politicorum libri VIII latine ex versione Leonardi Aretini* [Roma: E. Silber, 1492]), which includes the commentary of St.Thomas Aquinas.

civil society to be perfect, acquisition and preservation are equally necessary.

These two great makers of the world, God and His servant Nature, mindful of the good, comfort and universal happiness of the human being, imposed different burdens upon those with a strong constitution and those with a pleasant and light one. The stronger, braver person cannot remain in the peace of the home because he cannot tolerate extended rest. By the same token, the more delicate and gentle person can tolerate neither excessive suffering nor travel and danger. Not everyone is like Mithridates's wife who, disguised as a man, followed her banished husband and, overcoming her nature, triumphed over hardship, adversity, and misfortune.[20]

Rejoice in your loneliness, my friends, and know that you enjoy a gift, namely, a happy life that is far from the world's troubles, a life in which resides God's greatness and that of sacred things, kings, emperors, and all those in positions of dignity and supremacy. They all avoid showing themselves to the masses and refuse to satisfy other people's desire to see them. They believe that by showing themselves, they will gain not in honor, but in obscurity, like small lights that appear to lose their splendor when overcome by a greater light.

Nature always keeps and shelters the best and most important parts in the best places, such as the heart which, being the noblest part, is the sensitive principle that rules over the senses' operations. As the origin and principle of life, the heart is more important than other parts, and this is why Nature put it in the safest and most protected part of the body. Man imitates nature by hiding and concealing gold and precious gems, which are desired and loved, from greedy hands.

In the same way, our soul, although it is said to be "entire in the whole body and whole in every part,"[21] nevertheless resides in the heart because of its dignity and purity.

---

20. Hypsicratea, Mithridates's wife, who followed her husband in the war against the Romans, was a proverbial example of marital love and courage. See for instance Giovanni Boccaccio, *Filocolo*, ed. Enzo Quaglio (Milano: Mondadori, 1967), I.23.

21. "Tota in toto et tota in qualibet parte," Marinella writes. Raymond B. Waddington summarizes the history of this concept, which can be traced back to Plato (*Sophist*, 244e–245d) and was discussed by St. Thomas Aquinas (*Summa contra gentiles*, 2.72). "By the beginning of the sixteenth century, this doctrine had crystallized in a standard Latin formula, *tota in*

Seclusion is desired not only by very wise men but also by an infinite number of the friends of heaven, such as Hilarion and Paul, the first hermit,[22] and many others who, like shining gems, adorned the beauty of Paradise in the solitude of abandoned hermitages. Far from noise and crowds, these happy men could devote their minds to God and know and desire the goodness of His eternal providence, which is the supreme contemplative happiness. In the same way, women, in the tranquility of their seclusion, can enjoy the rewards of contemplation and lift their minds to God, comprehending the greatness of His mercy in the products of His clemency. They should therefore praise, rather than despise, Gorgias of Leontini, who honored women so much that he wanted the reputation born from their actions to live within domestic walls, where all excellence is hidden and sheltered.

In regard to women's nobility, Francesco Patrizio said that women should rarely leave their homes because they are too precious.[23] He does not approve, therefore, of their going outside their homes. It is inside the home that the results of their activity must be witnessed, and here also that their reputations, which is based in preserving wealth with prudence and wisdom and without complaint, must be kept. They must consider that had God, the Great Master, formed men and women of equal physical strength such that both were capable of traveling and conducting business and neither ruled over wealth and acquisition, all gain would be in vain. But, as the

---

toto, et tota in qualibet parte, and become a philosophic commonplace. It was available, broadly speaking, through two lines of intellectual descent, one more scholastic and Christian in its bearings and the other more humanistic and Neoplatonic" (Waddington, *Aretino's Satyr: Sexuality, Satire, and Self-Projection in Sixteenth-Century Literature and Art* [Toronto: University of Toronto Press, 2004], 112–13).

22. Marinella might have been familiar with St. Jerome's accounts of the lives of St. Hilarion and St. Paul the Hermit. For a modern edition see *Vita degli eremiti Paolo, Ilarione e Malco* (Roma: Città nuova, 1996).

23. "Mulieres raro egredi e domo debent," Marinella quotes. I was unable to find the exact reference. Francesco Patrizi (1529-1597) studied medicine at the University of Padua, was an active participant to the literary and philosophical debates of his times, and spent several years in Venice, where he could possibly have met members of the Marinelli household. He is always quoted as an undisputed authority in *Exhortations*. See Lina Bolzoni, *L'universo dei poemi possibili. Studi su Francesco Patrizi da Cherso* (Roma: Bulzoni, 1980) 17–26, and Cesare Vasoli, *Francesco Patrizi da Cherso* (Roma: Bulzoni, 1989), IX-XIII.

home must also be ministered, women were formed such that they adjust to tranquility and are satisfied with ruling over the accumulated wealth, while men were granted strength and vigor, that they might make their households happy and prosperous with their toil and with women's help, prudence, and skills.

Households are part of the city. If they are wealthy, well administered, and rich in virtue, so, too, will be the cities. It is necessary for the parts to correspond to the whole. Therefore, for the city to be strong and praiseworthy, the households must be likewise strong.

You have heard me praise the excellence of solitude and seclusion. I also want you to know that men envy the tranquility of your peace. Tell me in faith, my most beloved ladies: Do you think that Achilles would have donned a woman's skirt had he not loved seclusion? But as he desired your peace and rest, he found refuge among the daughters of King Lycomedes. That Thetis hid him to shelter him from the Trojan War is false.[24] Your peace, my friends, which is the goal of labor and effort, is too sweet. We labor that we might rest, just as we fight that we might enjoy peace. But you, without much effort, enjoy the peace that God gave you at creation.

Even Hercules, who held the skies on his shoulders, retired in Omphale's sweet seclusion, and took more pleasure in that woman's solitary peace than in her beautiful face.[25] Many other men retreat to solitude with women and learn embroidery and quilting, taking pleasure in this art and in the rest it provides. If not publicly, then at least privately, they can enjoy womanly glory and consolation.

---

24. See Statius's unfinished epic *Achilleid* where Thetis, afraid that her son Achilles will die in the Trojan war, hides him among the daughters of King Lycomedes. Notice however that Marinella, departing from Statius, attributes Achilles's stay among women to his choice. See Statius, *Thebaid, Achilleid*, trans. D. R. Shackleton Bailey (Cambridge, MA: Harvard University Press, 2003), I.207ff (Loeb, 329ff).

25. Apollodorus narrates how the oracle of Delphi condemned Hercules, guilty of murder, to live as a slave. Omphales bought him, dressed him as a woman, and obliged him to perform domestic chores. In this case, as in that of Achilles, Marinella attributes the hero's adoption of a woman's lifestyle to his personal and free choice, a departure from her sources. See Apollodorus, *Library*, trans. Sir James George Frazer, 2 vols. (Cambridge, MA: Harvard University Press, 1977, 1979), vol. 1,II.vi.3–4 (Loeb 241–45).

2. FROM THIS ADVICE YOU WILL LEARN THAT IT IS LAUDABLE TO ATTEND TO ONE'S ACTIVITIES AND TASKS AND THAT THE STUDY OF LITERATURE IS A USELESS VANITY OF LITTLE PROFIT.

When, on occasion, I recall the maxim of the great legislator Gorgias, "may a woman's reputation never abandon the protection of the home,"[26] I cannot but praise it as the saying of a prudent and wise man. Inspired by the affection and love I feel toward my sex, I will express my opinion without ever straying far from that of such a great man.

Some women are not happy for their success to remain all but buried within domestic walls; they want their names to appear worthy of glory and praise among the people because of their learning and wisdom. They hope this will bring them great honor. It is true that knowledge, were it appreciated, would make us happy in all human endeavors, but this is not the case. Many women, blinded by vain hope, devote themselves to studying. Some succeed, some do not—the same is true of men—but I will nevertheless exhort women to avoid this torment of the mind and look after their own virtue in order to escape disappointment, fatigue, and afflictions of the soul.

If every woman could have what she wants—that is, fame and praise—then she should pursue her ambitions, for nothing is sweeter than obtaining what one anxiously desires.

> Every man is accomplished in his own art and fails in the others.[27]

Similarly, Plato maintains that everyone must attend to their own art. Therefore, she who devotes her mind to learning—a domain that does not belong to her—will rarely be happy. Her mother and sister, seeing her turn her thoughts to something unusual, will reproach her. They will scold and chastise her for refusing to lay her hand to feminine tasks and womanly chores and choosing instead to use her intellect to pursue the vanity of difficult disciplines. They will there-

26. This exhortation, too, begins with a reference to Gorgias: "nesciat fama mulieris exire e septu domus." See above, n7.

27. "Omnis homo in arte propria perficitur, in aliena depravatur." Unknown source.

fore mock her and grudgingly withstand the sight of her wasting time on occupations of which they do not approve.

If she becomes learned, then sleepless Envy will turn its livid and malevolent eyes on her. Her neighbors and friends will persecute her. While pretending to praise her, they will in fact pierce her with malevolent tongues, believing she wants to raise herself above others. She will therefore hear not a single kind or encouraging word, but only insincere words and deceitful lies. The pangs will gnaw at her heart, and the wisdom she gains will bring her no joy, even if it chases sadness away.

But if you attend to knitting and other womanly occupations, then your family and others will praise you because they will know that you are not trying to rise above them with new ideas. You will therefore always be happy and content, your face serene and your heart satisfied, far from emulation and reproach.

To avoid writing tasteless and dull compositions, you must put hard work and suffering into learning poetry and philosophy. Your work requires sweet words and a peaceful countenance, rather than wrathful sentences and a scornful appearance. As Guarino says:

> The soaring swan requires an easy nest,
> A sky unclouded and sweet food, to sing.
> None climbs Parnassus with a load of cares.[28]

If, day after day, you progress in your studies, then animosity will rise with its angry spurs against you, like a terrible storm. Your family will insult you with hostile words, mock you, and flee you. The more praiseworthy you are, the more they will hate you without reason. Knowledge may well be divine, and finding something worthier and more noble and graceful would be impossible, if it were appreciated by the world. However, since it is not, it generates such difficulties. So far, your virtuous efforts have yielded great stress and little happiness and peace, as you are scorned and hated by your relatives

---

28. Giovan Battista Guarini, *Il pastor fido* (Milano: Mursia, 1977), Act V, Scene 1: "Lieto nido, esca dolce aura cortese / Bramano i Cigni; e non si va in Parnaso / Colle cure mordaci." For the English translation see Battista Guarini, *The Faithful Shepherd*, trans. Thomas Sheridan (Newark, NJ: University of Delaware Press, 1989), 152–53.

and friends. These are the fruits literature bears, and this is why many people wisely avoid it.

When your works begin to circulate in men's hands, some will make unpleasant faces when reading them, as if they had tasted a bitter fruit. Others will neither praise nor criticize you, but rather say that you are not too bad, for a woman. Hearing that you are not too bad "for a woman" will pain you. You infer from these words that you know very little, since, for the most part, women do not attend to such things. Therefore, to be declared "not bad for a woman" is tantamount to being declared "not bad for someone who has little or no expertise in literature." These remarks make you suffer and deprive you of the praise that you so eagerly seek and that is your due for having overcome ordinary limits.

Others, after barely looking at your compositions, put them aside and declare them womanly writings of little wisdom and no wit. Hearing this, someone who has started reading your work stops and puts it aside. All of your efforts, therefore, are useless, and, much to your sorrow, your books become the prey of moths. This also happens to many works written by men, however replete with wisdom and learning.

Some will read your works but out of envy refuse to praise them. With scornful and malevolent eyes they will put them aside, no matter their worth, to give you no reason to rejoice in your heart. I do not know whether envy causes them to behave this way, but may God forgive them.

Others will take one of your writings and at a glance, having read none of it, pronounce that since it was written by a woman, it cannot be good "for you can't give to another what you don't have yourself."[29] They will laugh and move on. I can't imagine your outrage and sorrow at hearing these contemptuous words, and how your heart burns with resentment and rage.

If you point out that many praise you and call you the wonder of your century, others will answer that your admirers are simply flatterers and liars who want you to believe things that are not true. They torment you with these words and lead you to believe that the praise

---

29. Plato's *Symposium* (197A) is a possible source of the Latin proverb Marinella quotes: "Nemo dat, quod non habet."

is false flattery intended to inflate your opinion of yourself. You, who believed you could amaze the world with your talent and your writings, are left disappointed, regretful, and almost scorned. Your heart receives nothing but poison and sharp arrows. After so many sleepless nights, and so much sweat and labor, you reap thorns and bitter fruits instead of honor and rewards. You now come to understand that cultivating one's own art and talent is laudable and fair.

If your works are acute, philosophical, and noble, people will say that a woman, whose weak mind does not reach the heavens, could not have written them and that a man endowed with wisdom and learning must have. They will not be able to even imagine that a woman may possess enough knowledge as to compete with them. Therefore, they will not want to admit that a well-written and well-structured poem may have been written by a woman. They will say that it must have been written by her friend or lover, who ascribed the work to her just to please her. "I am surprised; this is not a woman's work. It is a disguise. A donkey can wear a lion's skin, and even the crow showed up dressed in eagle's feathers."[30] This is how you remain deprived of the glory that you deserve because of your efforts, suffering, and many sleepless nights.

Still others will barely glance at one of your works. Without even reading it, they will put it aside and say: "This woman should lay her hand to the spindle and the needle rather than to the pen. Things that lie outside of one's nature cannot be done well; if shoemaker did a blacksmith's job, he wouldn't do it well. A carpenter's efforts at the art of a jewel-maker would be laughable, as would a sailor's at that of a carriage-builder. Masters are great in their own arts, but they do not gain merit in those of others."

Such sayings and critiques will bring you neither glory nor satisfaction. Therefore you who thought you were glorious and noble will find yourself deprived of the honorable prize you so desired; you who thought yourself equal almost to the divine Muses, your qualities appreciated and honored by princes, lords, and kings, will be sent away,

---

30. Quoting an imaginary detractor, Marinella refers to two of Aesop's fables. In the first, a donkey dressed in a lion's skin does not succeed in scaring a fox; in the second, a crow wears other birds' feathers to look more beautiful. See Aesop, *The Complete Fables*, trans. Olivia and Robert Temple (New York: Penguin, 1998), 199 and 119.

despised, and persecuted by avarice and the lack of appreciation that befalls virtuous people.

Women in particular, who should honor you, will behave even worse than men; this is why you should not pursue learning, my beloved women, even though knowledge is happiness itself. When you are rich in knowledge, you do not need anything else. Knowledge itself is the root of all good and all consolation.

I will never believe that any woman writes in order to accumulate wealth, because such gain is trivial compared to her worth, and too lowly a reward for the greatness of her virtue. Rather, women have written to gain honor, a prize worth the immense effort it requires. Maecenas no longer lives, and ancient munificence is dead; no longer do you find poets who, like Horace, are made rich by princes. Gone are the splendors of Rome, which brought light to every corner of the world. For this reason, the learned and gentle Stigliani regretted the meagerness and avarice of our times in an ingenious sonnet:

> I misunderstood the Muses at first;
> For they are false and sterile Virgins,
> And the laurel brings forth but bitter fruit.[31]

Ariosto, too, complained about his times while praising the old ones and showed how important it is for rulers to be honored by learned people:

> What has brought them their sublime renown have
> been the writers honored with gifts of palaces and
> great estates donated by these heroes' descendants.[32]

---

31. "Mal seppi de le Muse intender pria; / Perché finte sian vergini infeconde, / né frutto altro che amaro il lauro dia." Stigliani's sonnet is in *Delle rime del signor Tomaso Stigliani, parte prima. Con breui dichiarationi in fronte à ciascun componimento, fatte dal signor Scipione Calcagnini* (Venetia: Ciotti, 1605), 52. This poem is addressed to Celio Magno and is followed by a sonnet in praise of Lucrezia Marinella.

32. Ariosto, *Orlando Furioso*, XXXV.25. "Ma i donati palazzi e le gran ville / Da i descendenti lor, gli ha fatto porre / In questi senza fin sublimi honori / Da l'honorate man de gli scrittori." Lodovico Ariosto, *Orlando furioso*, trans. Guido Waldman (New York: Oxford University Press, 1974), 425.

Guarino complained about the courts—and perhaps even more about those who rule them—when he said in his *Faithful Shepherd*:

> But in this age (inhuman age!)
> The art of poetry is made too base.[33]

The world does not appreciate those who deserve praise and despises rather than honors them. We can learn this from the fact that Homer, though a very worthy and learned man, was neither made rich nor received any favors. On the contrary, he was left in the straits of poverty, and asked the Milesians to give him the food sufficient for a frugal life. Their assembly did not accept this honest request. In spite of his fame, they refused to allow the citizens to feed him. Homer was understandably overcome with pain and contempt for such ingratitude, and said:

> Milesians are not fools, yet they behave like fools.[34]

Gifts number among the honors that rulers distribute to reward other people's virtue, according to their merits (*secundum merita*). Aristotle mentions this practice in his chapter on justice when he discusses retributive justice and shows that rulers must distribute gifts and honors according to merit. For them to be distributed differently because of the rulers' flaws (*propter vitium Principum*) would be unfair. Nevertheless, evil men are often pleasing to princes, as Ariosto says of

> Those who infest the courts and are better welcomed
> there than men of integrity and worth.[35]

---

33. Guarini, *Il pastor fido*, Act V, Scene 1.181–82. "Ma oggi è fatta (oh secolo inumano!) / l'arte del poetar troppo infelice."

34. "Milesii quidem prudentes sunt, sed tamen agunt ea quae imprudentes solent." St. Thomas Aquinas expresses a similar concept: "Milesii non sunt stulti, sed operantur similia opera operibus stultorum" (St. Thomas Aquinas, *Sententia Ethicorum*, lib. 7 l. 8 n. 8) and also "Milesii quidem stulti non sunt, operantur autem qualia stulti" (*Quaestiones disputatae de malo*, q. 8 a. 2 s.c. 7). All the references to St. Thomas Aquinas are from http://www.corpusthomisticum.org

35. Ariosto, *Orlando furioso*, XXXV.20: "che viveno alle corti e che vi sono / più grati assai che il virtuoso e il buono." Trans. Waldman, 424.

These days, the liberality of patrons has been forgotten, as I said earlier. I do not know whether to attribute this to the great number of writers or to the avarice of our time, but I must tell you this: not only will you not receive the rich rewards Maecenas gave to his friends the writers; you will be deprived even of the favors and concessions that could effortlessly be granted to deserving people and that instead are enjoyed by many who are without virtue, and yet obtain what should be the reward of virtue.

When you think of this, you cannot help but complain. Disdain and grave sorrow, quite understandably, will torment your soul when you see that vice is rewarded and virtue chased away. Although I speak here in terms of prizes and gifts that are the due of human virtue, I mean to imply neither that the reward of knowledge is gold, silver, or something of that sort, nor that noble minds would undertake such a difficult enterprise to gain them. They are inspired rather by their desire for fame, which is a light, like a precious gem, so desirable that no soul is too rough, no mind too removed from civilization that it does not desire to be like Argus and admire its beauty with a thousand eyes.[36]

What will I say then, my beloved ladies? I will say "With what is too much for you meddle not."[37] Do not desire something that raises the mind to great things, only to let it precipitately fall afterward.

You are mortal, but you aspire to things that are immortal.[38]

I trust that in your low condition you will not be afraid of falling, nor will you imitate the fate of Phaeton who, eager for glory, fell and died.[39] Let us put knowledge aside; it is hazardous to our health. It is rare that those who pursue knowledge enjoy the treasure of glory, although it is dearer and more desirable than gold and pre-

---

36. Argus is the one-hundred-eyed giant of Greek mythology.

37. Ecclesiasticus 3:22: "Altiora te ne quaesieris." All references to the Bible are from http://www.vatican.va/archive/ITA0001/_INDEX.HTM

38. Ovid, *Metamorphoses*, II.55: "tua sors mortalis, non est mortale, quod optas." Trans. Frank Justus Miller, 2 vols. (Cambridge, MA: Harvard University Press, 1971), 65.

39. In Ovid's version of the story (*Metamorphoses* II.154–358), Phaeton loses control of the chariot he had borrowed from his father Helios and is eventually struck down by Zeus.

cious stones. To return to the disadvantages knowledge entails, I will say that if you progress in philosophy and poetry, many will despise you for fear of being surpassed by you; therefore Envy, armed with Malevolence, will hate and persecute you with the poisoned knife of its tongue and will prevent you from enjoying the rewards of your decision to study literature—a discipline from which I beg you to stay away as from something bad and dangerous. Plato writes that nobody wants their friends or lovers to become philosophers, for fear that they will become more learned than they are. To avoid being offended and neglected, men use all kinds of tricks to keep their friends and lovers devoid of all knowledge, inept and ignorant. However, I would not want you to believe that I am trying to discourage you from pursuing literature because I am afraid of being surpassed by you. This would be the act of an envious soul, not that of a heart that truly loves you as I do. As I faithfully love you, I desire that you put aside your vain passion for literature and thereby escape the damage, distaste, and resentment that always accompanies it. This way you will live happily and will care more for yourself than for a vain and fleeting shadow.

I will always exhort women to practice the virtues of temperance, goodness, justice, and religion and to attend to their natural womanly works because I know that the virtues that earn women praise and glory are industriousness, diligence, and parsimony. Everyone appreciates these qualities, whereas no one appreciates those of a woman of letters. While she is adorned by the qualities that allow her to climb the mountain of glory, men dislike her because they think, as I said, that she wants to become equal or superior to them. Therefore, they denigrate everything good and learned in your compositions in order to clip the wings of your glory that is beginning to soar. They will not even consider whether your works are good because humans naturally tend to destroy each other's reputation. This is why Seneca says that men's tongue is hasty in its judgment.[40]

Men will not be alone in denigrating your rare qualities. Your female friends, relatives, and sisters, touched by silent spite, will look at you with malevolent eyes for fear of appearing inferior next to you.

40. This sentence ("Lingua hominum ad iudicia praeceps") is attributed to Seneca in a sixteenth-century compendium of maxims (Pierre Lagnier, *Ex M.T. Cicerone insignium sententiarum [...] compendium* [Lyon: Jean de Tournes and Guillaume Gazeau, 1552] 345).

Therefore, you will be avoided rather than loved and appreciated, by both women and men, who are dominated by ignorance.

A learned man does not want to compete with a learned woman. I can almost hear him reason in his heart: how can I with all my knowledge be equal to a woman whose only prerogatives are the distaff and the thread that adorns it? He feels despised and unappreciated. He feels that his knowledge is diminished, as it happens when two enemy plants are placed side by side. Men do not realize that a woman's intellect may be equal to theirs, nor do they understand that women can become learned as easily as men.

This is why women's works do not receive glory or appreciation, although they are better than, or at least equal to, those written by men. Men do not want a woman as their partner in knowledge, and thus you are left almost forsaken. Other women are hostile, too, because they are jealous of men's favors and fear that you will be honored and admired for your knowledge, while they, neglected, will be left behind. Therefore, they will not love and honor you, but rather look at you malevolently.

Therefore, I will exhort the woman who wants to live happily, contentedly, and far from envy, to cherish and follow her own virtue, without trying to surpass other women in inappropriate ways. This way you will be appreciated and well regarded by both sexes. Attending to the business of the household is worthy of praise. Women who love science are called monsters and marvels because they are so rare, but matrons who bring honor and prosperity to their households deserve to be loved, honored, and appreciated. If you desire glory, you can obtain it without consuming your intellect in things that are dangerous. It is not necessary to torment your mind and body and become livid, thin, pale, and full of melancholy, like those Harpies who, according to Ariosto, came to soil the Ethiopian King's table. Listen, in faith, o my beloved:

> They were a swarm of seven, all with pale, wasted
> women's faces, emaciated and wizened by constant
> hunger, ghastlier than death's hands.[41]

41. Ariosto, *Orlando furioso*, XXXIII.120. "Erano sette in una schiera e tutte / Faccie di donna avean pallide e smorte / Per lunga fame attenuate e asciutte / Orribili a veder più che

Please consider the seriousness of this damage. Your beauty disappears and turns into something as ugly as anything Ovid has ever described. Unbeknownst to you, your praised grace and countenance flees. Your gracious color, your features, your serene forehead, all disappear; they are ruined and turned into melancholic sadness because of your thinness and pallor. You are no longer considered beautiful, but rather ugly and disagreeable.What's worse, studying brings little benefit. Many have neglected it and loved life and health more than knowledge and wisdom. People who care not for life and health deserve to be included as dimwitted minds of low caliber in Garzoni's discourse,[42] or in Plato's *Gorgias* and his other works.

Some say that women who attend to literature, rather than being useful, are useless to the home and the city. Ariosto confirms this:

> Many of you have left, and are leaving, your needles
> and fabrics to visit the Muses at the source of Hippo-
> crene.[43]

They left the needle and the cloth. Therefore, one can conclude, they are useless because women should handle the loom and the needle, which are womanly tools.[44] The household suffers if this essential work is not performed, and women cannot imitate Minerva by pursuing knowledge while also attending to womanly tasks:

> There are twelve hours in a day.[45]

---

la morte." Trans. Waldman, 409–10.

42. Marinella is probably referring to Discourse XIX ("De' pazzi disperati" [On Desperate Madmen]) in Tomaso Garzoni's *L'ospitale de'pazzi incurabili* (The Hospital of the Uncurable Madmen), first published in 1586 in Venice. See pp. 113–16 in Stefano Barelli's modern edition (Rome-Padua: Antenore, 2004).

43. Ariosto, *Orlando furioso*, XXXVII, 14: "Poiché molte lasciando l'ago e 'l panno/ [...] Al fonte d'Aganippe andate e vanno" (trans. Waldman, 442). The fountain of Aganippe (or Hippocrene), on Mount Helicon, was sacred to the Muses, and drinking its waters was believed to induce poetic inspiration.

44. Marinella misrepresents Ariosto's lines which praise, rather than criticize, learned women.

45. "Sunt duodecim orae diei," Marinella writes, paraphrasing Christ's question in John 11:9: "Nonne duodecim orae sunt diei"("Are there not twelve hours in a day?").

Many say that devoting oneself to two arts that demand time and intellect is an arduous and difficult enterprise. I say, on the contrary, that it is easy to attend to both, because ruling over your household is a pastime compared to the study of intellectual disciplines.[46]

We will practice our rule over the household in order to relax (*gratia relaxationis*), because Minerva is not only the goddess of wisdom and arms, but also the goddess of sewing and spinning, which are of little consequence to her great intellect. Therefore, it should not be surprising if women pursued knowledge while remaining diligent and industrious in the affairs of the home, because this goddess, in whose footsteps women want to follow, proves herself perfect in many domains. Many, however, say that "a heart that goes two ways shall not have success."[47] You cannot properly apply yourself to two tasks because, inevitably, you will like one and despise the other. It is like lighting two fires at a short distance from one another: neither one will give light. Some say that if a woman devotes herself to both activities she will not shine in either one. Therefore, to avoid this problem, I maintain that women should practice the art that comes naturally and is proper to them. If they attend to both occupations, one will suffer while the other prospers. It is impossible to divide one's heart in two.

Therefore it is appropriate for you to remain content within the walls of your home, with a tranquil soul. Like a solitary sparrow,[48] distant from everybody and happy with yourself, you will attend to your duties while enjoying the sweetness of your song, without envying other people's fame. With a tranquil soul, you will enjoy within the boundaries of domesticity the reputation that springs from goodness, chastity, and other necessary virtues. Glory is similar to the sound of a timbal or a harmonic concert. Nothing is left when the music stops. Pride is like a shadow: once its cause is taken away, it, too, disappears;

---

46. Marinella's argument becomes condensed and obscure at this point. She seems to admit that women can take care of their household as well as practice literature, but then she inserts a Latin sentence ("Ex duobus in actu non fit tertium in natura nisi unum fit tamquam materia") inspired by the Aristotelian law of the excluded middle (see in particular *Metaphysics*, IV.vi [1101b24–1012a28]), which implies the exact opposite.

47. Ecclesiasticus 3:28: "Cor ingrediens duas vias non habebit successus".

48. From Psalms 102:8, the image of the solitary sparrow reached Petrarch (*Canzoniere* 226) to fly all the way to the 19th century and Giacomo Leopardi.

pride is vanity and the childish blabber of people of little value and intellect—rather than people of deep knowledge and wisdom. Glory is a dream that, like an image impressed in water, does not retain that which created it. Tasso in his *Goffredo* compares it to dreams:

> What men call praise and valor—a mere name,
> an idol only, no reality!
> That fame which so attracts your pride, O men,
> which sounds and seems so sweet, what can it be
> but an echo, a dream, or even a dream's shade—
> with every wind it must dissolve and fade.[49]

Therefore, I invite you to flee this mutable wind, this echo that does not correspond to your desires, this dream full of fallacies, this fleeting and vain shadow, and instead pursue truth—something firm, useful, stable, and laudable. Pursuing knowledge and poetry—which are mere blabber—is not a real task, and besides, success can only rarely be achieved. It is an exhausting, harmful, laborious, and problem-ridden task because, when the mind is busy studying, the senses and the vegetative and sensitive soul cannot exercise their faculties. Learned speculations generate in the mind either near slumber or ecstasy. Hence, the nutritive virtue is oppressed and almost asleep, leading to poor physical health. Furthermore, intense studying propels you toward old age.

I continue to learn many things as I grow old.[50]

Listen, my friends, and especially you who spend the whole day trying to make yourselves more beautiful. Studying makes you

---

49. Tasso, *Gerusalemme liberata*, XIV.63: "Nomi senza soggetto, idoli sono, / Ciò che pregio, e valore il volgo appella. / La fama, che invaghisce a un dolce suono / Voi, superbi mortali, e par si bella, / È un eco un sogno, anzi di un sogno, un'ombra, / Che in picciol tempo si dilegua e sgombra." Trans. Esolen, 282.

50. Pseudo-Plato, *Rival Lovers*, 133C, trans. Jeffrey Mitscherling, in Plato, *Complete Works*, ed. John M. Cooper and D. S. Hutchinson (Indianapolis, IN: Hackett Publishing Co., 1997), 620. The exact sentence Marinella quotes ("Discenti assidue multa senecta venit") can be found in *De philosophia vel amatores*, in *Omnia divini Platonis opera*, trans. Marsilio Ficino, ed. Simon Grynaeus (Basil: Froben, 1546) Cf. Plutarch, *Vitarum parallelarum* 1761–62, 241.

old, deprives you of beauty and health, and gives you a pale, sad, and melancholy countenance. Add to this the sorrow that is brought by the criticism of your work, which wounds your soul with the sharpness of a spear. After working so hard, you will not be happy and content, but live in pain and sorrow, sad and burdened by a thousand illnesses. Sometimes you will accuse your bad luck, sometimes envy; sometimes you will complain that virtue is not appreciated and your works not welcomed—although this fate also befalls the works of wise men, so you have little reason to complain. Competition and ambition, which fill the minds and souls of learned people, will torment you. Your desire that other people's learning be considered inferior to yours will persecute and torment you so much that you will deem happy those who are free from such feelings and lead a calm and contented life, far from envy and emulation.

If sometimes you enjoy some word of praise, glory, and consolation, you will say:

O honey scarce, all vinegar and aloe.[51]

Encouraging words will raise you to the stars, but you will remain like the tortoise who wanted to fly and was carried by an eagle into the sky. When the tortoise saw itself so high above the ground, it said: "Let me go, and I will fly for myself." Once released, it fell to the ground and died.[52]

One sentence in your praise lifted you to the stars. Sentences that criticize you—which are numerous, due to our natural inclination toward evil—will slap you and make you fall down with an immortal blow. Little trace will be left of your glory. How many men who exposed themselves to danger in the midst of horrible battles of fire and arrows thought they had gained immortal glory with their wonderful deeds, but are now forgotten! This is why Petrarch, when considering faded glory and the brevity of life, said in his *Triumphs*:

---

51. Petrarch, *Canzoniere*, 360: "O poco mel, molto aloe con fele." Trans. Musa, 499.

52. See Aesop, *The Complete Fables*, trans. Temple, 257.

I saw our glory melt like snow in the sun.[53]

Elsewhere, he sighed over the fleeting course of fame:

> If the span of this life of yours were not so brief,
> You soon would see them fade away in smoke.[54]

Man is mortal and so is his glory. The Gods disdain having companions on this earth. Who assures you that your little glory will survive? Not everyone has swans to carry their names out of the waters of Lethe, that the beautiful nymph might put them in the temple of immortality. Often names are taken from Lethe by crows and vultures, which lack the strength to lift their burden and are forced to drop these magnificent spoils into the dead water.[55] This will make you suffer, and your soul will never be happy. Hector compared an ignorant person to a learned one, saying:

> A bad person and a wise man die the same way.[56]

Wise and prudent women who follow their virtue, however, do not envy other people's writings and fame, nor are their hearts pierced by angry emulation. They are always satisfied, happy, and content; they keep their life and beauty for a long time and enjoy as much glory as is sufficient to them, without that accursed sin of envy that always rules among writers. This is why a good writer, famous not only for his skills but also for his mercy toward the female sex, composed the following sonnet. As he knew how damaging literature is, and how useful and good the arts of Minerva, he encouraged women to pursue peaceful activities:

---

53. Petrarch, *Il trionfo del tempo*, 130: "Vidi ogni nostra gloria al sol di neve." Trans. Wilkins, 100.

54. Petrarch, *Il trionfo del tempo*, 125–26: "Se'l viver nostro non fosse sí breve / Tosto vedresti in fumo ritornarle" (Marinella writes: "in polve ritornarle"). Trans. Wilkins, 100.

55. See Ariosto, *Orlando furioso*, XXXV, 13–14.

56. "Eque moritur tam malus, quam multa sciens." I was unable to determine the precise source. Marinella could be referring to Hector's words to Andromache in *Iliad* VI, 488–89.

To the needle, the reel, the distaff, and spindle
May the woman lend her wise hand,
Nor may desire of fame ever fill her with the vain thought
Of proudly handling pen, books, and papers.
"It is good," Gorgias said, "for woman's honor
To remain confined, and not to know
How to go farther than the home." He thought
Popular renown to be insane and worthless.
This is the reasoning of that great mind, to whom Nature
Revealed the meaning of its most hidden secrets,
And thanks to whom Stageira lives forever.
We must heed the advice of these men.
We should go out of our way to follow them
On the straight path that their genius prescribes.
For even the Holy Goddesses
Embraced distaff, reel, and needle
Which brought them fame, and a happy and satisfied soul.
Neither was fame less fond
Of Lucretia and Arachne, when they made
The world pleased and happy with the needle and thread.[57]

In the tail of the sonnet, the author praises the virtues of many women and goddesses. This noble, learned, and famous soul urges women not to pursue the glory that is born of pride in knowledge. He recommends that women's glory and pride be limited to the narrow confines

---

57. "A l'ago, a l'aspo, a la connocchia, al fuso, / Pieghi la donna la prudente mano. / Né mai per fama evolga il pensier vano / Di penne, libri, e carte al superb'uso. / —Buono è—disse Gorgia—che l'honor chiuso / Stia della donna; ne gire più lontano / De la casa egli sappia.— E stimò insano / E di nissun valor grido diffuso. / Così stimò quel Grande, a cui natura / Di suoi più chiusi arcani il senso aperse; / Onde per lui Stagira eterna viva. / Al parer di costoro deasi haver cura. / Più tosto errar seguendoli, che è pieno / Dritto andar, dove il Genio a noi preserve, / Che anchor le sante Dive / Abbracciar la connocchia, il fuso, l'ago, / E n'ebber fama, e 'l cor contento, e pago. / Ne men fu il grido vago / Di Lucrezia e d'Aragne allhor che 'l mondo / Fer co l'ago e col fil lieto, e giocondo." More precisely, this is a "sonetto caudato," or "sonnet with a tail," which features six additional lines. In light of the similarities between this poem and *Exhortations*, it is possible that the unidentified "good writer" is none other than Marinella herself. She could have been tempted to present similar concepts in prose and in verse, as she did in *Vita di Maria Vergine*.

of the domestic walls, something Gorgias and Aristotle, those great and famous men, also praised.

Fame is like a flame that spreads widely by its own nature. It is a noble quality that proceeds from a noble origin, and a woman may enjoy enough of it to be satisfied. If she wants her glory to fill a good part of the world, she should act rightly and prudently, without fearing that her fame will not spread throughout the city like that of the mother of the Gracchi, Lucretia, and others like them.[58]

Honor is like a quiet whisper that reaches every ear; it is like the sun that cannot be enclosed. It brightens not only the surrounding air but every place, however distant and remote.

Women can be famous even if they simply attend to their occupations, as we learn from many women who did not have to sweat and struggle, and yet are remembered in history and poetry simply for their industrious and diligent rule over their households. Those who would like to know the valor, prudence, and virtue of women may read my book *The Nobility and Excellence of Women and the Defects and Vices of Men*, in which I discuss these issues at length.

I would not want you to believe that everyone always honors philosophy and knowledge. I will make this clear through the authority of great and learned men, and particularly famous philosophers, because no one can discuss something better than those who have experienced it. This is why Claudian, when speaking of Vertumnus, says:

> But you should not believe what other people say about me, but what I myself say. Not all tongues are inclined to truth.[59]

---

58. Marinella draws these two proverbial examples of feminine virtue from Roman history: Cornelia, loving mother of the Gracchi brothers (second century BCE), and Lucretia (fifth century BCE), who committed suicide out of shame for having been raped.

59. "Ma tu non a quel che dicon le persone / di me, ma quel ch'io stesso dico credi, / Ch'al ver non son tutte le lingue buone." The passage is found in Propertius (*Elegiae* IV), not in Claudian as Marinella claims. Marinella has probably taken the vernacular translation from Vincenzo Cartari's highly successful *Le immagini degli dèi*, first published in Venice in 1556. The lines appear in chapter VIII (Nettuno). See Caterina Volpi's modern edition of Cartari's work (Rome: De Luca, 1996), also available at http://www.bibliotecaitaliana.it/xtf/view?docId=bibit000718/bibit000718.xml.

We must trust the word of the experts in the field. Discussing women's virtues, Plato said:

> Woman's virtue consists in the just rule of the household.[60]

This, my beloved women, will be your philosophy and your science, and of this you must be proud. You should also know that the aforementioned philosopher does not approve of philosophy even in men; you can only imagine what he would have said about women philosophers, had someone asked him! I am sure he would have repeated what he said in his *Gorgias*:

> Philosophy is no doubt a delightful thing, Socrates, as long as one is exposed to it in moderation at the appropriate time of life. But if one spends more time with it than he should, it's a man's undoing. For even if one is naturally well favored but engages in philosophy far beyond that appropriate time of life, he can't help but turn out to be inexperienced.[61]

How is it possible that such a noble science can make man ignorant in everything? How can we interpret this? As these sayings suggest, knowledge is detrimental and destructive, although it grants honor and greatness with its beauty. Thanks to the words of this learned man, we realize that men diminish all virtue in themselves when they practice philosophy.

What we consider laudable this philosopher considers damaging, a path that leads to the harbor of ignorance. Therefore, if knowledge does not deserve praise, why struggle, if praise is what you desire?

60. "Virtus mulieris est recte domum gubernare." Unknown reference.

61. Callicles's invective against philosophy is in *Gorgias* 484C, which Marinella quotes in Latin: "[Nam philosophia quidem, Socrates,] res est et venusta si iuvenis moderate attigerit. Si autem in ea tempus contriverit, hominum est corruptela, se diutius filosofetur necessarium est omnium rerum imperitus evadat." Plato, *Gorgias*, trans. Donald J. Zeyl, in Plato, *Complete Works*, 828–29.

This learned man thinks that those who devote themselves to philosophy are crazy, simple, and of no caliber. They are mocked and offended by others and are considered dim-witted, as Boccaccio says.[62] *Quoties ad aliquam rem gerendam vel publicam vel privatam se conferunt, videntur ridiculi*, meaning that whenever these people go out to handle public or private affairs, they are considered laughable, rough, simple, and useless.[63]

If you take this into account, who can praise intellectual disciplines, knowing that they lead their practitioners to ridicule, mockery, and scorn? For God's sake, who can possibly recognize their own demise and shame and still love what causes them?

Therefore do not be surprised if your works, however worthy, are not appreciated. I believe that if any of you had any inclination to learning, once you heard the opinion and the words of such a great man, you would abandon your desire and turn your intellect to happier and more laudable occupations—womanly arts and concerns. Therefore, we will not be surprised if, perhaps after reading Plato's contempt for knowledge, Emperor Licinius called the study of literature a public disease. So did Emperor Constantine—not the Constantine who gave Rome to Pope Sylvester, but another Constantine.[64] Similarly, many others have despised literature as a vain, light, and irrelevant thing, further confirming what I have already said.

62. "Di grossa pasta," Marinella says, quoting *Decameron*, III.4, 5 and VIII.3, 31. Marinella's references to Boccaccio's masterpiece are rare. Listed in the *Index librorum prohibitorum*, the *Decameron* circulated in censored editions during the seventeenth century. See Giuseppe Chiecchi and Luciano Troisio, *Il Decamerone sequestrato: le tre edizioni censurate del Cinquecento* (Milano: Unicopli, 1984).

63. Callicles, in Plato's *Gorgias*, continues his invective against philosophy by claiming that when philosophers "venture into some private or political activity, they become a laughing-stock" (484D). Trans. Zeyl, in Plato, *Complete Works*, 829.

64. Valerius Licinius Licinianus was the Roman emperor from 308 until 324, when he was defeated by Constantine. Marinella still seems to give credit to the authenticity of the Donation of Constantine, in spite of Lorenzo Valla's evidence to the contrary in his *De falso credita et ementita Constantini donatione declamatio* (*Discourse on the Forgery of the Alleged Donation of Constantine*), published in 1517. For a modern English translation with the Latin on facing pages, see *The Treatise of Lorenzo Valla on the Donation of Constantine*, trans. Christopher B. Coleman (New Haven: Yale University Press, 1922; rpt. Toronto: University of Toronto Press, 1993 [for the Renaissance Society of America]). The reference to the "other" emperor Constantine is not clear.

Therefore I exhort you over and over again— and I believe that each one of you will bend your soul to my advice, not to apply yourself to such vanity in the belief that it will lead to honor and fame. I have shown you that you will have to face so many obstacles that your desire will never be fulfilled.

We have often seen scientists and learned men in the straits of poverty because knowledge is considered something vile, and therefore they are despised by the world. This is the proof: if a wise and learned man aspires to a high office, even the inexperienced and the felons will shamelessly compete with him. They will obtain the favors that were due to the learned man, while he with all his knowledge will be left neglected and scorned. This happens because the powerful men who dispense favors hate him. This is why Ariosto, the swan of Ferrara, speaks of

> Those who are reputed gentlemen at court because
> they can emulate the donkey, the scavenging hog.
> Now when just Fate (or rather Venus and Bacchus)
> have wound up their master's life-thread, all these folk
> I mention, supine cravens that they are, born only to
> feed their bellies...[65]

These people are often more appreciated and cherished by the rulers than are the lovers of virtue. This is why Ariosto says that they are dearer than worthy and good men.[66] They are the ones who enjoy the gifts and favors that should be given to worthy people. Considering how knowledge is chased away, scorned, despised, trampled on, and put down, Petrarch wrote in one of his sonnets:

65. Ariosto, *Orlando furioso*, XXXV.21: "E son chiamati cortigian gentili / Perche sanno i-mitar l'asino e'l ciacco, / De lor Signor. Tratto che n'habbia i fili / La giusta Parca, anzi Venere e Baccho. / Questi di ch'io ti dico inerti e vili / Nati solo ad empir di cibo il sacco." Marinella's quote is incomplete. Ariosto continues: "Portano in bocca qualche giorno il nome / Poi nell'oblio lascian cader le some" ("carry his name on their lips for a day or two, only to let the burden fall into oblivion"). Trans. Waldman, 424.

66. Ariosto, *Orlando furioso*, XXXV.20: "Piú grati assai che'l virtuoso e'l buono." Trans. Waldman, 424.

> In poverty and naked goes Philosophy,
> The masses bent on making money say.[67]

Common and corrupt people despise knowledge. As such people are numerous, I encourage you to pursue womanly arts and occupations and to disregard everything that can damage your rule over the household. If you do this with diligence and love, then, as you make your household increasingly richer with beautiful embroidery, you will gain fame and praise. I give you this advice because I love you. As I love you, I desire welfare and happiness for your body and soul, and I urge you to recall often my advice about the evil the study of literature causes.

I will also say, as I did earlier, that focusing on knowledge causes many different illnesses of the head, stomach, and eyes. Your countenance, made sad and melancholy by your many speculations, grows pale, weak, and thin. Furthermore, as you realize that you are not appreciated—but rather are despised and scorned—pain and indignation will gnaw at your unhappy soul. You will regret and repent for having wasted a good part of your life pursuing useless vanities and wish that you had spent it in more profitable occupations. You will be indignant that women, who should celebrate, praise and cherish you, show on the contrary very little love, which I do not know whether to attribute to ignorance or to envy.

You will also be appalled to find that many silly and insipient compositions are praised and cherished, while many full of art and knowledge are soon forgotten. You are right in feeling sorry when you see that evil is rewarded and good is scorned. If you write a good or perfect and praiseworthy work, you will not see it in print for long, I can assure you of that. Why have many ancient books written by men been preserved, while none written by women have? And yet, we can certainly believe that there must have been some, if not many, who wrote works that deserve eternal glory. Nevertheless we have no record of them and must turn to historians, who often embellish their narration with stories to make it more appealing. This proves that men do not want to favor your compositions, whether they are good or not.

67. Petrarch, *Canzoniere*, VII.10–11: "Povera et nuda vai Philosophia. / Dice la turba al vil guadagno intesa." Trans. Musa, 8.

They do not want women to compete with them. They have gained power in the kingdom of glory, and therefore all your works are destined to oblivion.

As is evident in his letter to Orazio Ariosto,[68] Torquato Tasso believes that the life and death of books derives from good or bad luck, for many men who deserve eternal life are instead neglected and receive no attention. Therefore, they quickly sink and are absorbed by the River Lethe. Meanwhile, you see some worthless little works published over and over, which again is only the effect of good or bad luck. This luck, according to Aristotle, is a hidden force, unknown to us, that makes everything either appreciated or not appreciated. I am not speaking here of things that are different in nature, but of things that are the same. That hidden force works such that it brings out difference in things that are intrinsically similar. This is why we see that worthless works, devoid of wisdom, are appreciated, whereas others full of doctrine and knowledge quickly fall into disgrace. This amazing phenomenon, Tasso says, can derive only from a friendly or an unfriendly destiny. Therefore the Philosopher says: "Where intelligence and good judgment are lacking, fortune abounds; where they are present, fortune is scarce."[69]

Fortune is a blind goddess who distributes favors according to her limited understanding and denies, at will, rewards to those who deserve them. I would not want the wisdom of those of you with a passion for knowledge to be tricked by Aristotle's words, which say that all men by nature desire to know.[70] He uses the word "scire," which means "to know," but there are many different things that can be known. Wisdom is knowledge and comprehension of the most beautiful things in nature.[71] This definition of knowledge can be ap-

---

68. This passage is absent from the only letter to Orazio Ariosto (Ludovico Ariosto's nephew) included in Cesare Guasti's edition of Tasso's correspondance (*Le lettere di Torquato Tasso*, ed. Cesare Guasti [Napoli: Rondinella, 1857] I.235–43).

69. "Ubi deest mens, et ratio, ibi fortuna plurima: ubi est mens, et ratio, ibi fortuna minima." Aristotle, *Magna Moralia* II (1207a4).

70. First lines in Aristotle's *Metaphysics*, echoed by Dante in *Paradiso*, IV.124–25, and quoted by Marinella as "Omnes homines natura scire desirant."

71. "Sapientia est rerum praestantissimum natura [*sic*] scientia et intellectus." Unknown source.

plied to literature, but people can be defined as "learned" also because they excel in their occupation. Phidias, for instance, excelled in carving marble. Polyclitus was considered learned because he excelled in sculpting statues.[72] Many others who exceed the norm in different occupations are considered learned. Knowledge pertains to many arts and occupations, and we even read of someone who was an expert in warfare (*sciebat bellica opera*).

When Ulysses enumerates the gifts Agamennon offered to Achilles to compensate for the loss of Briseis, he mentions "women skilled in noble handiwork."[73] By this he means women who were good at embroidery and other womanly tasks. Similarly, Pluto knew all of the languages.[74] Therefore, we understand that to be "learned" can mean many different things:

> Him did the gods make neither a digger nor yet a ploughman nor wise in anything else.[75]

From this you will understand, my beloved, that "knowing" does not necessarily mean knowing literature, but can refer to knowing any art. Knitting, sewing, playing an instrument, knowing music, and just about anything that requires intellectual work can be considered knowledge.

It is apparent that everybody desires to know, but we must know *ad sobrietatem*, as Saint Paul says,[76] meaning that each person needs to know only those things that are appropriate to his state, his condition, and his nature.

---

72. Marinella could have found the examples of Phidias and Polyclitus in Aristotle, *Nicomachean Ethics*, VI.vii (1141a5).

73. *Iliad*, IX.270: "Dabit autem foeminas proestantissimas opera scientes." Cf. *Iliad*, IX.129.

74. "Et is omnes linguas sciebat," Marinella writes. It is not clear where she might have found this reference to Pluto's linguistic skills, unless this is how she interpreted Pluto's mixing of Hebrew, Latin, and Greek in Dante, *Inferno*, VII.1 ("Pape Satàn, Pape Satàn Aleppe"). I thank Benedetta Colella for this suggestion.

75. "Is nec fossor erat, nec erat robustus arator, aut alia re aliqua sapiens," Marinella writes. These lines from the pseudo-homeric poem *Margites* are quoted by Aristotle in *Nicomachean Ethics*, VI.vii (1141a15).

76. Romans 12:3.

I want you to know that, according to some wise men, you have possessed the knowledge you desire since before your birth, because such knowledge is intrinsic to the souls that are united with our bodies.[77] Therefore, you should not be surprised if some wise and learned men, when asked why we take pleasure in hearing musical harmony, answer that our souls learned the sweetness of its pleasing ways in heaven, before they were born to the world. Therefore, we possess the science and pleasure of music in ourselves, without struggling to learn it.

Therefore, my friends, if you lend your ears and judgment to the opinion of these special men, you will know that you have enough knowledge and science in yourselves. It is not necessary to know literature. If it were necessary, no part of the world would be without it, while there are, on the contrary, many countries, in the East and elsewhere, where people either ignore or do not appreciate literature. If you want to understand just how dangerous intellectual disciplines are, consider that many who loved them too much went crazy, disregarded and destroyed the patrimony that other people envied, and led a retired and solitary life in order to contemplate the secrets of nature and the abstract substances.

Many believe that such people are fools because, instead of fleeing knowledge, they loved it too much. Literature really is to be despised, as we learn from the very judicious Paris, Priamus's son. He revealed his opinion, and almost simultaneaously pronounced that literature was not to be appreciated, when in the Idean Valley three naked goddesses appeared before him that he might decide which was the most beautiful and graceful. Each promised great and noble gifts to influence the judge, as wise and expert quarrelers do. Juno promised ample kingdoms and infinite wealth; beautiful Venus promised him the most beautiful woman under the sky, equal in beauty and nobility to the goddess herself; Minerva, meanwhile, confident that knowledge was greater than both wealth and beauty, was already rejoicing in her impending victory. She assured him that he would become master of all possible knowledge.

77. Marinella seems to be referring to the theory of knowledge put forth by Plato in *Phaedo* (see in particular *Complete Works*, pp. 75–76).

Paris, the judge, after carefully considering the three goddesses and their gifts, proclaimed Venus the most beautiful. With this decision, he showed that knowledge is less precious than mortal beauty. At this verdict, Juno was greatly saddened and perturbed, but even more so was Minerva, who went close to madness. Only then did she start to know herself and understand that she was not as appreciated as she had previously thought. She realized that, if Paris could neglect the gift of wisdom for something as perishable as human beauty, then knowledge and doctrine were not praised but almost scorned.[78] From that time on, she was angry and inconsolable and, together with Juno, did whatever she could to bring fire and destruction to Troy, as we read in Homer, who describes her taking up arms to wage war against the Trojans:

> But Athena [...] put on the tunic of Zeus the cloud-gatherer, and arrayed herself in armor for tearful war. Then she stepped into the fiery chariot and grasped her spear, heavy and huge and strong, with which she vanquishes the ranks of men.[79]

She would always burn with indignation at the Trojans, more because of the insult against knowledge—which she thought everyone honored—than because she was considered less beautiful than Venus. Beauty, in fact, should be given little consideration because it is as fleeting as daylight during winter.

Plato thought philosophy a youthful exercise, unworthy of a mature man. He was happy to see a young boy philosophize, but if the boy kept studying once he had grown up, he would despise and

---

78. Ovid gives an account of the judgment of Paris in *Heroides* (in *Heroides and Amores*, trans. Grant Showerman, rev. G. P. Goold [Cambridge, MA: Harvard University Press, 2d ed., 1977]), 16.71ff, to cite a source that was probably familiar to Marinella.

79. Homer, *Iliad*, trans. A. T. Murray, rev. William F. Wyatt (Cambridge, MA: Harvard University Press, rev. ed., 1999), VIII.384–91(Loeb, 379–81): "Haec autem loricam induens Iovis nebularum congregationis /Armis in bellum armatur lachrimosum. / In autem currum splendidum pedibus ivit, accepit autem lanceam / Gravem, magnam, fortem. Hac domabat turmas virorum."

hate him as a useless man of little value, deserving of punishment and beatings. Listen:

> When I see philosophy in a young boy, I approve of it [...]; But when I see an older man still engaging in philosophy and not giving it up, I think such a man by this time needs a flogging.[80]

Let us therefore all agree that since nobody possesses knowledge, you can rest assured that you will not have it either. This is the opinion of Plato and Pythagoras, says Marsilio Ficino:

> According to Pythagoras and Plato, only God is wise, that is, knowledgeable.[81]

True wisdom cannot be achieved because those who do not know the First Causes cannot be considered wise. Indeed, only when we master the essence of the First Causes can we believe that we have gained knowledge.[82] The same philosopher says that those who experience something know its effects, but not its causes. They know through their senses that fire is warm, but not the reason why it is warm. We cannot, therefore, reach the truth.

> As the eyes of bats are to the blaze of day, so is the reason in our souls to the things which are by nature most evident of all.[83]

---

80. Plato, *Gorgias* 485C ff. "In adolescente Philosophiam dum cerno valde delector sed quando grandiorem natu philosophantem animadverto, nec studia eius modi deferentem, verboribus iam hunc indigere censeo." Marinella attributes to Plato the words of Callicles, one of the participants in the dialogue. Trans. Zeyl, in *Complete Works*, 829.

81. "Apud Pythagoram et Platonem sophos, id est sapiens, solus est Deus" ("Marsilii Ficini Commentaria et Argumenta in Platonis Sophistam", in Ficino, *Opera Omnia*, II.1284).

82. "Scire putamus, cum causas, principia et usque ad elementa scimus." Marinella's Latin quote recalls Aristotle, *Physics* I.1 (184a12).

83. Aristotle, *Metaphysics*, II.i (993b9–10): "Sicut oculus hoctico [*sic*] aeris ad lumen diei, sic intellectus noster ad ea qua sunt manifestissima in natura."

Those who struggle to know the origins of things, know them only from their effects. Therefore, nobody achieves true knowledge. Together with Aristotle, we will conclude that they have no hope of achieving that knowledge (*ipsum scire perimunt*) because they cannot know its source. Origins cannot be grasped even in contemplation because everyone is sure to be mistaken when dealing with things he does not know (*circa namque illa quae non cognoscunt decipiuntur omnes*).

Therefore Anaxagoras, after considering the difficulty of pursuing knowledge, said that looking for the truth is no different from following birds (*Nam quaerere veritatem non esset nisi volucres sequi*). He thinks that knowledge varies according to each person's beliefs (*Talia eis entia erunt, qualia ea esse putarint*).[84] Therefore, following Democritus, we can say that the truth either does not exist or is not known to us.[85]

Therefore, let us be satisfied with our ignorance, my beloved, knowing that it is impossible to understand the first principles. It is enough to be learned and competent in your arts and skills to have your souls at rest.

84. Marinella is probably referring to Aristotle, *Metaphysics*, IV.iv (1009b25).

85. Aristotle, *Metaphysics*, IV.iv (1009 b10): "Aut verum nihil est, aut non est notum nobis."

3. WE EXHORT WOMEN TO REALIZE HOW NOBLE, USEFUL, AND APPROPRIATE WOMANLY ARTS ARE. EMPRESSES, QUEENS, AND GODDESSES HAVE PRACTICED THEM, AND THEREFORE I BELIEVE NO ONE SHOULD BE ASHAMED TO BE SEEN WEAVING.

A particular art or science is nobler and more respected than another either because it originated from a nobler inventor or because it deals with more precious material. Minerva, greatest among the goddesses, daughter of the peerless Zeus, invented womanly art. Lucian wrote that Pallas Minerva, Neptune, and Volcano competed among themselves. Neptune made a bull, while Minerva made a house.[86] This goddess also invented the reel, as Theocritus explains when he says that Minerva introduced embroidery, the art of adorning cloth with beautiful inventions and figures, and the spinning of wool.[87]

It is thus laudable for young women to attend to the loading of reels with wool and linen, and weave with pleasure and diligence, thus imitating the powerful goddess.

> When once they have won the favor of Pallas, let girls
> learn to card the wool and to unload the full distaffs.
> She also teaches how to traverse the upright warp with
> the shuttle, and she drives home the loose threads
> with the comb.[88]

I believe that this goddess was more proud when she showed off these examples of womanly art than when, armed with shining

86. The competition among the three gods is narrated in Lucian, *Hermotimus* 20, trans. K. Kilburn (Cambridge, MA: Harvard University Press, 1961), vol. 6, 297.

87. Theocritus mentions the distaff as Minerva's gift in his poem "The distaff" (in *The Greek Bucolic Poets*, trans. J. M. Edmonds Cambridge, MA: Harvard University Press, rev. ed. 1928, rpt 1996), 349. But Marinella's reference to the Goddess is much more complex: "Eiusdam inventum est colus, haec acu pingere telam texere et omnes lanifitium."

88. Ovid, *Fasti*, trans. Sir James George Frazer (Cambridge, MA: Harvard University Press, 2d ed., 1989), III.817–20 (Loeb, 180): "Pallade placata lanam mollire puellae / discant et plenas exonerare colos. / Illa etiam stantis radio percurrere telas / erudit et rarum pectine denset opus."

weapons, she waged war against the Trojans or when the Palladium fell from the sky and, to everyone's surprise, immediately started to walk. Minerva carried a spear in her right hand, a distaff and spindle in her left. She thereby showed that the honors originating from the distaff and the spindle were as praiseworthy as those derived from war. Both arts were, in fact, equally dear to the Gods, as Apollodorus states:

> It was three cubits in height, its feet joined together;
> in its right hand it held a spear aloft, and in the other
> hand a distaff and spindle.[89]

Since the Palladium fell from the sky and brought the distaff and the spindle, we can only infer that these tools had been made in heaven. I do not believe that Volcano made them because excessive heat would have scorched them. They are, I believe, celestial tools.

So there you have it: Minerva, a most noble and honored goddess, offspring of the divine, taught us an art whose tools she brought from heaven. She invented this art which is therefore worthy of honor and not, as some say, a vile exercise that is familiar even to the lowliest women and widespread among the masses and people of no account. I concede that common people also practice this art, but this does not lessen its importance. On the contrary, it makes it even better and more noble and laudable. The sun doubles its brightness when it shines over golden roofs, yet it also casts the beauty of its rays over mud and other rubbish. It certainly cannot be blamed and condemned for conceding its grace to everything and not wanting to leave any spot neglected and deprived of its favors. Similarly, God spreads the goodness of his mercy everywhere, because good is diffusive (*quia bonum diffusivum suipsius*).[90] In fact, the more good is spread, the greater its dignity.[91]

---

89. Apollodorus, *Library*, 3.12.3 (Loeb, vol. 2, 39). Marinella quotes the passage in Latin: "Palladium eccidit trium cubitorum, quod sponte deambulare videbatur dextera astam tenens, ac sinistra colum et fusum." The Palladium (or Palladion) was the effigy of Minerva that fell from the sky for the protection of Troy.

90. St. Thomas Aquinas, *Summa contra Gentiles* I.37.5.

91. St. Thomas Aquinas, *Super Sententiis* IV.49.1: "Quanto aliquod bonum est communius, tanto divinius."

God and nature made man and woman skilled at different operations for their common benefit. This was God's desire, not some human invention. One of them was made independent and valiant in the face of the dangers and inconvenience of travel, cold, heat, and other bothersome accidents. The other one was created delicate, weak, and gentle, that she might, without complaining, find her peace in the seclusion and solitude of her home. As she puts her thoughts to rest in the tranquility of her household, she can compete for praise with her husband. He enriches his household with everything he collects with his labors, and she does the same by preserving what he has gained. He makes the household more prosperous from the outside; she does the same from the inside. Their tasks are different, but equally laudable, because preservation is not inferior to acquisition.

A woman must not be seen idle, but rather always at work, so that her household may be rich in cloth and other things that pertain to cleanliness and civility. She will make her household abundant in beautiful and delicate cloth, so that everyone may enjoy it. Even if she is noble, she will not disdain lending her hand to the needle and spindle. She will find ingenious ways to draw images of wild beasts with the subtle thread and endow them with as much spirit and life as possible by adorning them with wonderful white shades. People who admire them will be as surprised as those who saw Nausicaa's beautiful and rich robes. This daughter of Alcinous and Arete had decorated and made them more precious with her own hands.[92]

This is how wise and honorable women become famous and laudable. The handling of the needle, the spindle, and the loom is suitable not only to common women, but also to queens and goddesses. Although some fools disregard this art, every woman must know its excellence and praise Nature, which has bestowed such happiness upon them.

This is what Solomon, the wisest of men, said when talking about a great and much-praised woman:

She sought wool and flax and worked by the counsel
of her hands.[93]

92. "Nausicaa of the beautiful robes" is first introduced in Homer, *Odyssey*, VI.49.

93. Proverbs 31:13: "Quaesivit lanam et linum et operata est consilio manuum suarum."

By this, he means that this laudable woman sought wool and linen and transformed it with the industriousness of her hands. Thus, he shows us that she did not waste her time in idleness. And by adding that "her fingers grasp the spindle,"[94] he means that she spun the fine wool herself because she wanted to do something useful and good. And she was so diligent and successful that, as Solomon says,

> She shall not fear, in the cold of snow, for her household. For all those of her household have been clothed twofold.[95]

She was so good that everyone in her household wore two layers of clothing.

> She has made embroidered clothing for herself.[96]

We cannot praise enough the divine industriousness of such a woman, and we should lift her diligence to the stars. The woman Solomon describes was famous, wise, and mature, but she received praise in particular for her womanly art. From these words, we can understand how useful and noble this art is, if such a wise king praises this lady for her womanly occupations.

The Greeks cherished and worshiped a statue of Minerva that showed the goddess as a venerable matron sitting on a high marble chair. She held with both hands, as a dear and precious thing, the reel loaded with wool or linen. In doing so, she invited women to their tasks.

In Rome, this occupation was considered so laudable that a festival in honor of the goddess was celebrated in March. On that occasion, the ladies of the house honored the servants, because more utility and profit derived from the servants than from the mistresses.[97]

94. Proverbs 31:19: "Digiti eius apprehenderunt fusum."

95. Proverbs 31:21–22: "Non timebit domui suæ a frigoribus nivis; omnes enim domestici eius vestiti sunt duplicibus."

96. Proverbs 31:22: "Stragulatam vestem fecit sibi."

97. A reference to this Roman festivity can be found in Cartari, *Le immagini degli dèi XI* (Minerva).

Minyas's diligent daughters loved this art so much that I do not want other women to be deprived of such a joy. Ovid says they are either

> spinning wool, thumbing the turning threads, or keep
> close to the loom, and press their maidens with work.[98]

In Lydia, there once lived a girl named Arachne. She was of humble birth and came from a poor city. She thought she was the best in womanly tasks and the pride of her land. She boasted that she was better not only than all the other women who devoted themselves to such tasks, but even better than Minerva herself, and she often wished to compete with her. Hearing such pride and contempt, Minerva disguised herself as an old woman and invited the girl to surrender to the goddess:

> Do not scorn my advice: seek all the fame you will
> among the mortal men for handling wool; but yield
> place to the goddess, and with humble prayer beg her
> pardon for your words, reckless girl.[99]

Arachne blushed, her eyes aflame with proud disdain. She was barely able to keep her hands from hitting the disguised goddess. She thought she was a senile and crazy woman and answered with an irate voice:

> Doting in mind, you come to me, and spent with old
> age. And it is too long life that is your bane.[100]

---

98. Ovid, *Metamorphoses* IV.34–35: "Aut ducunt lanas, aut stamina pollice versant / aut haerent tela, famulasque laboribus urgent." Trans. Miller, 181. The Minyades—Minyas's daughters—were turned into bats by Dionysus when they chose to perform their traditional tasks rather than take part in the Dionysian Mysteries.

99. Ovid, *Metamorphoses* VI.30–33: "Consilium ne sperne meum: tibi fama petatur / inter mortales faciendae maxima lanae; / cede deae veniamque tuis, temeraria, dictis / supplice voce roga: veniam dabit illa roganti." Trans. Miller, 291.

100. Ovid, *Metamorphoses* VI.37–38: "Mentis inops longaque venis confecta senecta, / et nimium vixisse diu nocet." Trans. Miller, 291.

The goddess burned with scorn for the girl who had insulted her. She felt deprived of the most beautiful and honored virtue she possessed. She could not bear the thought of having a partner and rival in such a noble and useful art. But Arachne challenged her, without the least fear of confronting such a powerful deity.

Unsure of her victory, Minerva removed her disguise, and they both started weaving. Minerva drew herself among many figures, as the above-mentioned poet describes:

> To herself the goddess gives a shield and a sharp-pointed spear, and a helmet for her head; the aegis guards her breast.[101]

Arachne finished her work, which was perhaps more beautiful and perfect than Minerva's. The goddess was stupefied and filled with pain and indignation. She could not stand such excellence; she understood that she had been defeated and destroyed the web of her industrious adversary.

> Not Pallas, nor Envy himself, could find a flaw in that work. The golden-haired goddess was indignant at her success, and rent the embroidered web with its heavenly crimes; and, as she held a shuttle of Cytorian boxwood, thrice and again she struck Idmonian Arachne's head.[102]

This story shows how proud Minerva is of this art. She is the goddess of knowledge and war, yet she thought that, if defeated, she would be deprived of her greatest attribute. Indeed, were spinning not of great reputation and excellence, she would not have deigned, as a goddess, to compete with a mortal woman. This is all the more re-

---

101. Ovid, *Metamorphoses* VI.78–81: "At sibi dat clipeum, dat acutae cuspidis hastam, / dat galeam capiti, defenditur aegide pectus." Trans. Miller (Loeb), 293–95.

102. Ovid, *Metamorphoses*, VI.129–33: "Non illud Pallas, non illud carpere Livor / possit opus: doluit successu flava virago / et rupit pictas, caelestia crimina, vestes, / utque Cytoriaco radium de monte tenebat, / ter quater Idmoniae frontem percussit Arachnes." Trans. Miller (Loeb), 297.

markable if you consider that Minerva was no ordinary goddess, but the goddess of intelligence and knowledge, who had made with her own hands a dress and a veil of celestial beauty, which she removed when she took up arms against the Trojans:

> But Athena, daughter of Zeus who bears the aegis, let fall on her father's floor her soft robe, richly embroidered, that she herself had made and her hand had fashioned.[103]

Hercules's actions show how dear this womanly art was to him. He was not satisfied with having strangled snakes while still in the cradle, or with having killed Caco and many others as the Tamer of Monsters. He realized that he was restful and at peace only when he put the distaff at his side. This was the culmination of his glory. To become even more famous he wore a female skirt. He was not ashamed to turn the spindle and spin the fine carded wool, as Ovid shows in his epistles:

> Do you draw off with stalwart thumb the coarsely spun strands, and give back to the hand of a pretty mistress the just portion she weighed out?[104]

Varro, according to Pliny's testimony, said that the distaff and the spindle of Tanaquil, Tarquinius Priscus's wife, were kept in a vestibule sacred to the gods as a sign of honor and reverence. Tanaquil was a famous woman who ruled over her household with wisdom and common sense. It is said that for Servius Tullius, her son-in-law, she sewed with her own hands a royal robe of wonderful artistry, which was placed in the temple of fortune as an excellent and priceless artifact.[105]

---

103. Homer, *Iliad*, V.733–35: "Sed Minerva, filia Iovis Aegiochi, vellum quidam deposuit subtile partis in pavimento, pulchrum, quod ipsa fecerat manibus." Trans. Murray (Loeb), 261. See also *Iliad*, VIII.385–36.

104. Ovid, *Heroides*, IX.76–80: "Crassaque robusto deducis pollice fila / aequaque famosae pensa rependis erae?" Trans. Showerman (Loeb), 115.

105. See Pliny the Elder, *Natural History*, VIII.lxxiv.194, trans. H. Rackman, 10 vols. (Cambridge, MA: Harvard University Press, 1938–63), 3.137.

I do not want my discourse to be deprived of your name, faithful Andromache, wife of Priamus's son Hector, who was so valiant that "he did not seem the son of a mortal man."[106] Although you were the wife of such a great man, you were not ashamed to lend your hand to womanly tasks. Hector himself encouraged you to do so when he told you to go back to the royal palace:

> But go to the house and busy yourself with your own tasks, the loom and the distaff, and tell your handmaids to ply their work: and war will be the concern for men.[107]

"Go back to your secluded palace and exercise your womanly task of the loom and the spindle. Give orders to the maids, so that they not waste time but attend to their tasks. War belongs to men:" this is how Hector spoke to his wife.[108] He was not ashamed to have a companion who would lend her hand to the thread and the loom, although she would also sometimes—and perhaps often—show herself with a golden scepter. After Hector's death at Achilles's hand, those who related the sad news to Andromache did not find her in front of the mirror, combing her hair or smoothing her face, as many women do, but in a secluded place, next to her loom.

> She was weaving a tapestry in the innermost part of the lofty house, a purple tapestry of double fold, and in it she was weaving flowers of varied hue.[109]

---

106. "Non hominis videbatur filius," Marinella writes, condensing a passage in Homer, *Iliad*, XXIV.258.

107. Homer, *Iliad*, VI.490–93. Marinella writes: "Sed in domum iens tui ipsius opera cura; / Telamque, columque et ancillis iube / opus adire. Bellum autem viris cura erit." Trans. Murray (Loeb), 311.

108. Quoted above, n107. Here Marinella uncharacteristically quotes the passage in Latin and then provides her own paraphrase in Italian.

109. Homer, *Iliad*, XXII.440–42: "Sed telam texebat concavi domus altae, / duplicem, splendidam, in autem pigmenta spargebat." Trans. Murray (Loeb), 485.

These lines show that she was weaving in the most internal part of the royal palace and that she made rare and wonderful images appear in the perfection of her art. Although she took part in important meetings, it is nevertheless for her diligence and wisdom that she is sung and remembered in Homer's song, which brings immortality. The poet shows us that, in spite of being married to the son of Priamus, the wife of such an important hero did not waste her time in vain idleness. She was not a lowly and common person, but a great woman and a queen. I offer her example as a rebuke to those who maintain that spinning and sewing are a plebeian and unworthy occupation. I hope they will now be quiet and realize their mistake. While this is an occupation of common people, I will say it also suits goddesses and honored and noble women.

> In fact, goodness is even nobler when it is enjoyed by many.[110]

I offer these examples so that women of high rank and condition will not avoid this art and ornament.

Plutarch wrote in his *Problems* that when a bride entered the house of the groom for the first time, she brought with her the distaff and the spindle, which are the tools of a revered and noble woman.[111] This act showed that her life was not to be devoted to idleness, laziness, and vanity, but that she would spend her days adorning her house with delicate and soft cloth, with industry and ingenuity. These things are indeed as necessary and useful as they are beautiful and appreciated, and they are desired by all civil people. This art is so precious that it certainly suits queens and empresses. Therefore we should not be surprised that a certain Asinius of Pozzuoli placed a golden reel and spindle in a little temple, along with the inscription: "From this derive the nobility and the wealth of my household."[112] In doing

110. St. Thomas Aquinas, *Super Sententiis* IV.49.1: "Quanto aliquod bonum est communius, tanto divinius."

111. This custom is described in "Life of Romulus," in Plutarch, *Lives*, trans. Bernadotte Perrin (Cambridge, MA: Harvard University Press, 1914–1926), 10 vols: 1.15.4–5 (p. 133).

112. "Ab hac nobilitas et divitia domus meae." Marinella could be referring to Gnaeus Asinius, son of the Roman senator Gaius Asinius Pollio and Vipsania Agrippina. Gnaeus Asinius

so, he showed that the prosperity and honor of his household derived from the reel and the spindle. Who, then, could disparage such an occupation? Many honorable but unfortunate women fed and sustained entire families with this useful art alone. Beyond spinning linen and wool, they spin gold and silver with great profit and gain. Therefore, many households are supported by the industrious hands of diligent women, who in peace and rest bring people comfort and happiness.

I want to embellish my little book with the beauty of your womanly pride, Nausicaa, and I trust that you will not refuse to honor my writings with the diligence of your pleasant and useful virtues. Nausicaa, daughter of king Alcinous and of queen Arete, was rich in both womanly wisdom and many different linens. Regarding her shirts, which she made herself, Homer says:

They make other people wonder in amazement.[113]

This is how delicate and rich they were. Her mother Arete, Alcinous's wife, did not wander here and there, like many women of our times. This is what the above-mentioned poet says about her:

She sat at hearth [...] spinning the yarn of purple dye.[114]

She did not believe that her greatness as a woman who carried crown and scepter would be diminished if she had the reel at her side. There are many who would, on the contrary, be ashamed because they believe that unloading the heavy distaff of its thread does not suit nobility. Yet, the queens I have mentioned rejoiced when their excellence was honored by the distaff and spindle. These virtuous women were

---

was in fact the patron of Puteoli—modern Pozzuoli. See Ronald Syme and Barbara M. Levick, "Asinius Gallus, Gaius," in Simon Hornblower and Antony Spawforth, eds. *The Oxford Classical Dictionary* (Oxford: Oxford University Press, 2003) 191–92.

113. "Che fanno altrui stupir di maraviglia," Marinella writes, probably alluding to Nausicaa's description in *Odyssey* VI.49: "Nausicaa of the beautiful robes." Trans. Murray (Loeb), 223. However, Homer does not mention Nausicaa's ability at the loom.

114. Homer, *Odyssey* VI.52–54: "Di fina lana di porpora tinta / A la rocca traea torcendo il fuso."

ingenious silkworms who brought forth precious threads to make beautiful dresses and ornaments that would last for eternity.[115]

The goddess Calypso, that beautiful and graceful nymph who loved womanly arts, will not refuse to share her noble qualities with the other women I have mentioned. She wanted to make Ulysses immortal because she loved him and did not want him to leave her. When Zeus sent Mercury so that Ulysses could return to his house in Ithaca, the God found her busy perfecting her web. The lines with which Homer describes her, translated in the vernacular, are thus:

> She was singing with a sweet voice as she went to and
> fro before the loom, weaving with a golden shuttle.[116]

This womanly task was so dear to Augustus that he took indescribable pleasure in seeing his wife and daughters with the distaff at their side, spinning the reel and taking enough thread to make themselves precious clothes with their royal hands. Who can claim that this art suits common people alone? Not even a Roman empress thought that spinning detracted from her greatness or from that of her daughters, the princesses. Knowing the honor, praise, and reverence that is due to the distaff, nobody can but bless Midas's servant. Unable to keep silent about his master's ears, he dug a hole. But perhaps some among you, my beloved ladies, do not know the story.

Midas was a king who believed he was greater than others thought he was—which is a common mistake among men. Confident in his prowess, he entered a singing competition with Apollo. The God won because of Marsias's biased judgment and turned Midas's ears into those of a donkey that they might show his ignorance and foolishness.[117] Midas hid his ears as best he could, but was discovered

---

115. Here Marinella indulges in a bizarre Baroque metaphor.

116. Homer, *Odyssey* V.62–63: "Essa dentro cantando in chiara voce / Movea la bella e vaga spola d'oro / Tra le fila sottil di ricca tela, / Quella tessendo con mirabil arte." Trans. Murray (Loeb), 187.

117. Marinella's summary is confusing. Tmolus, judge of the musical contest between Apollo and Marsias (or Pan), assigned victory to Apollo. Midas criticized the verdict and Tmolus's integrity, and for this he had his ears turned into a donkey's by an enraged Apollo. The story is narrated by Ovid in *Metamorphoses* XI (Loeb, 131–33).

by one of his servants, a chatterer like other people of his kind. He could not be quiet and keep his tongue from revealing the secret of his master's ears. Being cautious and clever, however, he found a way to hide himself while satisfying his desire to tell the truth about the king's ears. He dug a deep hole, put his head in it, and satisfied his desire by repeating over and over that his master had donkey ears:

> [He] went off and dug a hole in the ground and into
> the hole, with low, muttered words, he whispered of
> his master's ears which he had seen. Then by throwing
> back the earth he buried the evidence of his voice and,
> having thus filled up the hole again, he silently stole
> away.[118]

From that spot much cane was born, and from it reeds were made, as we read:

> But a thick growth of whispering reeds began to spring
> up there.[119]

From that time on, they started making tools with light and beautiful reeds. Before that time, they must have used something different, perhaps some kind of roll that spun the thread and forced the spinner to sit all the time. That way, she could do nothing else. Reeds, on the other hand, are so comfortable that many can do countless chores in the house with the distaff at their side and without ever leaving their work. We must praise Midas's servant, who was the source of so much good.

A life without linens would be almost unhappy. Without them, people would be wearing clothes as harsh as a cilice. The beauty and usefulness of linen clothes are almost impossible to describe. The beauty and excellence of embroideries elicit amazement. Civil and no-

---

118. Ovid, *Metamorphoses* XI.184–89: "Humumque / effodit et, domini quales adspexerit aures, / voce refert parva terraeque inmurmurat haustae / indiciumque suae vocis tellure regesta / obruit et scrobibus tacitus discedit opertis." Trans. Miller (Loeb), 133.

119. Ovid, *Metamorphoses* XI.189–90: "Creber harundinibus tremulis ibi surgere lucus coepit." Trans. Miller (Loeb), 133.

ble souls who love cleanliness and neatness desire these delicate joys. I have heard many say that they prefer a thin and beautiful shirt over a silk dress.

In my hometown, when the burning lion races across the sky blowing blazing breath from its nostrils and setting the surrounding air aflame, it is wonderful to see gracious and noble women in halls and on high balconies show their own pride and excellence. Their sleeves and smocks are adorned with priceless needlework. Fine veils are enriched by an embroidery known as "air stitch" because it is made without being attached to cloth. There you can admire leaves, branches, flowers, and fruit formed by industrious hands and equal to the most beautiful gardens in the Tyrrhenian Sea, desired by Achelous's daughters.[120]

You can see embroidered and decorated tablecloth and most noble sheets. As wonderful stitches make them dear and precious, they embellish and decorate royal chambers, and with their softness and whiteness convince even the most reluctant people to enjoy a sweet rest. These are the things the hands of valiant women bring forth. Without the comfort this art offers, I would consider our lives next to miserable. Cloth keeps the body clean, and such cleanliness is indispensable to our lives. It serves our welfare and bestows beauty and grace upon our houses, which are the small parts from which cities are formed, as I said earlier. This is why Aristotle, Plato, and others insist that husband, wife, and children be good, well-mannered, and moderate. This will cause cities, which comprise these small units, to be good, right, and praiseworthy.

I cannot stress enough, my dear ladies, how noble this art is. Polybius's wife, a woman of great wisdom, wanted to honor Helen with a beautiful and appropriate gift, as she was similar in face and countenance to a goddess (*similis deabus*), as Homer reports. Of the many things that came to her mind, Polybius's wife found none appropriate for this beautiful queen. After her mind had wandered here

---

120. The transformation of Achelous's daughters into sirens is narrated by Ovid in *Metamorphoses* V. Embroidery had a strong tradition in Venice and particularly on the island of Burano. The "punto in aria" (air stitch) described by Marinella was in fact also known as "punto Burano" (Burano stitch).

and there, she remembered a golden distaff with all the accessories, as Homer reported in the *Odyssey* (in Gerolamo Bacelli's translation[121]):

> And besides these, his wife gave to Helen also beautiful gifts—a golden distaff and a basket with wheels beneath did she give, a basket of silver, and with gold were the rims thereof gilded. This then the handmaid, Phylo, brought and placed beside her, filled with finely-spun yarn, and across it was laid the distaff laden with violet-dark wool.[122]

This gift was truly noble and appropriate to Helen's worth, although she was a queen and King Menelaus's wife. Therefore, worthy women will not be ashamed to spin thread, because this art was an ornament to queens, goddesses, and other sublime women. What can we say about Penelope? She worked all day at the loom, and at night she undid her work to ward off the harassment of the Proci. She performed all that useless work to escape their annoying temerity and gall. When her son Telemachus saw his mother sad and idle, he urged her to resume her neglected work, saying:

> Now go to thy chamber, and busy yourself with your own tasks, the loom and the distaff, and bid your handmaids be about their tasks.[123]

121. Girolamo Bacelli is remembered by Ugo Foscolo as a fine translator ("Intorno alla traduzione de' due primi canti dell'*Odissea* ec." in *Opere*. Vol. II. [Florence: Le Monnier, 1883] 209). His versions of the *Odyssey* and of the first seven cantos of the *Iliad* were published in Florence in 1581–82 (Melchior Cesarotti, "Catalogo delle principali edizioni e versioni di Omero," in *Opere*, vol. XVI, Appendix [Pisa: Tipografia della società letteraria, 1800] 14–15).

122. Homer, *Odyssey* IV.129–34: "Indi la moglie sua cortese diede / Molti gentili, e gratiosi doni / Ad Helena gentile e gratiosa. / Tra quali era una vaga rocca d'oro / E la gentil panaretta d'argento / Ritonda e bella che su l'orlo estremo / Tra l'argento intrecciate molte fila / Aveva d'or forbito a maraviglia. / Questa la vaga filò. Ancilla adorna / Seco portava e presso lei la pose. / Ch'era di egual e sottil fil ripiena. / E sopra essa distesa si vedeva / La bella ornata rocca che la chioma / Aveva di lana fina, il cui colore / A quel de le viole era simile." Trans. A. T. Murray. Rev. George E. Dimock (Cambridge, MA: Harvard University Press, 1995), 129.

123. Homer, *Odyssey* I.356–58: "Tu dunque vanne dentro, a le tue stanze / Là dove ad opere femminili intenta / Quella cura e sollecita le ancille / Comanda ch'a l'oprar veloci sieno."

Telemachus and his mother so honored this art that they did not want
to waste time. Time is precious, particularly when spent in attending
to womanly tasks. I want to end this line of reasoning and instead
describe the usefulness and welfare that derives from this occupation,
which is not undignified and vile as many people of little wisdom believe. While it is true that many common people devote themselves to
this occupation, the same is true of empresses, queens, and goddesses,
who are worthy of honor and fame.

If Venus does not weave or spin or practice any laudable occupation, it is because she is a vile, lazy, vain, and worthless goddess.
This is why in Guarini's *Faithful Shepherd* Silvio, indignant, dishonors
her with these and other words:

> O Goddess, most unjustly called a Goddess except of
> persons vain, remiss and blind.[124]

With this in mind, we will not be surprised if her little bastard son
wanders around raving without a shirt on, as reported by a pleasant
poet (*absque braga*).[125]

Sober and diligent goddesses attend instead to good works,
like Minerva, who not only delights in handling the spear and the
sword and ruling over wisdom and knowledge but, unsatisfied still,
lends her honored hand to the spindle, the needle, and the loom, and
invites women to do the same. And if some of you have already devoted yourselves to intellectual disciplines, you should nevertheless
practice womanly virtue, which is appreciated by everyone and enjoys
great consideration and dignity. This way, you will make your virtue
shine with a double light, to use the words of Solon the wise:

Trans. Murray, rev. Dimock (Loeb), 39.

124. Guarini, *Il pastor fido*, Act IV, Scene 8: "O dea, che non sei dea se non di gente / vana,
oziosa e cieca." Trans. Sheridan, 136.

125. Marinella is quoting Cupid's description in Teofilo Folengo, *Zanitonella sive Innamoramentum Zaninae et Tonelli*, trans. Franco Loi (Milano: Mondadori, 1984), I,18. However,
the expression used by Folengo and quoted by Marinella ("absque braga") seems to indicate
that Cupid is not wearing any pants.

The longer you live, the longer you learn.[126]

The prudent and diligent woman builds her house. She industriously makes it bigger, richer, and more wonderful in comfort and appearance, with cloth and precious works. Not any one virtue, my beloved women, but many are needed to make a person famous and worthy of glory. As it is said, "One swallow does not make a summer, nor does one fine day."[127] Therefore, I exhort you to attend only to the governance and enrichment of your house, and this will be sufficient.

Circes, daughter of the Sun, is calling me. She, too, desires womanly glory and wants to be offered as an example. I will then say that, although this most beautiful nymph is a goddess, she does not scorn these works and the distaff. On the contrary, she adorns her excellent dignity with their beauty. As she weaves she sings most sweetly, drawing sweet rest from her toil. Homer says of her:

> Circes […] went to and fro before a great imperishable web, such as is the handiwork of goddesses, finely-woven and beautiful, and glorious.[128]

And Virgil wrote, when singing her praise:

> While she drives her shrill shuttle through the fine web.[129]

---

126. A sentence similar to the one Marinella quotes ("Tam diu discendum quam diu vivitur") can be found in Seneca, *Moral Epistles* LXXVI: "tam diu discendum est, quam diu nescias et, si proverbio credimus, quam diu vivas" ("You should keep learning as long as you are ignorant—even to the end of your life, if there is anything in the proverb"). See Lucius Annaeus Seneca, *Moral Epistles*, trans. Richard M. Gummere (Cambridge, MA: Harvard University Press, 1917–25), vol. II,148–49.

127. This proverbial sentence also appears in Aristotle's *Nicomachean Ethics* I.vii (1098a15). Marinella quotes it in Latin: "Una hirundo non facit ver, nec una dies."

128. Homer, *Odyssey*, X.222–24: "Circe, ch'ivi tesseva una grande tela / immortal, qual conviensi a altre dee, / sottile, vaga, rilucente e bella." Trans. Murray, rev. Dimock (Loeb), 375.

129. Virgil, *Aeneid* VII.14: "Arguto tenues percurrens pectine telas." Trans. Fairclough, rev. Goold (Loeb), 3.

With true love I invited, and invite, the female sex to seek glory for their own arts, because things outside one's domain are worth little or nothing. This is my opinion and my advice: become illustrious and famous in your own art, not in someone else's, notwithstanding the great philosopher who said that men and women are naturally skilled at the same things.

> Women share by nature in every way of life just as men do.[130]

Although men and women are fit for the same actions, I nevertheless will not exhort women to fight, organize armies, dig the trenches and the vallum, and protect cities, as Plato would have them do. Listen to what he says, that you might give credit to my words:

> Men and women will campaign together. They'll take the sturdy children with them.[131]

He wants women to take their children to battle that they might grow accustomed to terrible scenes. He also says that women are naturally inclined to protect the city, as men are:

> Men and women are by nature the same with respect to guarding the city.[132]

This wise man also says:

> We said that women's natures should be made to correspond with those of men, and that all occupations, whether having to do with war or with the other as-

---

130. Plato, *Republic* V.455d: "Omnium quidem operum natura compos est femina omnium, et vir compos est." Trans. G. M. A. Grube, rev. C. D. C. Reeve, in Plato, *Complete Works*, 1083.

131. Plato, *Republic* V.466e: "Militabunt communiter tam mares quam feminae. Mulieres adducunt filios in proelium."

132. Plato, *Republic* V.456a: "Mulieres itaque et viri eadem haec natura ad civitatem custodiendam."

pects of life, [should be common to both men and women].[133]

He wanted women to engage in wars and protect their cities as much as men. He says that both male and female dogs protect the shepherd's flock because both are good at the same things.

Nevertheless, I will advise women against this, because their delicate nature is unfit for these tiring tasks. Furthermore, as it is necessary to preserve one's gains, trying to attend to both activities would be useless and uncomfortable. It would also be almost impossible to achieve because those who use their intellect in two different domains always cherish one more than the other. It is impossible to attend to both: you will either attend to neither or, at the very least, neglect one. We must strengthen our welfare, and preservation is no less important than acquisition. Otherwise, it would be like drawing water with a sieve: it escapes as soon as it is drawn.[134]

Therefore, you will rule over your household with diligence and industriousness, and you will make it richer. You will not attend to military art, which does not aim at the preservation and growth of households and cities, but rather their damage and destruction. You will run your household peacefully and benevolently. There your royal palace will be. There you will hear the sound of your praise and glory.

And when you arrive at the end that is common to us all, the one determined by nature and necessity, the one which not even Jupiter can fight (*Nec Jupiter pugnabit*), you will leave the world with the honor of your household, the glory of your children, and praise for you and your actions. You will rise to heaven to spin silver and golden threads to make dresses for the angels and adorn the beautiful walls of Paradise with delicate cloth. Therefore, my dear ladies, do not disdain these memories of me, that is, these exhortations that you can practice

---

133. Plato, *Timaeus* 18c, trans. Donald J. Zeyl, in Plato, *Complete Works*, 1226. For Marinella's (incomplete) Latin quote ("Naturam praeterea mulierum non aliter quam virorum effingi praecepimus; studiaque omnia, tam belli quam pacis, mulieribus [cum viris esse communia]") see *Omnia divini Platonis opera*, 701.

134. The comparison is in Aristotle, *Economics* I.vi.25. Trans. Forster, in *The Complete Works*, II.2133.

with a quiet soul and a peaceful and well rested body. You can thank the heavens that you had someone to show you the truth.

4. WE EXHORT THOSE WHO DESIRE PRAISE TO
    BE CAUTIOUS WHEN SPEAKING, UNLESS THEIR
    ARGUMENTS ARE TO PROVIDE SOMETHING
    GOOD, USEFUL, OR WORTHY TO THE LESS
    FORTUNATE.

Silence is laudable when imposed by duty or circumstances. Some people consider it superior to any learned argument.[135] He who does not know how to stay silent, does not know how to think either. This is the logic behind the saying "he who does not know how to keep quiet, does not know how to speak" (*nescit loqui, qui tacere nesciet [sic]*). Speaking is as useful and noble when necessary as it is ugly and shameful when unecessary.[136]

We know the worth of a person by the way he speaks. It makes his mind, knowledge, and intelligence known to others. As speech is the herald of all feelings, it makes every passion, whether good or bad, known to other people, and publicizes virtues no less than vice.

The tongue has been useful to many, but it has also been a source of damage and sorrow to many more, as we can infer from infinite events that occurred to many people. Overall, it has brought more evil than good.

Knowing how dangerous speaking can be, the mysterious Egyptians, according to Apuleius and Martianus, worshiped a God named Harpocrates. He resembled someone at the end of childhood, who is just beginning to enjoy the grace of youth. With a finger on his mouth, he signified silence.[137] He was a good friend to just men and philosophers. As we are not, by nature, straight and good, however, he began to move away from laudable and virtuous habits and, changing

135. Marinella stresses the concept by repeating it in Latin: "Silere cum tempus postulat, iactat se super omnia docta verba."

136. A passage in the margins refers to Ecclesiasticus 4:29: "In lingua sapientia dignoscitur" (By the tongue wisdom is discerned).

137. A child with a finger on his mouth, Horus represented for the Egyptians the hieroglyph for "child." Greeks and Romans, however, misunderstood his meaning and made him Harpocrates, the God of Silence. References to Harpocrates can be found in works by Varro, Ovid, Apuleius, and Martianus Capella.

his inclination, devoted his friendship and conversation to men of little worth, as Eridano's son[138] reports:

> When there were no philosophers or holy men left to keep him on the straight and narrow path, he forsook his virtuous propensities and threw in his lot with the wicked. He began consorting with lovers at night, then with thieves; he was party to every sort of crime.[139]

The statue of this god was covered entirely in eyes and ears, symbolizing the dictum to listen and look, but be slow to talk. The Egyptians also chose the wolf as the hieroglyphic of silence, because he moves slowly and silently through the deep shadows of the night. If it has reason to make noise, it bites its legs instead. Knowing its nature, Tasso says: "Then as a silent wolf slinks to his lair."[140] Minerva, the goddess of knowledge, chased away the crow, the twittering and loquacious bird that was changed from white to black because of its speech, as Ovid reports:

> Thy plumage, talking raven, though white before, had been suddenly changed into black.[141]

Infinite is the damage that derives from the tongue. In vain nature, as if foreseeing the evil it could cause, confined it to a harsh prison. Although surrounded by the well-ordered sharpness of hard teeth, the tongue is still a source of offense and sometimes death.

Battus, however silent, was still a great chatterer. His silence did not derive from his virtue, but rather from his fear of Mercury. But fear did not prevent his fingers from acting like a tongue. This

---

138. Marinella seems to refer to Ariosto as the son of the Po River—known in ancient times as Eridanus.

139. Ariosto, *Orlando furioso*, XIV.89: "Mancati quei filosofi e quei santi / che lo solean tener pel camin ritto, / dagli onesti costumi ch'avea inanti, / fece alle sceleraggini tragitto. / Cominciò andar la notte con gli amanti, / indi coi ladri, e fare ogni delitto." Trans. Waldman, 147.

140. Tasso, *Gerusalemme liberata*, XII.51: "come lupo tacito, s'imbosca." Trans. Esolen, 241.

141. Ovid, *Metamorphoses*, II.535–36: "Cum candidus ante fuisses, / corve loquax, subito nigrantis versus in alas." Trans. Miller, 97.

is why the wing-footed God transformed the perjurer into a flinty stone called Index.[142] This man of little faith was not the only one to be turned into stone. The same fate befell some garrulous women known as magpies.[143]

Tongues that cannot restrain or control themselves are the cause of the dissensions, offenses, rivalries, and insults that we see every day. They instigate injuries and death and, though small, are offensive and fierce. So writes Angelo Sagrino in the *Life of Saint Benedict*:

> Among the different parts of the body, the evil tongue
> is apt to butt.
> It is bellicose, insincere, worthless, rebellious, unstable.
> Among the small parts of the body, although the
> tongue is weak,
> soft, and insignificant, nevertheless it breaks the
> strongest bones.[144]

The unfaithful tongue reveals to others most of what a person thinks and will soon do, hence "it breaks the strongest bones" (*ossa durissima frangit*).

Regarding this matter, Xenocrates the philosopher recommended that men—particularly those who want to pursue virtues and knowledge—do much listening and little talking.[145] There is nothing

142. Ovid, *Metamorphoses*, II.705-6: "periuraque pectora vertit / in durum silicem, qui nunc quoque dicitur Index". However, Ovid's Battus uses speech, and not gestures, to betray Mercury. Perhaps Marinella combined this figure with that of another Battus, who had a speech impediment (Herodotus, *Histories* IV.154).

143. In *Metamorphoses* V.24-678, Ovid narrates the story of Pierides, who challenged the Muses to a singing contest. The Pierides refused to accept the verdict of the nymphs which assigned victory to the Muses, and were transformed into magpies as a punishment for their insolence.

144. "Lingua mala est membrum, varia inter membra, petulcum. / Belligerum, mendax, vile, rebelle, vagum; / Lingua licet membrum, parva inter membra, pusillum / Labile, molle sit ossa tamen durissima frangit." No information is available on Angelo Sagrino.

145. Xenocrates of Chalcedon's love for silence is described in Diogenes Laertius, *Lives of Eminent Philosophers* IV.2.11, trans. R. D. Hicks, 2 vols. (Cambridge, MA: Harvard University Press, 1972), I.385-87.

more noble and valiant, however, than a speech whose river of words originates from a learned mind and calmly and wisely irrigates the countryside of hearing, bringing mature and peaceful waves of sweet water. This is what we read about Nestor:

> The clear-voiced orator of the men of Pylos rose up, he
> from whose tongue speech flowed sweeter than honey.[146]

Menelaus was a man of few words which were, however, wise and full of maturity, as we read in the *Iliad*:

> Menelaus to be sure spoke fluently, with few words,
> but very clearly, since he was not a man of lengthy
> speech, nor did he indulge in rambling.[147]

These are words that deserve to be heeded and appreciated, as historians say of Alcibiades, who was so powerful in his reasoning that he dominated other people's will. This is why the Florentine poet said:

> Alcibiades, who so many times
> Turned Athens back and forth, to suit his will
> By his fair face and by his honeyed words.[148]

Writing of Madonna Laura, Petrarch shows that she thought in silence:

> Attitude that speaks out in its silence.[149]

Elsewhere he writes:

146. Homer, *Iliad*, I.249–51: "Suaviloquus surrexit suavis Pyliourum concionator, cuius etiam a lingua melle dulciore fluebat sermo." Trans. Murray (Loeb), 31.

147. Homer, *Iliad*, III.213–15: "Certe quidem Menelaus succincte dicebat. Pauca quidem, sed valde acute, quoniam non multorum verborum, neque in verbis peccans. " Trans. Murray (Loeb), 145.

148. Petrarch, *Trionfo della fama*, II.25–27: "Alcibiade, che sí spesso Atena, / come fu suo piacer, volse e rivolse / Con dolce lingua, e con fronte serena." Trans. Wilkins, 79.

149. Petrarch, *Canzoniere*, 215.11: "Et un atto che parla con silentio." Trans. Musa, 315.

> In her silence she said, it seemed to me:
> "Who takes away from me my faithful friend?"[150]

And in another passage:

> Silent and alone.[151]

By this he means that she reasoned more with her mind than with her speech, as wise people do, because by sitting and resting a person becomes judicious and wise.[152] The poet of the Arno River wrote of Madonna Laura:

> In silence, like those words skillful and wise.[153]

When we are silent, in tranquil rest and taciturnity, we understand how sweet is a tongue that, full of knowledge and eloquence, silently reflects upon many useful and noble things, as did Scipio, who used to say that

> He was never less idle than when he had nothing to do
> and never less lonely than when he was alone.[154]

This is the experience of that great man who dealt with the most pressing matters of government—to distinguish between the opportune and the inopportune, the reasons for and advantages of war and of peace—when he developed his thoughts in silence. In this way, he did more for the republic than did those who used their strength.

---

150. Petrarch, *Canzoniere*, 123.13–14: "Et tacendo dicea, come a me parve: / Chi m'allontana il mio fedele amico?" Trans. Musa, 187.

151. Petrarch, *Trionfo della morte*, I.122: "Tacita, e sola."

152. "Quiescendo fit vir prudens et sciens," Marinella writes, echoing St. Thomas Aquinas, *Summa contra Gentiles* I.4.4.

153. Petrarch, *Canzoniere*, 105.61: "In silenzio parole accorte et sagge." Trans. Musa, 163.

154. Cicero, *De officiis*, III.1: "Numquam se minus otiosum esse, quam cum otiosus, nec minus solum, quam cum solus esset." Trans. Walter Miller (Cambridge, MA: Harvard University Press, 1913, 1961), 271.

The eloquence of a wise mind resonates in silence and appears sweeter than the murmuring of waves that break against stones in a pleasant river. Delivered at the appropriate time, the speech of a wise and learned man is like the sweet harmonies of musical notes in the silence of the night. They sweeten our bitter thoughts and cheer our melancholic souls. They are the best possible thing to hear. These people deserve to make their ideas known and their speech heard, for their words are like the delicate beauty of the snow, moving in a windless winter through calm air. This is how Homer describes Ulysses's words:

> But when he projected his great voice from his chest,
> and words like snowflakes on a winter's day, then
> could no other mortal man rival Odysseus.[155]

Nobody could imitate the wisdom and sweetness of his speech. One could say of him what Tasso says in his *Goffredo*:

> The birds were hushed, intent to hear him sing,
> and even the breezes ceased their whispering.[156]

Regarding the power and sweetness of a polished and learned speech, this poet says:

> From her delightful lips a golden chain
> puts their souls under her will's spur and rein.[157]

To put souls under one's will is indeed very powerful. Elsewhere Tasso says of Armida:

---

155. Homer, *Iliad*, III.221–23: "Sed quando vocem magnam ex pectore mittebat / et verba nivibus similia hiemalibus, / non post ea cum Ulysse contendebat homo alius" Trans. Murray (Loeb), 145.

156. Tasso, *Gerusalemme liberata*, XVI.13: "Tacquero gl'altri ad ascoltarlo intenti / E fermaro i sussurri in aria i venti." Trans. Esolen, 302.

157. Ibid., IV.83: "Esce da vaghe labra aurea catena / che l'alme a suo voler prende ed affrena." Trans. Esolen, 88.

Confident, she unfolded her deceit,
binding their senses by a sound so sweet.[158]

He shows us the power of sweet reasoning, even when it is treacherous. It could not harm Goffredo as he was not the right target (*subjectum adequatum*), but it did harm the other knights and the best men of the Latin army.

There are also certain arguments that contain nothing wise or sensible and might better be called blabbering.[159] They contain little substance and many words. They fill the ears with chatter and the heart with satiety.

We exhort those who cannot reason wisely and maturely to keep silent or talk very little, for slowness hides the dullness of ignorance. Just as speech reveals the value of a learned tongue, so too does it reveal the futility and vanity of a dumb or crazy one. Therefore, reading between the lines, we conclude that silence is always more laudable than speech.

Mindless speaking is crazy. First, we should consider what we intend to say and then we should imitate the rooster who, before singing, flaps its wings three times. Similarly, we should evaluate the quality of what we are about to say, in order to avoid other people's sneers. This is why the ancients worshiped a Goddess named Nemesis and depicted her with a brake in one hand and a wooden measuring stick in the other. This image urges us to think and consider, before speaking, what we want to say. That is why this goddess says, by way of an intelligent poet:

With this brake and with this measure
I, Nemesis, signify that every one
Must control his tongue, and never do
anything without weighing it well first.[160]

<hr/>

158. Ibid., IV.38: "Sí, che i pensati inganni al fine spiega / In suon, che di dolcezza i sensi lega." Trans. Esolen, 79.

159. The word used by Marinella, "infrascamenti," evokes the confusion created by a heap of leaves.

160. "Con questo freno, e con questa misura / Io Nemesi dimostro che frenare / Debba ciascun la lingua, né mai fare / Cosa, se prima ben non la misura." This representation of Nem-

We must practice taciturnity because it is highly appreciated and laudable. A man who was cautious in his speech said:

To restrain one's tongue is not the least of virtues.[161]

A man who listens a lot and speaks only a little can be regarded as the treasury[162] of wisdom, because in the wise man hearing is the way and the door to knowledge. A young man who does not possess this treasure must gain it by listening much and speaking little: the speech heard from the teacher's mouth is a source of learning for the pupil (*sermo auditus ex ore docentis causa est disciplinae in sciente*).

Words carry, carved upon themselves, the good and evil of the soul, knowledge and ignorance, good and its opposite, virtue and vice. Speech is like the water of a river that bears traces of its source and its bed. If it springs from or flows on a sulphurous place, then it carries a sulphurous odor and other similar qualities. Therefore, since words retain that quality of the heart, it is reasonable to consider, before speaking, whether your words are appropriate and good. This way, your listeners will not think that you are a person of little wisdom and worth, worse than Calandrino when he went to the Mugnone river looking for pebbles.[163]

Plato detested useless conversations. He who spends his time on idle chatter deserves not only to be laughed at, but also punished. He is considered a chatterer, an annoying person, someone to avoid and despise. This is why the above-mentioned philosopher says:

---

esis is found in Vincenzo Cartari's *Le immagini degli dèi XIII* (Fortuna). The verses Marinella quotes can also be found in Cartari, who attributes them to an unspecified Greek source.

161. "Linguam compescere, virtus non minima est," Marinella writes, perhaps quoting once again Pierre Lagnier's *Compendium* (345).

162. According to the *Grande dizionario della lingua italiana*, ed. Salvatore Battaglia (Torino: Utet, 1961–), the word "erario" (treasury) was not employed as a metaphor before the eighteenth century. However, Elissa Weaver points out that Arcangela Tarabotti had a particular fondness for this metaphor. See Francesco Buoninsegni and Arcangela Tarabotti, *Satira e antisatira*, ed. Elissa Weaver (Roma: Salerno, 1998) 75, n150.

163. *Decameron*, VIII.3. See n62.

> There is a very heavy penalty for careless and ill-con-
> sidered language; Retribution, messenger of Justice, is
> the appointed overseer of these things.[164]

This means that the goddess Nemesis watches over vain, vola-
tile, and light words, which contain no knowledge. She passes judgment on such errors and imposes grave punishments upon the sin-
ners. Excessive talk is abhorred and avoided by all. It is said that nature
gave us two ears and one tongue that we might listen a lot but speak
little. Heaven did not grant everybody the grace, sweetness, and power
of speech it granted Xenophon, who was called "The Attic Muse" for
his pleasing eloquence.[165] Therefore men must be patient in their listening. Answers will be brief, modest and sententious. They will fall
from the lips as precious dew falls from the sky to water and revive the
beauty of the flowers and the green of the grass. Always keep in mind
that he who is slow and tardy in speaking always receives more praise
than he who is quick and ready. This is why James the Apostle says:

> Everyone should be quick to hear, slow to speak.[166]

Paucity of words is attributed to women in particular, as they do not
have much experience and therefore cannot talk about many things.
Experience, like a wise master, schools man in his life, deeds, and
speech. This is why Gorgias of Leontini, that great legislator, said that
silence bestows glory upon a woman but not upon a man (*mulieri decus affert taciturnitas, non ita viro*).[167] Seclusion brings little knowledge
of human life, and therefore silence bestows glory upon a woman.

    Silence is not to be praised when time, place, and circum-
stances call for speech. To keep silent when speaking is required will

---

164. Plato, *Laws*, IV.717d: "Levium volatiliumque verborum gravissima imminet poena,
nam omnibus praeposita est Nemesis, iuditii angelus, huiusque consideratrix." Trans. Trevor
J. Saunders, in Plato, *Complete Works*, 1403.

165. The reference to Xenophon as "Attic Muse" is in Diogenes Laertius, *Lives of Eminent
Philosophers* II.57 (Loeb, I.187).

166. James 1:19: "Sit omnis homo velox ad audiendum, tardus ad loquendum." http://www.
vatican.va/archive/bible/nova_vulgata/documents/nova-vulgata_nt_epist-iacobi_lt.html

167. Cf. Aristotle, *Politics* I.13 (1260a30).

be attributed to ignorance, stupidity, and dullness of mind. This is why that good poet says:

> When it is time to speak, to keep silent is not a sign of wisdom.[168]

When times and need call for eloquence, silence is shameful. Nestor gained glory with his prudent and clever arguments, whose wisdom and sweetness forced Agamemnon to say:

> I wish […] I had ten such counselors.[169]

The king wished to have ten advisers like Nestor, rather than ten men as strong in battle as Achilles. His words were stronger than weapons, which is why it is said

> Let violence give place to the law.[170]

Those who imitate Nestor do not bury meaning under a multitude of words; indeed, they barely decorate it. One should not listen to deadly tongues, which are like poisonous arrows. They bring death by mixing sweetness with poison. Often, when you think you are loved, you become victim of unforseen disgrace. These pernicious tongues belong to the flatterers, whom the philosopher considers slaves by nature (*servus a natura*). Elsewhere he says that they come from the common people (*adulatores sunt de gente minuta*).[171]

Their hearts harbor the opposite of their tongues. This is why Tasso says in the *Aminta*:

> Mopso, who
> Has honeyed words forever on his tongue

168. Marinella writes: "Ubi tempus loquendi est, silere non est prudentiae signum." Unknown source.

169. *Iliad*, II.371: "Utinam decem essent mihi tales consultatores." Trans. Murray (Loeb), 89.

170. Cicero, *De officiis*, I.22: "Cedant arma togae" (lit: "may the arms yield to the gown").

171. Marinella is probably referring to Aristotle's characterization of flatterers in *Nicomachean Ethics*, IV.iii (1125a).

While on his lips he wears a friendly grin
And carries fraud within his breast and blades
Beneath his coat.[172]

And when, in *Goffredo*, Argante goes with Alete to meet Goffredo, he reveals that Alete is a great flatterer:

Poet of slanders dressed in such strange ways,
he most accuses when he seems to praise.[173]

This is the talent of a false and flattering tongue. Regarding this matter, one poet said:

He resembles a flatterer, who throws
His poisonous arrows at you
The more he praises you with his words.[174]

Therefore, we agree with the wise man who says:

The man who speaks what is right is loved.[175]

172. Torquato Tasso, *Aminta*, trans. Charles Jernigan and Irene Marchegiani Jones (New York: Italica Press, 2000), I.2, 215–19: "Di quel Mopso / C'ha la lingua melate parole / E ne le labbra un amichevol ghigno / E la fraude nel seno, et il rasoio / Tien sotto il manto."

173. Tasso, *Gerusalemme liberata*, II.58: "Gran Maestro di calunnie adorne in modi / Novi, che sono accuse, e paion lodi." Trans. Esolen, 47.

174. Francesco Berni, *Il primo libro dell'opere burlesche di m. Francesco Berni, di m. Gio. Della Casa, del Varchi, del Mauro, di m. Bino, del Molza, del Dolce, e del Fiorenzuola* (Usecht al Reno: Jacopo Broedelet, 1726), 199: "Ha de l'adulatore, il qual ti scocca / Nel cor le sue saette venenose / Quanto piú ti lusinga con la bocca."

175. Proverbs 16:13: "Qui recta loquitur diligetur."

5.   THE ORIGIN OF ORNAMENTS AND LUXURY, AND
     HOW THEY BECAME INCREASINGLY IMPORTANT,
     IS DISCUSSED. WE EXHORT WOMEN TO USE THEM
     WITH MODESTY AND MODERATION.

At the beginning Prometheus, Iapetus's son, saw that the world was
rich in ornaments and beauty. It was almost like a cute and childish
boy who laughs in the midst of such happy abundance and full of joy
discovers fields adorned with infinite riches. With a serene mind and
a pleasing murmur, it seemed to invite a master who would rule over
such greatness and excellence. Knowing its desire, Prometheus took
some soil that had just been separated from heaven and still retained
some celestial quality, mixed it with river water and formed man, as
Ovid says:

> That earth which the son of Iapetus mixed with fresh,
> running water, and moulded into the form of the all-
> controlling gods.[176]

Prometheus so extolled his creature that he wanted it to resemble
the Gods. While all the other animals were prone and looked at the
ground, this one raised his head to the dwelling place of the eternal,
that he might contemplate his place of origin.

> And, though all other animals are prone and fix their
> gaze upon the earth, he gave to man an uplifted face
> and bade him stand erect and turn his eyes to heaven.[177]

Therefore, this rational animal, thanks to the excellence of the divine
presence still in him, ruled over all the things created and disposed of
them according to his will. In his innocent simplicity, he led a happy
life full of justice and love. He lived without fear of the harsh threats
of the law, the unjust verdicts of a corrupt judge, or the cruel and mer-

176. Ovid, *Metamorphoses*, I.82–83: "Quam satus Iapeto, mixtam pluvialibus undis, / finxit
in effigiem moderantum cuncta deorum." Trans. Miller (Loeb), 9.

177. Ibid., I.84–85: "Pronaque cum spectent animalia cetera terram, / os homini sublime
dedit caelumque videre / iussit, et erectos ad sidera tollere vultus." Trans. Miller (Loeb), 9.

ciless schemes of an evil tyrant. Cities were safe without protection, trumpets did not announce the deaths of brave captains with a bloody song, and rivers did not carry deadly poison in their pure waters. Everything was full of peace, justice, and love.

But as man turned toward injustice and lacerated the clothes of innocence that covered his nudity, giants appeared on the earth (*apparverunt Gigantes super terram*). Shouting and raging, proud man began to blast the lightning of scornful lies and the flames of insidious hatred against the sky. He placed Ossa over Olympus, and Pelion over Ossa, in a crazy attempt to defeat the highest kingdom and draw the celestial dwellers under the power of his scepter.[178] Although his plan was ultimately fruitless and in vain, man nonetheless retained his desire to be equal to the Gods. He longed to be divine and looked with envy at the Gods' eternal dwelling. If he could not equal them in strength, he believed he could compete at least in ornaments and beauty.

Seeing the sun shining with a crown of rays over the world, he decided to imitate it by wearing a different kind of crown. Sharp-minded, he penetrated Mars's home and discovered that the god armed himself with a helmet and a golden cuirass and presented himself proudly in a silver mesh. In this attire, Mars appeared remarkable and superb among the other gods. Similarly, Minerva was proud not only of her weapons, but also of her beauty, which she highlighted with a golden veil. In man's mind, Chloris appeared in a dress of privets and roses. She had deprived the celestial gardens of lilies and other flowers to make herself more graceful. Man considered the greatness of the Gods, and wished to be their equal in some way. He was sorry to be less excellent than they were, but he did not know how to become their equal. And so, in the great sea of the mind, he wavered between envy and pain.

But what can remain hidden from our intellect? It occurred to him that he could find something comparable to their greatness in the mysterious ocean or in the womb of the untouched earth. This greed and pride—this desire to emulate the gods—inspired man to take shining pearls from seashells, reddish corals from the depths of the

---

178. In Marinella's account, man's rebellion is more successful than in Ovid's *Metamorphoses* (I.151-62) and Homer's *Odyssey* (XI.313-16).

sea, and gold, silver, and precious stones from the most secret recesses of the earth. With these, man began to make ornate artifacts, such as gilded crowns, necklaces, golden globes adorned with pearls, and various enamelware, belts, and other objects shaped in countless ways.

Unsatisfied with merely shaping gold and silver into different guises, man has beaten these metals to make them thinner, and used their fine threads to weave rich and precious webs that are superior to Arachne's. Man's skill is so refined and industrious that one can say

> The workmanship was more beautiful than the material.[179]

As man began to adorn himself with all these jewels, his pride increased, and he began to think himself similar to the Gods. However, despite all their efforts to embellish—or rather burden—themselves with riches of all kinds, women could not satisfy their desire. Therefore they created for the head—which until that moment had maintained an honest and modest appearance—a new style involving the addition of great amounts of hair. But this addition makes the hair on both sides of the head extend to or beyond the shoulder, creating an ugly and misshapen countenance. As it is easy to add to things already invented (*facile est inventis addere*), artificiality and luxury increase every day. Women strew so many flowers over their hair that they would surpass the gardens of Genoa and Naples, as well as of King Alcinous's.[180] Some women, although these strange and unreasonable ornaments—which should rather be called "disornaments— make them no prettier, still want to use them. Forgive me for saying this, women, but they do not realize how much uglier they are, with their little beauty confused and lost among that mixture of flowers and ribbons and silk of different colors.

Some women's pride, luxury, and folly are so great that they devote all their attention to their personal hygiene and make up. They do not believe that there is anything in the world more important than artificial countenance. So powerful is this servitude, which they mis-

179. Ovid, *Metamorphoses*, II.5: "Materia superabat opus." Trans. Miller (Loeb), 61.

180. The orchard of Alcinous, king of the Phaeacians, is described by Homer in *Odyssey*, VII.112–31.

take for happiness, that when they are all made up, they think themselves superior to noble, rich, and virtuous women. Following the latest fashion, some have even begun to imitate the plumed helmets of famous knights and valiant captains by waving colored feathers over their heads. But let's move on.

A hair style that extends to the width of the shoulders and a dress that reaches the breast without any shape create before our eyes a misshapen countenance that is disagreeable to the mind. Noble women used to wear their dresses tight around their hips, which gave them wide shoulders and a beautiful and well-proportioned womanly shape. Today, there is no shape at all. The head, shoulders, and dress are all of a similar size, hiding from view that beautiful bodily countenance women used to have.

The more they searched for new items of luxury and vanity, the worse they looked. Superfluity and embellishments increased daily, and the mind grew tired of inventing new fashions. When Jupiter, our common father, turned his eyes from the eternal dwelling place and gazed at Venice, my hometown, he saw that its luxury and vanity had risen to the extreme. He saw that the works of gold and the abundance of precious stones and gems had surpassed anything one could desire. He saw Adria's beautiful daughters[181] compete among themselves to see who could spend the most and consume the greatest quantity of gold. He realized they had so much gold and precious metal shining on their heads and in their veils, dresses, and belts that the golden age that had long passed had taken the shape of those necklaces, belts, handles, and golden globes. He thought that the reason for the decline of the golden age was that gold had been transformed into ornaments of so many different shapes.

The Father of the Gods and of humans was rather disgusted. He summoned Maia's son,[182] who appeared immediately, and told him: "Go to the Queen of Cities, Venice, which is equal or superior to Rome, where justice, religion, peace and other virtues shine. Make it known to those very prudent and invincible Patricians that they should moderate their excessive luxury, superfluous ornaments, and pleasure. They should restrain such license through prohibition."

181. The Adriatic Sea is believed to have been named after the Etruscan town of Adria.

182. Hermes or Mercury, messenger of the Gods.

Those very wise lords heard, appreciated, and cherished this message. They quickly proclaimed a ban. Barely had the town crier divulged the interdiction than it spread at the speed with which the sun's rays shine over the world. His were not words, but sharp-arrowed spears, which pierced without pity the hearts and souls of the city's beautiful daughters. Many were so melancholic that they made their internal pain and sorrow known not simply with words, cries, and laments, but by striking their chests and faces while sobbing, unable to find a remedy for their desperation and pain. Hence, the favorable Muses inspired a merciful friend of Phoebus whose name I have forgotten to compose two sonnets, his heart having been struck by the sweet hand of gentle pity and the hope of consoling and advising Adria's sorrowful daughters. I transcribe the sonnets here, that all women might read them and receive solace from their painful concerns.[183]

A vain torment afflicts and wounds the heart
Of Adria's beautiful daughters.
Gems are forbidden to them, and the beautiful work
That is the glory and reward of a woman's mind.
And yet, kind nature gave you the praise and
Beauty of ivory, purple, and gold,
In your hair and face, by far a richer treasure
Than any that effort and art provides you.
Now every woman over the rich spoils,
Almost like beautiful Venus over dead Adonis,
Melts clouds of tears from her beautiful eyes.
May women and girls adorn themselves with such ornament
That is not subject to someone else's desires,
Or to the threats of an insidious star.[184]

183. This mysterious "merciful friend of Phoebus" could very well be Marinella herself. The two sonnets complement each other: the first is moralistic (women should turn their thoughts toward God's eternal gifts, rather than worry about earthly and transient treasures); the second—which significantly begins with "but"—is a gallant celebration of women's power to bend the will of the sternest legislators.

184. "Vano tormento il cor travaglia e fiede / D'Adria a le belle figlie; poiché a loro / Son le gemme interdette, e'l bel lavoro / Del feminil sapere gloria e mercede. / Pur la natura a

But if magnanimous women cannot placate
Or calm their inflamed hearts
To the placid rigor of the supreme command,
They need to imitate the Patricians of Rome.
Feeling, as they did, no less harsh a sorrow,
Indignant they took, with manly soul,
every crossroad, square, and path
that the Quirites travel to the magistrate.
With firm faces and gracious words
The stolen honor of the removed ornaments
They sternly asked of those stubborn minds.
In the end, the princes and rulers of Rome
Granted the gems to their laments,
And together with the gems their hearts in chains.[185]

I believe that these consolations and exhortations will please women's souls, which will be satisfied with what is right and will praise natural beauty as their own gift, however fleeting. Ornaments are not part of a person, and nobody can be proud of something that does not belong to them. All artificial things are superfluous.[186] This is why Venus was born naked. A beauty without ornament and unnecessary vanity is nobler than one adorned. True beauty does not need luxury or decoration, but is laudable for what it is. This is why the prince of philosophers recommends that women keep well within the limits set

voi cortese diede / il pregio e 'l bel d'avorio, d'ostro, e d'oro / Nel crin, nel volto, assai piú bel tesoro / Di quant'industria et arte a voi concede / Or di esse ognuna su le ricche spoglie / Quasi su 'l morto Adon Vener bella / Nembi di pianto da begli occhi scioglie / S'orni di fregio tal Donna e donzella / Che soggetto non resti a l'altrui voglie, / né al minacciar d'insidiosa stella."

185. "Ma s'addolcir, se racchetar non sanno / Le magnanime donne il petto altero / Al placido rigor d'eccelso impero / Le romane patritie a imitar s'hanno. / Sentito anche esse un non men duro affanno / Preser sdegnose, e con viril pensiero / Ogni trivio, ogni piazza, ogni sentiero / Onde i Quiriti al magistrato vanno / Con fermo viso e gratiosi accenti / Di lor fregi inconcessi i tolti onori / Chiedean severe a l'ostinate menti. / Al fin di Roma i principi, e i rettori / Concessero le gemme a i loro lamenti / E con le gemme incatenati i cori."

186. Here Marinella repeats the same concept in Latin, borrowing the phrase used in a completely different context by St. Thomas Aquinas (*Summa contra Gentiles*, I.38.3): "Est aliquid additum."

by the law upon ornaments.[187] Nothing deserves praise more than the modesty and dignity of an honest and virtuous life.

I do not criticize the *pianelle*,[188] although they make noise and perhaps bother some people. For some mysterious reason, the Ancients depicted Venus wearing them. They wanted to signify that women must not wander around, but rather stay in their homes to attend to children and family. The *pianelle* are weights that prevent women from running and bestow gravitas and decorum upon them, which suits special people deserving of honor. The height of the *pianelle* is such that those who want to admire a woman's beauty must gaze upward, as if looking at a goddess. This is a good thing because it removes men from terrestrial vileness. If things were different, only rarely would they turn their eyes toward the sky. Nobody can deny this good result.

I find no reason to criticize the noise of the *pianelle*. Momus, who chastised and corrected the action of the Gods, found Venus to be flawless. To mention just one defect among her perfection, however, he said that her *pianelle* made too much noise.[189] The little noise they do make, however, will not perturb our souls. Those ancient wise men wanted to show women that practicing seclusion is laudable. They knew that there were some women who not only wanted to spend all day wandering around but also wanted to attend comedies and similar pastimes at the theater at night, with little pride and profit to themselves and their households. However, I would not go as far as saying that all honest pleasure should be denied to them.

Many believe that women wear high heels because they have not forgotten the pride of the Giants. Unable to imitate their deeds and place Ossa over Olympus and Pelion over both of them, they try to get closer to the sky by imposing these heavy weights upon themselves. Whatever the reason, I do not despise them. Many men used to wear them, although they have since given them up. Perhaps they

187. Cf. Aristotle, *Economics*, III.1. Marinella writes: "Utantur minori ornata quam permiserint leges civitatis."

188. Renaissance travelers marveled at the sight of Venetian women wearing the *pianelle*, platform shoes whose heels could reach two feet.

189. Vincenzo Cartari refers to Momus's criticism of Venus's noisy *pianelle* in *Le immagini degli dèi XIII* (Fortuna).

have realized that theirs was a vain attempt to rival the height of towers and mountains.

Just as men once loved the *pianelle,* they now love excessive hair and strive to imitate women. Long, curly, and abundant blond hair is indeed a beautiful thing, but it must be one's own. I hear that some try to remedy their natural deficiency by obtaining hair from poor corpses. This hair seems to me more horrible than that of Medusa or Megaera, as the good Satyr of the *Faithful Shepherd* says of Corisca:

> You should have despised it
> much more than Megaera's
> viperous, monstruous locks.[190]

They do so because they want women to believe that they too are loved and sufficiently endowed by Nature. Although Hercules and Achilles did wear women's dresses, I haven't heard that they wore *pianelle* or augmented their hair artificially. To do so would be truly inappropriate for a man, who must show manly dignity, as Tasso says when speaking of Goffredo:

> and yet true valor is its own decoration,
> shines on itself, and needs no special care.[191]

The true and laudable ornament of any woman is the modest use of make up and jewels, and a sober, clean, and genuine style of dress. It is wrong to believe that an excessive, unreasonable style, the profusion of silky clothes and colorful ribbons increase one's beauty and glory. Rather, they violate the dignity and honesty of a woman's reputation. Much more could be said about this subject, but let us put it aside.

Many men—and not necessarily only those of little importance and wisdom—believe they are showing respect for a woman by calling

---

190. Guarini, *Il pastor fido,* II.6: "Che aborrire / dovevate assai piú, che di Megera / Le viperine e mostruose chiome." Megaera, one of the three Furies, had snakes for hair, like Medusa.

191. Tasso, *Gerusalemme liberata,* II.60: "Ma verace valor, benché negletto / è di se stesso a sé fregio assai chiaro." Trans. Esolen, 48.

her "dama."[192] If they knew what the word meant, however, I doubt they would use it to address a worthy person. I—who desire glory and pride for women— would never use that word. If I did, I would fear that women would rightly become angry at me. "Dama" does not suggest power and excellence, but rather servitude and subjection, as the works of many historians and learned writers make clear. They use the word "dame" to refer to women who accompany queens, princesses, and other women of high rank. We read for instance: "Leonora, Duchess of Mantua, went to church with her 'dame.'"[193] Here, "dame" refers to the girls who were in her service. Elsewhere, we read that the queen came with her "dame" and countesses. Boccaccio uses the term similarly when he speaks of Madonna Beritola and her honest damsel.[194] In the *Filocolo*, the queen sends away her damsels ("damigelle"), and the princess arrives at the tournament with her damsels, meaning with her servants. Indeed, you never find a princess or lady without a damsel, that is, a servant.

"Dama," then, does not imply superiority. Rather, a woman should always be referred to by the word "donna," which seems always to indicate superiority and power. In fact, whereas "dama" derives from and always suggests the state of servitude and subjection, "donna" derives from the state of dominion and rule. I need offer no further examples, for the connection between "dama" and servitude is abundantly clear. Etymologically, I believe it derives from the verb *do-das* (to give). The imperative, in the vernacular, is *dammi* (give me). Here, the subject is the lady or the princess and the object is

192. Here Marinella begins an etymological disquisition on the term "dama" (lady). This aside does not fit very well into the general structure of this chapter and is based on erroneous etymology. Far from being a contraction of the imperative "dammi" (give me), as Marinella claims, "dama" derives from the Latin word for lady, "domina," through the mediation of the Provençal "dom'na." It is therefore very close to "donna," the Italian word for "woman," which Marinella always correctly interpreted as a sign of distinction. The confusion seems to stem from Marinella's interpretation of "dama" (lady) and "damigella" (damsel) as synonyms. See Ottorino Pianigiani, *Vocabolario etimologico della lingua italiana* (Genova: I Dioscuri, 1988). Marinella's passion for etymology figures prominently in the opening chapter of *The Nobility and Excellence of Women*, titled "On the nobility of the names given to the female sex."

193. Unknown source.

194. Boccaccio, *Decameron*, II.6. See n62.

the damsel or servant, who must obey the subject's order. As Horace demonstrates in his *Poetics*, words often change; first, an "m" was subtracted from "dammi," and then the "i" was changed to "a." These simple changes left us with "dama." This, then, is the true etymology of the term. "Dama" is a sign of submission and obedience. Those who doubt this can infer this truth from the results, as causes are known by their effects.[195] Indeed, as I have said already, a "dama" serves and obeys, whereas a lady commands. Therefore, since, as I contend, the meaning of the appellation "dama" is a person under someone else's control, it is not appropriate to use this word when referring to a great woman worthy of respect.

195. Marinella's Latin quote ("Ab effectu cognoscontur causae") seems to imply a reference to Aristotle's *Metaphysics*, V.1 (1013a15).

6.   WOMEN'S PRUDENCE.

According to Aristotle, prudence is a true and reasoned state of capacity to act with regard to matters that are subject to change.[196] There are several kinds of prudence. The kind that pertains to a president is known as architectonic prudence; another kind of prudence concerns the self; yet another, known as household management, relates to the household and its members.[197] The latter pertains to women.[198] Although Aristotle denies that prudence can be found in women, he does speak of the "prudence of the household" (*prudentia rei familiaris*).

In his opinion, the governance of a household belongs to the woman. But how is she to govern without prudence? To deny that a woman and a mother possesses prudence is to deprive her of all virtues, which would be unfair, in spite of her lack of experience. Just because she does not know about everything that happens in the world

196. Aristotle in the *Nicomachean Ethics* discusses the concept of *phronesis*, commonly translated as "prudence" or "practical wisdom." Unlike theoretical wisdom (*sophia*), which concerns universal truths, practical wisdom deals with matters that are subject to change and leads humans to operate properly in their lives (*Nicomachean Ethics*, I.v [1140a–1140b30] and VI.vii [1141b8]). See David Arnaud and Tim Le Bon, "Key Concepts In Practical Philosophy Series: Practical and Theoretical Wisdom," in *Practical Philosophy* 3.1 (March 2000), 6–9. http://www.practical-philosophy.org.uk/Volume3Articles/practicalwisdom.htm

197. Marinella switches to Latin to indicate the practical wisdom addressed "ad plures, ut in domo, quae dicitur prudentia rei familiaris." The closest reference appears to be Aristotle, *Nicomachean Ethics*, VI.viii (1141b30): "Practical wisdom also is identified especially with that form of it which is concerned with a man himself—with the individual; and this is known by the general name 'practical wisdom'; of the other kinds one is called household management, another legislation, the third politics [...]." Trans. W. D. Ross, rev. J. O. Urmson, in *The Complete Works of Aristotle*, ed. Jonathan Barnes (Princeton: Princeton University Press, 1984), II.1802–3.

198. Marinella writes in the margins that, according to Aristotle's *Poetics*, practical wisdom does not suit a woman or a child ("prudentia non convenit nec mulieri nec puero"). This passage, however, is absent from standard editions of the *Poetics*, the closest reference being the philosopher's recommendation that characters in a tragedy behave according to their gender: "The character before us may be, say, manly; but it is not appropriate in a female character to be manly, or clever" (*Poetics*, 15, 15 [1454a20]) (Trans. I. Bywater, in *The Complete Works*, II.2327). Women are absent from the discussion of practical wisdom because such a virtue belongs to rulers, who, in Aristotle's thought, are by definition men. See Leah Bradshaw, "Political Rule, Prudence and the 'Woman Question' in Aristotle," in *Canadian Journal of Political Science / Revue canadienne de science politique* 24:3 (1991), 557–73.

does not mean she is without prudence. She is an expert in everything that happens within her house and knows which things to pursue and which to avoid, just as she knows what is useful and what is harmful.[199]

Prudence comes from experience. Experience is made of actions repeated over and over again, and prudence is made of many experiences.[200]

Women, I am certain, do not know what belongs to the military or equestrian arts, but they do have great experience in the various operations of the domestic sphere, which are infinite. This is because a large household is similar to a small city, which comprises many different parts.[201] If a city is to be ruled by a prudent prince, so, too, is a household to be governed by a prudent woman. Prudence is necessary in those who rule over many. Nature, which never exceeds in what is superfluous or lacks in what is necessary, gave hands to man because he is most prudent. Since a woman also has hands, we can conclude that she, too, is most prudent, rather than simply prudent.

The philosopher concurred with Anaxagoras, who said that hands are the tools Nature gave to the prudent man, that he might do and operate whatever he pleased. Hands do not make man the most prudent animal. Rather, he was given hands because he is more prudent than any other animal.[202] He who possesses such prudence can use many tools and practice many arts. In the words of Aristotle:

---

199. Here Marinella extrapolates principles from Aristotle's different works to reach an original conclusion. She combines the idea that practical wisdom applies to the household (a premise derived from *Nicomachean Ethics*, see note above) with the notion that household management pertains to women. This allows her to conclude that women are endowed with practical wisdom, something Aristotle did not contemplate.

200. The original is in Latin: "Prudentia est ex experientia. Ex multis actibus iteratis fit experientia, ex multis experimentis fit prudentia." Unknown source.

201. A gloss in the margins reads: "Aristotle, *Politics*, I: 'A large household and a small state are almost identical'" ("Domus magna et parva civitas quasi nihil differunt"). If read in its entirety, however, that passage conveys a very different meaning: "Some people think that the qualifications of a statesman, king, householder, and master are the same [...] as if there were no difference between a great household and a small state [...] But all this is a mistake." (*Politics*, I.i [1252a9–18], trans. Benjamin Jowett, in *The Complete Works*, II.1986).

202. A quote in the margins refers to Anaxagoras's idea that hands were given to man because of his prudence ("Datae sunt manus homini quia prudentissimus est"), following Aristotle's interpretation of the philosopher's thought: "Now it is the opinion of Anaxagoras

> Hands are instruments. Nature, like a prudent man, gives to each the things that he can use. Man is not the most prudent of all the animals because he has hands, but because he is the most prudent of all the animals he has received hands. As he is the most prudent, he can use many instruments.[203]

If hands are a sign of prudence, and if women also have hands, how, then, can one deny that women are prudent, given that man received hands because he is most prudent? And yet some say that prudence is a habit that does not suit a woman.[204] But women, like men, obtained hands from nature, and are most prudent. Therefore, we can't deny that the management of the household belongs to women, who can thereby show their prudence and competence.[205]

The philosopher in some passages denies that women can be prudent. However, when he says that everything in the household must be governed by only one person, namely, the woman— he implicitly admits that she is prudent.

> The rule of the house is a monarchy, for every house is under one head.[206]

---

that the possession of these hands is the cause of man being of all animals the most intelligent. But it is more rational to suppose that man has hands because of his superior intelligence" (*Parts of Animals*, 687a8–10, trans. W. Ogle, in *The Complete Works*, I.1071).

203. Marinella's Latin quote seems to summarize a passage in Aristotle, *Parts of Animals*, 687a10–20. Cf. Aristotle, *Parts of Animals* IV.x (687a): "Manus sunt instrumenta naturae utique homo prudens tribuerat cuique rem, quam uti possit. Homo non propter manus prudentissimus est, sed quia prudentissimus omnium animalium manus obtinet, et quia prudentissimus est, plurimis instrumentis uti potest." Another Aristotelian quote in the margins stresses the concept, albeit by mistakenly referencing to the *Poetics*: "hand is a tool of tools" ("manus est organum organorum") (*On the Soul* 432a, trans. J. A. Smith, in *The Complete Works*, I.682).

204. Marinella writes: "Prudentia est mos non convenit mulieri."

205. A note in the margins reads: "A good wife should be the mistress of her home, having under her care all that is within it" (Aristotle, *Economics*, III.i: "Oportet probam mulierem omnibus dominari quae intus sunt"). Trans. Armstrong, in *The Complete Works*, II.2146.

206. Aristotle, *Politics*, I.vii (1255b20): "Unius est imperium, nam ab uno regitur omnis domus." However, the rest of Aristotle's argument makes clear that the master of the house-

This cannot be achieved without prudence. Without prudence, no one can govern a household full of boys, girls, parents, brothers, servants, and others, each devoted to different tasks and occupations. This is why Aristotle says in the *Politics* that a large household is no different from a small state.[207] However small, a town requires a prudent prince. Likewise, a household needs a prudent woman, who with the right means and laudable ways can not only manage the wealth the man has gained, but also distribute punishments or rewards, praise or blame each person according to their merits or shortcomings, which pertains to domestic prudence.

Prudent people need to ponder which things are good, useful, and honorable for themselves and for their household, and this is precisely what the prudent woman does. The philosopher says that there cannot be prudence without experience. According to this logic, a young person cannot be experienced, as only length of time brings experience.[208]

Women reveal their prudence through their repeated experiences in the home. They become queens of this virtue and understand which things are profitable and which are detrimental, which are useful and which are dangerous. I believe that Pericles and men like him have practical wisdom because they can see what is good for themselves and what is good for men in general.[209]

I believe this virtue consists of using our intellect to make a mature assessment of the good and the bad that might proceed from various circumstances. We do this without any experience. Once we have made our assessment, we turn our minds to the fulfillment of our needs. I call this kind of assessment prudence, even if it requires no experience. We have seen Alexander, Hannibal, and Scipio lead very

---

hold is the man, not the woman as Marinella claims. "A husband and father, we saw, rules over wife and children [...] The male is by nature fitter for command than the female, just as the elder and full-grown is superior to the younger and more immature." (*Politics*, I.v [1259a38–1259b3]). Trans. Jowett, in *The Complete Works*, II.1998.

207. "Non differt magna domus a civitate parva," Marinella repeats.

208. Marinella writes: "Iuvenis expertus non est, experientiam temporis affert longitudo." Cf. Aristotle, *Nicomachean Ethics*, VI.viii [1142a10].

209. Aristotle, *Nicomachean Ethics*, VI.v (1140b): "Periclem, et eiusmodi viros prudentes appellamus, quia qua sibi, et aliis hominibus sint bona, possunt contemplari."

powerful armies at a young age. They won dangerous battles with uncertain outcomes that others of more maturity and experience might not have been able to win.[210] Their judgment was sufficient to overcome their enemies. With new military stratagems and inventions, they defeated enemy armies of almost insurmountable power, to the amazement of the world and to their own glory, and they achieved this without any experience. These invincible captains proved their worth in the first days of their youth, regardless of the fact that military struggles require experience and prudence. They proved the philosopher incorrect in his belief that the young, being inexperienced, are also necessarily imprudent. I conclude that, for many, good judgment is a natural virtue that, like the experience of many laudable things, belongs to man.

We know that even without experience we can perform deeds equal to those of experienced people. Therefore nobody can deny that women exercise prudence in spite of their lack of experience. There is a certain natural light that replaces experience in showing women what to follow and what to flee. This constitutes their good judgment.

Although Aristotle is sometimes hostile toward the female sex, he nevertheless allows women to exercise authority over everything in the household (*omnibus, quae intus sunt*).[211] Therefore, he implicitly concedes that women possess household prudence, as he makes her the administrator of everything that man has gained with his labor. Nor would it be fair for the Philosopher to consider spiders and bees most prudent[212] while deeming prudence impossible for women, given that Nature has granted women, like men, hands that they might show the excellence of their intellects. I am not claiming that women must be as prudent as Semiramis when she devised how

210. The connection between practical wisdom and experience is explored by Aristotle in relationship not to women but to young men, whom he believes incapable of prudence: "[...] It is thought that a young man of practical wisdom cannot be found. The cause is that such wisdom is concerned not only with universals but with particulars, which become familiar from experience, but a young man has no experience, for it is length of time that gives experience" (*Nicomachean Ethics*, VI.viii [1142a10]). It becomes therefore necessary for Marinella to break this connection between prudence and experience, which she tries to do in the last part of this chapter.

211. Cf. Aristotle, *Economics* III.i.

212. Aristotle, *Physics*, II.viii (199a20).

a well-protected city could be conquered[213] or many other things that I mentioned in my book *The Nobility and Excellence of Women*. We will be content if they be prudent in womanly tasks and manage their families and households in devoted and endearing ways.

213. Marinella's positive assessment of Semiramis recalls Christine de Pizan's praise of the Babylonian queen in *The Book of the City of Ladies* (trans. Rosalind Brown-Grant [London: Penguin, 1999], 35). Both Dante (*Inferno* V.52–60) and Boccaccio (*De Mulieribus Claris* II) had instead stigmatized Semiramis for her alleged lust.

7. WE EXHORT HUSBAND AND WIFE TO LIVE IN HARMONY. THIS BRINGS HONOR AND PROSPERITY TO THE HOUSEHOLD, PRAISE TO THE HUSBAND AND WIFE, GLORY AND SATISFACTION TO THEIR CHILDREN, AND UNIVERSAL HAPPINESS.

We have invited women not to fall in love with literature and not to neglect womanly tasks. On the contrary, they should attend to these tasks with great passion and diligence because they are useful, comfortable, and honorable. It is good and appropriate that we turn now to the life and habits of men and women together. It is necessary that we unite these two who cannot remain separate.[214] Eternal wisdom, which knows what is necessary to human happiness, ordered the union and companionship of these two individuals, as these words make clear:

> Thus the nature both of the man and of the woman
> has been preordained by the will of heaven to live a
> common life.[215]

As these two individuals must come together, we must give mature consideration to their union, that they might live happily in peace, calm, and serenity, for the glory of the heavens, the praise of their household, and the honor of themselves and their city.

To avoid error, it is wise to rely on the opinions of wise men. Therefore, I believe that everybody will appreciate our continuing our exhortations under their escort. It would certainly be stolid and ignorant to ignore the voices of learned and wise men. Therefore we invoke the words of Hesiod. Regarding the union of these two, he said that a man should choose a maiden as his wife, so that she may diligently learn his ways. Were he to choose a widow, he would find her habits

214. A gloss in the margins refers to Aristotle, *Politics*, I.ii (1252a25): "In the first place there must be a union of those who cannot exist without each other, namely, of male and female" ("Necessarium est combinare eos, qui non possunt esse nisi simul seu marem et feminam ad societatem"). Trans. Jowett, in *The Complete Works*, II.1986.

215. Aristotle, *Economics*, I.iii [1343b25]: "Sic divina providentia utriusque natura ordinata est, scilicet viri et mulieris ad societatem." Trans. Forster, in *The Complete Works*, II.2131.

difficult to change, for she would already have grown accustomed to the habits of another.[216] It is difficult to move to something foreign to us (*Ad aliena difficilis est transitus*).

The habits one acquires at an early age cannot be changed easily. Furthermore, it is possible that your wife will prefer those habits over yours. A silent jealousy would gnaw at your soul, and you would never be certain of her love. Therefore, we must praise and uphold Hesiod's opinion as just and laudable. If a woman adopts your habits, then you will be like two bodies with one soul. Aristotle agrees with Hesiod, and recommends:

> Take thee a maiden to wife, and teach her the ways of discretion.[217]

Following Hesiod's opinion, the honorable and wise philosopher adds:

> Dissimilarity of habits tends more than anything to destroy affection.[218]

If you obey these great men, then I am sure you will enjoy happiness. Differences in habit and disposition, especially between a husband and a wife, lead only to disagreement, misunderstanding, and unhappiness.

Considering the peace and love that harmony between a husband and a wife brings to a household, this wise poet invites men to choose a maiden, someone who has yet to receive external influences. If you follow Hesiod's advice, then, like Aristotle says of the mind, your wife will be

---

216. Cf. Hesiod, *Works and Days*, 695–705 (quoted by Marinella as "Virginem habeto, ut tuos sedula discat mores"). However, Hesiod says nothing here about marrying a widow. A Latin quote in the margins supports this reliance on established authorities: "To dissent from learned men is evidence of ignorance" ("Dissentire a viris sapientibus esset inscitiae argumentum").

217. Aristotle, *Economics*, I.iv [1344a15]: Aristotle is quoting Hesiod's advice. Trans. Forster, in *The Complete Works*, II.2132.

218. Ibid.: "Nam dissimilitudines morum non sunt aptae ad conciliandas amicitias."

A writing-table on which as yet nothing actually stands written.[219]

She will be like a white cloth that can take on any color and will receive your habits, which is laudable and dignified. Similarity generates peace and love, both of which are necessary if your household is to be ruled, governed, and enriched by both of you. If one works against the other, you will ruin and destroy rather than build and establish. You will be like two contrary rivers, which noisily and forcefully break their furious waves against one another.

When your desires are similar, your habits consonant, and your thoughts the same, your household will be ruled and enriched as if by one mind, for consonance of will is of great importance. This is why Tasso says of Erminia and the shepherd:

and brought her to his aged spouse, whom heaven
had given him, one heart and soul to share.[220]

To achieve this consonance, Hesiod recommends:

A man should marry a maiden, that habits discreet he
may teach her.[221]

If you heed this advice, your wife will be like a young plant whose branches an experienced gardener can bend into the forms of different wild beasts and other figures. Likewise, you will bend the soft and simple girl according to your desires. Seeing the partner you have formed according to your desires will bring incredible happiness and consolation. Indeed, different lifestyles cannot result in stability and peace.

---

219. Aristotle, *On the Soul*, III.iv [430a1]: "Est tam tabula rasa, in qua nihil est scriptum" (trans. Smith, in *The Complete Works*, I.683). Although Aristotle does not mention Hesiod here, Marinella merges the two.

220. Tasso, *Gerusalemme liberata*, VII.17: "E la conduce ovè l'antica moglie, / che di conforme cor gli ha data il Cielo." Trans. Esolen, 137.

221. Hesiod, *Works and Days*, 698–99, in *Theogony. Works and Days. Testimonia*, trans. Glenn W. Most (Cambridge, MA: Harvard University Press, 2006), 55.

When tranquility reigns between husband and wife, friends rejoice while enemies worry and suffer, pierced by Envy's poisonous teeth. Aristotle, Hesiod, Plato, Homer, Francesco Patrizio, and others, whose opinions I will quote, are so knowledgeable that I do not believe anyone will ignore their advice, especially on such an important matter.[222]

One could say that those who do not desire a sober, modest, just, temperate, and honest wife do not care about God. The woman is the one who protects the household's honor and cares for its preservation and growth. She is the one who raises your children and disciplines and educates them. Think of the care and consideration you must devote to choosing your wife, knowing that she must assimilate your habits and constantly refer to you, as if she were your double. I want you to know that you must set the example for her life. If you are good, then you will admire in your wife, as in a reflection, every laudable virtue. She will exemplify your distinctive rare qualities, for a girl is no different than basic matter and can take on any form. She will be, as I said earlier, like a blank slate, on which nothing is written.[223] Like the rainbow that reflects the image of the sun, she will reflect your honorable countenance.

But if you have no goodness or virtue, she will reflect your imperfections, evil ways, and flaws. Therefore, you should consider this carefully. First, you should summon the divine powers and ask them for advice, that with the help of the celestial light you might examine yourself with a lynx's eyes, for you must set an example for the woman. Therefore I always recommend that he who wants to take a wife not ignore Hesiod's opinion. He should behave as one who has repented for his past life and wants to confess his sins to a wise and prudent priest. First, he should withdraw from the world and retreat to his bedroom, and then from his bedroom he should retreat inside himself and frequently and carefully examine his conscience. He should judge himself with a fair and objective eye, not with self-interest, but with the same attention that finds the smallest flaws in one's neighbor. He should examine his past and present life, his habits, deeds, and words, and remember that he must be a mirror and an example to the woman

222. On Francesco Patrizio, included here in an impressive cohort, see above, n23.

223. Aristotle, *On the Soul*, III.iv [430a1]: "Tamquam tabula rasa, in qua nihil est scriptum."

he marries. A man's self-restraint ensures his woman's honesty. According to a wise man, a husband should not allow a woman to hear or see any dishonest words or deeds. If he desires a faithful, honest, and good wife he should separate himself from anything suspicious.[224]

This is what he said, following Hesiod: "Habits discreet he may teach her." When we want to see our face, we look in the mirror, but when we want to know ourselves, we must look at our friends. Similarly, a husband can see his face in his reflection, but if he truly wants to know himself, then he must look at his wife, who is the best friend he can have. If you are good, then you will find that she, too, is good. If you are vicious, she will bear the same image.

You may discover that you are imperfect, that you are lacking in fairness and self-restraint, that you are devoted to gluttony and gambling, and that, even without Circe's poisonous drinks, you can transform yourself into animals as ugly as any Ovid described in his *Metamorphoses*. In this case, restrain your life, control your immoral actions, and avoid the consequences of your immoderate desires. Do not dream of taking a wife before you have adjusted and pacified your senses through reason. Do not turn your intellect, which is in part celestial, into something earthly and mortal by refusing to lead your life according to your divine side and by following instead in the footsteps and excesses of Sardanapalus and Lucullus,[225] believing like a new Epicurean that there is no pleasure after death.[226] If, however, you repent for your sins, you will either flee or submit to the yoke and correct yourself, so as to make yourself worthy of your desires.

---

224. A note in the margins indicates that the "wise man" is Francesco Patrizio. The concept is also repeated in Latin: "Uxori turpitudinis causam videat ne vir praebeat, proinde caveat, ne quid obsceni in uxoris conspectu loquatur, et se abstineat ab omni alieno congressu, si vult uxorem honestam."

225. Marinella quotes two proverbial examples of dissolute behavior: Sardanapalus, legendary Assyrian king famous for his lust, and Lucius Licinius Lucullus, lover of banquets. Sardanapalus is mentioned by Aristotle in *Nicomachean Ethics*, I.5 (1095b20); an account of Lucullus's life can be found in Plutarch, *Lives*, trans. Perrin, II.471–611.

226. "Post mortem nulla voluptas," Marinella writes. This proverbial expression can be traced to the epitaph of Sardanapalus in Strabo, *Geography*, 14.5.9, translated by Guarinus Veronensis and Gregorius Tiphernas at the end of the fifteenth century. See Harry Vredeveld, "Anthologia Latina 873e: Renaissance Latin from Strabo (*Geography* 14.5.9)," *Classical Philology* 93:4 (1998), 343–44.

I would like you to read Plato's *Republic*, where he expels from the city men who are unjust, spoil good habits, and cultivate vices rather than practice virtues.[227] You should not imitate Bacchus and crown yourself in vines, branches, and cups. You must not imitate Eurixeno, who desired to have the neck of a crane because he found glory and pleasure in filling his throat and stomach with food and set the throne of his virtue in the lap of vice.[228] You must not love the ugly deeds of Elagabalus and others like him.[229] Instead, you must blush and realize that such people deserve to be punished like unreasonable and ugly animals.

If you find yourself marked by one of these vices, change your mind; do not bend your freedom under an iron yoke. You have made yourself dirty with ugly pitch. That obscure darkness should not mix with light, for such confusion will produce no good and laudable results.

Rest assured that your wife will learn your ways. Many do not know themselves. The Delphic command "know thyself" does not resonate with them.[230] They do not even try to know themselves. Were somebody to ask these people who desire to marry if they wanted their wives to share their habits, they would say they would consider themselves lucky if they were to achieve such a result. They do not

227. Marinella could be referring to the famous expulsion of poets from the city in the tenth book of Plato's *Republic*. However, she inserts a Latin sentence ("qui insanabiles sunt, prorsus exterminare et poenas irrogare") that is closer to the statement made in *Laws*, IX.862e by the Athenian, who prescribes the death penalty for those who are "beyond cure" (the "insanabiles" Marinella mentions). Aristotle also says that "the incurably bad should be completely banished" in *Nicomachean Ethics*, X.ix.10. Trans. Ross, in *The Complete Works*, II.1865.

228. Marinella's reference to a man "qui cupiebat habere collum gruis" helps identify "Eurixeno" with Philoxenus, who is described in the same terms in Athenaeus of Naucratis, *Deipnosophists*, trans. Charles Burton Gulick (Cambridge, MA: Harvard University Press, rev. 1951, rpt 1997), I.6b (Loeb, 25). See n361.

229. Of Syrian origin, Elagabalus became emperor with the name of Marcus Aurelius Antoninus (218–222) and went down in history for his disregard of Roman religious and sexual mores. Marinella could have been familiar with the chapter Boccaccio devoted to Elagabalus and his mother Symiamira (*De mulieribus claris*, XCIX).

230. Pausanias reports that this maxim (quoted by Marinella in its Latin translation, "nosce te ipsum") adorned the entrance of Apollo's temple in Delphi (Pausanias, *Description of Greece*, trans. W. H. S. Jones [Cambridge, MA: Harvard University Press, 1979], XX.xxiv.1) (Loeb, vol. 4, 507).

know themselves and instead are blinded by their self-love, which is like a hallucination. Some wise men say that knowing oneself is the most pleasant but also the most difficult thing.[231]

Many who neither know nor want to know their flaws have mean and immoral wives. They see their wives' flaws, but they cannot see them in themselves. I do not know what makes them so blind. Their own vices appear disguised as virtues, unlike those of others. But let us move on. If you are unjust, proud, greedy, and ambitious, and your wife is pleasing, grateful, fair, honest, and wise, you will never be friends for you will not rejoice in the same things (*gaudebitis eisdem*), which is the sign of friendship. Different habits cannot bring you peace and unanimity. Even if she is good, over time she may change her nature and adopt your evil ways. Those who touch the pitch get stained. Listen to what Theognis says:

> Learn goodness from good men. By interacting with
> an evil friend, you will lose your common sense, if you
> have any.[232]

Even if a woman is good and lives with you in harmony and peace, eventually she will adopt your habits, however bad and despicable. Perhaps, being young and unaware, she will mistake for good what is actually evil. By imitating your vices, she will come to believe that such a lifestyle is noble and laudable. Sensations are concerned with the present (*sensus est praesentis*).[233] She will delight in the pleasures of your sensual life. She will think, perhaps, that she is acting properly

231. Aristotle, *Magna Moralia*, II.xv (1213a13): "[...] It is both a most difficult thing, as some of the sages have said, to attain a knowledge of oneself, and also a most pleasant." Trans. St. G. Stock, in *The Complete Works*, II.1920. Marinella writes: "Difficillimum est quidam dixere sapientes, se cognoscere, et suavissimum."

232. "A iustis disce bona. Si versaberi amico cum pravo, amittes mens bona si qua tibi est." The maxims of the elegiac Greek poet Theognis of Megara constituted a depository of practical wisdom. For an early seventeenth-century edition see *Poetae minores Graeci* (Cantabrigiae: Thomas Buck, 1602) 347–407. The maxim corresponding to the one quoted by Marinella is at p. 348.

233. Albertus Magnus, *Liber de memoria et reminiscentia* I, 3, in August Borgnet, et al., eds., Albertus Magnus, *Opera Omnia* (Paris: Vivès, 1891) IX,100. I would like to thank Marco Arnaudo for this reference.

and will be tricked by what only appears to be virtue. Moreover, by imitating you, she will lower your standing among wise people, and will pass on to your children the vices and lack of moderation that she has received from you.

Therefore, he who wants to subject himself to this indissoluble bond, which is far more difficult to untie than a Gordian knot, must employ great diligence and effort to adorn himself with noble and appropriate manners. Even he who considers himself to be good, virtuous, and irreproachable, must nevertheless be humble and refrain from reaching the conclusion that he is good. He should be uncertain and full of doubt, and say together with Plato, that great philosopher:

> If I actually had a soul made of gold, Callicles, don't
> you think I'd be pleased to find one of those stones on
> which they test gold?[234]

I translate this so that you, too, my women friends, may understand the meaning: if my soul were made of gold, don't you think I would like to find one of those stones that proves the nature of gold and, by getting close to it, test the perfection of my soul? This is what that divine prophet said. He did not trust himself very much, for we rarely see our own flaws, and the criticism of wise and experienced men reprimands and punishes us.

I cannot believe that Hesiod would have wanted a good woman to turn into a vain and mean one, exchanging her kindness for immorality. While he wanted husband and wife to be in agreement, he assumed the man to be self-restrained, just, and moral. It would be neither appropriate nor laudable for the woman to exchange her good habits for bad ones in order to live in peace. Indeed, when Hesiod said that a man must be the law and example for his wife's life, he assumed the man would be sober, discreet, and modest. He certainly would not have recommended that a liar or otherwise bizarre or vain person act

---

234. Cf. Plato, *Gorgias* 486d. Marinella paraphrases Socrates's words: "Si mihi aurea anima foret nonne arbitraris me libenter reperturum aliquem, ex his lapidibus per quos probari aurum solet optimum, ad quem lapidem animam admovens, approbaretur." Trans. Zeyl, in *Complete Works*, 830.

as a woman's guide and escort. The Philosopher agrees with Hesiod's opinion, which he supports and reinforces when he says:

> It is fitting that a woman of well-ordered life should consider that her husband's uses are as laws appointed for her own life by divine will.[235]

The Philosopher wants the wise woman to consider and imitate her husband's ways as the laws of her life. However, I do not believe that these learned men intended to say that she should become bestial and uninhibited just to be in harmony with her husband. These philosophers were referring to good, restrained, and laudable habits, and they presumed that a young, simple and inexperienced woman, having just left her parents' home, could only bend her mind to follow her husband's ways. Like a piece of iron responds to the magnet's invitation, so would she make these new habits the law of her life. It is necessary, however, that such habits be full of goodness and modesty. This is commendable, for the result of the good habits she will learn is a holy, chaste, perfect, peaceful, and honest union, as recommended by the Philosopher.

> Now to a wife nothing is of more value, nothing more rightfully her own, than honoured and faithful partnership with her husband.[236]

We must praise and appreciate the virtue of a moral and civil man as much as we rebuke the flaws of a vicious and careless man.

---

235. Aristotle, III.i.10: "Estimare debet mulieris mentis bene compositae, mores viri esse legem vitae suae impositam a Deo." Trans. Armstrong, in *The Complete Works*, II.2147.

236. Aristotle, *Economics*, III.ii, trans. Armstrong, in *The Complete Works*, II.2148. Marinella's Latin quote ("Nihil vero suum est uxori, nec magis illi a viro praestandum est quam sancta et intemerata societas") appears verbatim in Ludovico Settala, *De ratione instituendae et gubernandae familiae libri quinque* (Milano: Giovanni Battista Bidellio, 1626), 140.

> A bad man, whose desire is for pleasure, is corrected
> by pain like a beast of burden.[237]

He must be beaten and punished like an irrational animal, for perfection in a man's life proceeds from rationality and the intellect. A life ruled by instinct belongs to an ugly and wild animal. Nevertheless, there are some men who put aside virtue and fall into the sea of vice. They devote themselves completely to sensual pleasures. Caught as if in a shameful slumber, they do not consider the offense and damage their dishonesty causes to their wives, their homes, and their children. We should not be surprised that some women, given such an immoral example and careless with their honor and modesty, make a man's ugly behavior their own ("habits discreet he may teach her").

Many men spend their money extravagantly outside their homes. They waste their wealth in partying and gambling before their wives' very eyes, almost as a sign of contempt and neglect. This behavior must be avoided at all costs, as it is shameful and hurtful. The wife realizes that her household lacks even the most basic things and that she is left poor and in need. It should be no surprise if she becomes desperate and earns herself a bad reputation. Desperation, pain, and disdain make her turn her own hands against herself.

Men have no right to complain about this, given that they schooled their women in perverted and immoral actions and obliged them to lead an immoral life. These vicious men should hold themselves guilty, as well as their abominable habits, their awful deeds, and the little consideration they lend to those whom they should, on the contrary, praise and love. If your household has fallen into disgrace, it is your fault. You are the root of and the reason for the errors the desolate woman committed, her patience long challenged. She follows Hesiod and imitates your habits. Therefore, she is forced to be dissolute, dishonest, and out of control. The man is thereby able to look at his own flaws. He sees, as if in a mirror, his own indecency and shame, as well as that of his family and lineage, and how he has become the talk of the town. A man should appraise his lifestyle before entering marriage, that he might avoid similar misfortunes and disgrace.

---

237. *Nicomachean Ethics*, X.9 (1180a10), "Qui turpia appetit castigandum esse et temperandum non aliter quam iumentum." Trans. Ross, in *The Complete Works*, II.1865. See n362.

When the Philosopher joins Homer in saying that a woman must adopt a man's habits, they mean that both must be modest, just, and good. If the man lacks these qualities, he cannot blame the woman for likewise lacking them. Homer offers the example of Agamemnon, who did not remain faithful to Clytemnestra. When the Greek army assembled to return the prisoner Chryseis to her father, Agamemnon dared to call the unworthy, barbarian woman prisoner in no way inferior to Clytemnestra.[238] In doing so, he sinned against his wife (*in propriam peccavit uxorem*). This is how Homer records Agamemnon's words:

> I would far rather keep her at home. For in fact I prefer her to Clytemnestra, my wedded wife, since she is in no way inferior to her, either in form or in stature, or in mind, or in handiwork.[239]

Agamemnon sinned against his wife, but Ulysses did not. Atlas's daughter promised Ulysses eternal life in return for staying with her, but he despised the beautiful goddess and the promise of eternity. He chose to decline her invitation and refuse the gift rather than deceive Penelope and betray her faith and love.[240]

Aristotle and Homer praise the man who is faithful to his wife and vice versa. Neither can bear the sight of an unworthy companion (*Nec se videre deteriorem posse*). This is a sign of love. He who loves

---

238. Aristotle, *Economics*, III.iii: "Captivam mulierem, nec natura praestantem in nullo Clytemnestra esse deteriorem." Trans. Armstrong, in *The Complete Works*, II. 2149.

239. Homer, *Iliad*, I.113–15: "Quoniam multum volo ipsam domi habere. Etenim Clytemnestrae preposui puellari uxori, quoniam non est peior neque corpore, neque aetate, neque mentibus, neque item operibus." Trans. Murray (Loeb, 21).

240. "Ulisses roganti Atlantis filia ut secum maneret, ac sempiternitatem pollicenti. Nec ob id prodere voluit uxoris affectum, amorem et fidem." This opposition between Agamemnon and Ulysses is in Aristotle, *Economics* III.iii: "Agamemnon did wrong to his wife for the sake of Chryseis, declaring in open assembly that a base captive woman, and of alien race besides, was in no way inferior to Clytemnestra in womanly excellence [...] Ulysses on the other hand, when the daughter of Atlas besought him to share his bed and board, and promised him immortality, could not bring himself even for the sake of immortality to betray the kindness and love and loyalty of his wife [...]" Trans. Armstrong, in *The Complete Works*, II.2150.

does not allow himself or his friends to commit a sin. Why is that so? Because our natural instinct requires that we love ourselves more than others. Our desire for others to be like us is a sign of true and sincere love. As Aristotle says and as I have discussed, a prudent man wants his wife to learn his ways, that she might become the mirror in which he contemplates himself. If a man desires only to see his face, then he can look in a mirror. But if he wants to know himself, then he should look at his friend.[241]

If husband and wife are good, modest, just, and faithful, they will keep and improve their household in peace and happiness, as a Latin poet says:

> Nothing is better than when unanimous souls inhabit
> a house.[242]

Homer and Aristotle praise peace and harmony in man and woman and honesty in human affairs. These qualities enable us to preserve not only households, but also cities and kingdoms. Together with Homer, the philosopher who was the glory of Stageira praises the reciprocal benevolence of husband and wife, saying:

> [...] The unity that the poet commends is no mutual
> subservience in each other's vices, but one that is
> rightfully allied with wisdom and understanding.[243]

Elsewhere in the *Odyssey* Homer writes that Ulysses praised the goodness and worth of Nausicaa, King Alcinous's daughter, and wished her happiness and prosperity:

---

241. "Si vir cupit videre faciem suam respiciat in speculo. Si cupit videre se ipsum, respiciat amicum." Unknown source.

242. "Nihil potius et melius quam cum concordes animi domum habitant." Cf. Philipp Camerarius, *Operae Horarum Subcisivarum, Sive Meditationes Historicae* (Frankfurt: Ioannis Saurij, impensis Petri Korpffij, 1602), 232.

243. Aristotle, *Economics*, III.iv: "Laudat Poeta unanimitatem viri et uxori, non eam quidem quae circa improba obsequire sed quae animo et prudentia coniuncta est." Trans. Armstrong, in *The Complete Works*, II.2150.

> May the gods grant you a husband and a family to-
> gether with your husband—not any family, but an
> honest one.[244]

It is important here to notice the word "honest," which shows how
important honesty is. Ulysses resisted Circe's loving entreaties. She
wanted to marry him and promised to return his companions, whom
she had transformed into ugly beasts, to their original form. She also
promised Ulysses the gift of immortality. Ulysses loved his companions and considered eternity a prized and desirable treasure. Nevertheless, he could accept neither gift:

> In answer to her he even declared that in his eyes
> nothing could be more lovely than his native isle, rug-
> ged though it were; and prayed that he might die, if
> only he might look upon his mortal wife and son. So
> firmly did he keep troth with his wife; and received in
> return from her the like loyalty.[245]

Based on the opinions of Aristotle and Homer, two very wise
men, we can conclude that self-restraint, temperance, and other such
virtues pertain equally to men and women. According to these men
and to Hesiod, these virtues are even more necessary for men, for they
must set an example for women, while the opposite is not true. Therefore it is appropriate for a man to be perfectly good and to love virtue
entirely and sincerely, and not just partially.

A man should find the laws within himself (*vir reperiat sibi
leges*). The philosopher agrees with Hesiod and believes that a man
must serve as the example and the law for a woman's life. This is why

---

244. "Precatus est Deos, ut darent illi virum, et familiam unanimem cum viro, non qua-
mlibet sed honestam." The closest reference is Homer, *Odyssey* VI.178–81(Loeb, 233). Cf.
Aristotle, *Economics*, III.iv.

245. Aristotle, *Economics*, III.iii: "Nihil sibi dulcius videri posse, quam patriam incultam,
et asperam, magisque optavit mortalem uxorem et filium videre, quam fieri ipsum im-
mortalem. Sic firmam stabilemque fidem servabat, pro quibus merito ab uxorem eadem
reportabat." Trans. Armstrong, in *The Complete Works*, II.2150. Marinella inserts here an
Italian paraphrase of the passage.

he says a man should find those principles in himself. He must lead a just life, that his wife might diligently imitate his ways such that they can live together in friendly perfection with a single soul. Similar lifestyles generate harmony and unity, which bring happiness to their souls and prosperity to their household.

Although it may seem hard to believe, there are some men whose nature is so bizarre that they openly inform their wives of their shameful and immoral actions, yet expect them to remain wise, chaste, and modest. They do not understand what an ugly and inappropriate example they set for them. They do not know that chastity and temperance are as appropriate to men as they are to women. They do not fear that their long acquaintance may turn a laudable woman into a licentious and shameless one. Descending to Hell is easy.[246] Following one's instinct is easy. A reasonable man should fear such danger.

We reiterate what we have already said, as repetition is the best way to impress these fine exhortations upon your soul. With frequent blows, the blacksmith likewise perfects his work. He who wants forever to sacrifice his freedom must examine his actions and decide whether he hates vice and rejoices in practicing virtue. Virtue is a habit, rather than an end in itself. The end consists in putting virtue into practice. Practice is better than theory, and your goal is a virtuous life. Therefore, we assert that while it is our soul that grants us life and spirit, it is our soul's virtues that allow us to live honorably and reputably.[247]

As practice is better than theory, a man must show his wife how to put virtue into practice. If he walks the path of virtue sweetly and pleasantly, she will be happy and satisfied to follow in his footsteps and will not act out of obligation alone, like children who are well behaved not because they love goodness (*non virtutis amore*), but because they fear their teacher's beatings.

Therefore, because the man must be an example for the woman, he will lead his life on the good and praiseworthy path. In fact, there is nothing more glorious or honorable than the two, unanimous and united in their desires, ruling over their household with the scepter of justice and love. There will be no room for complaints, for they

246. Marinella writes "Facilis est descensus Averno," a proverbial rephrasing of *Aeneid*, VI.126.

247. "Anima vivimus, ob virtutem animae bene vivimus." Unknown source.

will lead their lives and behave virtuously, which is the source of true happiness.

I will never be persuaded that a man who loves wisdom, justice, and righteousness will rejoice in the viciousness of his wife and children. He who serves the enemies of reason chases from his home all glory and praise. I will never believe that a man could forget that his wife and children are reflections of him, like the rainbow is a reflection of the sun.[248] They retain his qualities, be they good or bad, and reveal to others his excellence or his flaws. If reprimanded, those who are careless with their honor will respond that temperance does not belong to men. They forget the many times Aristotle says in his moral works, in *Rhetoric*, and elsewhere that a man must be just, honest, and temperate.

Plato believed the same. He expelled immoral men from the city, as they endangered the health of good and moral people. Plato separated them from the others, like a shepherd keeps sick sheep aside, lest they infect the healthy.

Some people, when reproached for leading irrational lives, respond that resisting natural instincts is impossible because they are too strong, as if an abstentious and wise man could not resist the passions. They do not know that virtue is not something we are born with, but something we gain through tolerance and resistance to the passions. Virtue is to be praised precisely because it is gained not only with pleasure but also with suffering (*Non sine voluptate et dolore*).

Everyone can control their instincts and bring them to the just mean by refusing to indulge in excessive pleasure. We refuse to say that we cannot act against our desires, for were that true no one would ever have succeeded in doing so. Nobody is obliged to do impossible things (*Ad impossibilia nemo tenetur*). Were that true, the best philosophers would have dealt with this issue in vain. They would not have blamed and reproached those who spend their immoral days shamefully and follow their instincts for being unreasonable and ugly animals. Something that everyone can easily accomplish is hardly impossible. Virtue is, in fact, simply a happy medium between excess and

---

248. "La moglie e li figliuoli sieno come pararelli [*sic*] ritenenti le tue qualità," Marinella writes. It could be an allusion to the rainbows of *Paradiso*, XII.11, described by Dante as "two parallel arches" ("due archi paralelli"). I thank Benedetta Colella for this suggestion.

deficiency. A self-restrained person does not feel sensual pleasures, or feels them only insofar as honesty permits. A man must be adorned with laudable manners, that his wife might imitate him and thereby create the much praised unanimity. We must remember that different habits are unlikely to result in friendship (*dissimilitudines morum non sunt aptae ad conciliandas amicitias*). People with similar habits, on the other hand, will find pleasure and satisfaction in the same things, as is necessary, that they might rejoice in the same things, as the Philosopher says (*Ut gaudeant eisdem*). As the wife is obliged to learn her husband's ways, so should the husband be obliged to be good, if only for her sake. Listen to the Philosopher's words:

> It is fitting that a woman of well-ordered life should consider that her husband's uses are as laws appointed for her own life by divine will.[249]

Heaven imposes this upon her life. Therefore God and necessity force her to learn her husband's ways, be they good or bad. In heeding these philosophers' suggestions, women have no choice but to imitate their husbands' lives. I cannot stress how important this is. Every man who desires to have an honorable and laudable household will find out.

However, there were and still are women who refuse to follow Hesiod and Aristotle. These are wise, mature, and fair women who meet vain, dissolute, and vicious men. They tolerate their husbands' behavior and live chaste, modest, and patient lives, waiting for the men to realize their mistakes despite their poor judgment. Many of these men do eventually realize their wrongdoing and conform their lives and habits to those of their wise and prudent women. These men do the opposite of what the philosophers recommend. Therefore, intelligent women follow their husbands' habits only if they are good and laudable. If they are bad, however, these women disregard them, together with the disrepute they bring.

However, I cannot deny that there are also women who, like fronds in the wind, have poor judgment and little honor and are frivolous, vain, and immoral. This is not surprising, for even among the

---

249. Aristotle, *Economics* III.i. Marinella repeats: "Mores viri esse legem suae vitae, impositam sibi a deo." Trans. Armstrong, in *The Complete Works*, II.2147.

stars we can discern the poisonous scorpion, and among beneficial herbs the hemlock poses a deadly threat. Likewise, among honorable and glorious women we can find some who are immoral or out of control, female monsters who sacrifice their own chastity. Like flaws and ugly stains on a white dress, such women are not to be included among the good and the chaste. Therefore we will dispense with these despised creatures, whom everyone ought to scorn and not take into account. On this matter, the Florentine poet says:

> and who allows her honor to be taken
> is not a lady or alive—if some
> appear to be, their life is grim and harsh
> much more than death.[250]

The same poet, when praising good and temperate women in the *Triumphs*, says:

> Fairest of all was she who was most chaste.[251]

If you want to know just how much deformity and ugliness vice can bear, consider the republic of the Lacedaemonians and its legislators, who, according to the philosopher, neglected women. He says they provided inappropriate laws for women, who constituted half of the population,[252] and adds:

> The legislator wanted to make the whole state hardy, and he has carried out his intention in the case of the men, but he has neglected the women, who live in every sort of intemperance and luxury.[253]

---

250. Petrarch, *Canzoniere* 262: "Et qual si lascia di suo onor privare, / né donna è piú né viva; et se qual pria / appare in vista, è tal vita aspra et ria / via piú che morte." Trans. Musa, 366.

251. Petrarch, *Trionfo della castità* 174: "e la piú casta v'era la piú bella." Trans. Wilkins, 46.

252. Aristotle, *Politics*, II.ix (1269b19): "Male provisum est circa mulieres in ea putandum est mediatatem civitatis esse neglectam" (48r in Bruni's translation). Aristotle also criticizes the Lacedaemonians for their scarce attention to women's condition in *Rhetoric*, I.5 (1361a10).

253. Aristotle, *Politics*, II.ix (1269b20): "Legislator in viris quidem id fecisse constat, in mulieribus autem non fecisse; vivunt enim molliter ac in omnem licentiam dissolutae." (48v

He blames the legislators whose laws made men lead lives of virtue, but allowed women to lead dissolute, dishonest, and licentious lives of little honor. This is indeed wrong, and this philosopher, along with all who wish women to practice justice and other virtues, but above all temperance and chastity, condemns it as such.

Knowing that everyone avoids and despises immoral women, a prudent woman will be wary of anything that could leave a bad impression, including the excessive display of jewels. Her natural beauty and perfection will make her worthy of reverence and honor far more than the wealth that shines around her, which is not part of her soul or body but rather something additional brought by Fortune, as Boethius shows in *The Consolation of Philosophy*. I advise the good-natured and laudable woman to appear in church on the prescribed days, as well as in public assemblies and spaces, with less pride and vanity, wearing less make up and fewer ornaments such as gold and gems than the laws and customs of the city allow. She should hold clear in her mind that nothing is more precious than modesty, chastity, goodness, and purity of soul and behavior. These are the joys and riches that will make a woman shine in her beauty and take pride in herself. These are the ornaments and perfections that bring praise to her glory. Upon seeing her, people will thereby exalt her natural qualities. They will infer, from her outward honesty and wisdom, her intrinsic wisdom and beauty. Gold, silk, pearls, and gems do not belong to the women they adorn, but rather are the favors of good fortune.

Believe me, wise and learned men will always praise Penelope over Helen, even though the latter was like a goddess (*similis Deabus*). Cornelia, mother of the Gracchi brothers, will always be remembered and commended over Cleopatra and other such women. Honesty is so beautiful, my beloved women, and her manifestations so laudable, that it seduces even those who love vain and useless things. This is why that learned man says:

---

in Bruni's translation). Trans. Jowett, in *The Complete Works*, II.2015.

> A woman must not be loved for the beauty of her
> body, but for her personality and habits.[254]

Therefore, a woman must be loved for her excellent and just ways, rather than for her physical beauty, which, like a shadow, quickly fades and disappears. She must be loved not for superfluous ornaments, but for the beauty of her soul. Solomon praised some women for the virtues of their souls, which were more important than the beauty of their bodies. He said: "For that which lies hidden."[255] That internal beauty was the noble object of such a wise man's argument proves its importance. Seclusion and gravitas keep a woman's honor, which increases her greatness. Too many social interactions create suspicion and scandal, for people are inclined to believe the worst, and our evil nature pushes us to believe even things that appear impossible. Therefore a wise and prudent woman must be careful not to arouse even the slightest shade of suspicion, for honesty and chastity are the virtues that pertain to her. Knowing their importance, the divine Ariosto wrote in his *Furioso*:

> Just by virtue of her chastity Penelope was no lesser
> mortal than Ulysses.[256]

He equated Penelope's chastity with Ulysses's valor and prudence. Petrarch marvels that Lucretia had to resort to using the sword to end her life, given the pain she felt at losing her chastity. He says:

> Lucretia's story still surprises me
> because she needed steel so she could die,
> and that her grief alone did not suffice.[257]

---

254. "Mulier non est amanda propter corporis pulchritudinem, sed propter ingenium et mores." Unknown source.

255. Song of Songs 4:1: "Praeter illud quod intrinsicus latet."

256. Ariosto, *Orlando furioso*, XIII.60: "Sol perché casta visse / Penelope, non fu minor d'Ulisse." Trans. Waldman, 134.

257. Petrarch, *Canzoniere* CCLXII: "Né di Lucretia mi meravigliai, / se non come a morir le bisognasse / Ferro e non le bastasse il dolor solo." Trans. Musa, 366.

A woman's virtue and perfection lie in her chastity, which she must hold as more precious than her eyes and her very life.

I also recommend that, when bad fortune strikes a woman's husband with illness or some other disgrace, she not refuse to shoulder the burden of adverse destiny. As his companion in life, she should demonstrate her patience and silence in unfavorable as well as favorable times and wait for the end of adversity and misfortune. The philosopher also encourages you not to flee the uncomfortable burdens and misfortunes that befall families and men:

> If trouble should come it beseems the wife to consider that here a good woman wins her highest praise. Let her bethink herself how Alcestis would never have attained such renown nor Penelope have deserved all the high praises bestowed on her had not their husbands known adversity; whereas the troubles of Admetus and Ulysses have obtained for their wives a reputation that shall never die.[258]

Therefore, be strong and tolerant in adversity. By remaining honest, faithful and good, you will bear the offense of unfortunate events. You will be loved, respected, and honored by everyone who knows your perfection. Anyone can be good and balanced in the happiness and tranquility of prosperous times. Only in times of adversity will you know who is and who is not your friend. Experience is the real test, and we should not trust anyone before such a test, as Theognis says:

> You will know neither a man's nor a woman's mind before danger occurs.[259]

258. Aristotle, *Economics*, III.i. Trans. Armstrong, in *The Complete Works*, II.2147. Contrary to her normal practice, Marinella here provides not only a Latin version, but also its Italian translation.
259. "Neque viri nec mulieris ne mentem ante periculum cognoveris." Unknown source.

It takes time and experience to discover who loves us: "friendship requires time and testing."[260] Knowing how difficult it is to find a true friend, the philosopher recommends taking "a bushel of salt."[261]

I want to exhort men, once again, to remember the words of the oracle: "Know thyself" (*Nosce te ipsum*). You should always doubt your knowledge of yourself and deem yourself worse than you actually are. Do not heed the flattering voices of other people. Keep in mind that we cannot turn the eyes of knowledge on ourselves as an impartial and severe judge could.

The union of man and woman is of crucial importance. If my advice is sometimes repetitive, this derives not from a faulty argument, but from my warm desire to impress virtue upon other people's souls.

The constant drop hollows out the stone.[262]

Beating a nail over and over fixes it to a board forever.

As we have shown, Aristotle and Hesiod prescribe that a man's habits be the laws ruling over a wise woman's life, as ordered by God and Nature. Therefore he must be a clear and polished mirror, in which the woman can embellish and perfect herself. Consequently, if a man wants a chaste, abstentious, and laudable woman in charge of his household and his children, he must live in an irreprehensible way. As the great master of philosophical wisdom asked,

What could be more sacred than to beget children by
a noble and honored wife?[263]

---

260. "Amicus requirit tempus et experimentum." Unknown source.

261. "Modium salis," Marinella writes, alluding to the Latin proverb "Homini ne fidas nisi cum quo modium salis absumpseres" (Trust no man until you have eaten a peck of salt with him). (*Dictionary of Quotations* 159).

262. "Gutta continua cava lapidem." See Ovid's proverbial expression "Gutta cavat lapidem" (*Epistulae Ex Ponto*, IV.10.5, in Ovid, *Tristia; Ex Ponto*, trans. Arthur Leslie Wheeler [Cambridge, MA: Harvard University Press, 1988], 465).

263. Aristotle, *Economics* III.ii: "Quid sanctius esse potest, quam ex laudabilissima femina filios procreare." Trans. Armstrong, in *The Complete Works*, II.2148.

He finds nothing nobler than having children with an honest and just woman, whose qualities make her worthy of honor and glory.

Nothing under the sun is more desirable and pleasing than a woman who can add to her natural goodness, which proceeds from her nature and family tradition, the virtues and good habits of a temperate, moderate, and righteous husband—and many exist who deserve such praise and glory. Aristotle and Hesiod were referring to good men, not to some other dishonest, vain, and vicious men who are unworthy of being remembered and are not ashamed to keep foul prostitutes near and sometimes even in their own house—oh, the great shame of it!—or to squander their wealth on clothing and rewarding these wretched women. Meanwhile their wives, children, and their entire family must dress and eat poorly at little expense.

Tell me, Hesiod and Aristotle, what kind of example is this? Should the wife then learn her husband's ways? Tell me, you who want the husband's habits to become the God-given laws of his woman's life: how should she learn that life? Some households are so poor that necessity has forced their women, who were once rich, wealthy, and kind, to adopt their husbands' unworthy ways in order to sustain themselves and their children, thereby shaming themselves and their households, confusing their relatives and disgusting their friends. A husband of this sort is singled out and excluded from the society of honorable men. Therefore, it is not always laudable to adopt a man's ways; indeed, doing so can very well be a source of shame and dishonor. What would you say, Aristotle and Hesiod, if you saw the sad and abominable behavior of some men? This is the result of their failure to examine their lives and consciences before making this union. Had they done so, they would not have bound themselves with chains stronger than a diamond, but would have kept their freedom so that their disgraceful life and inner confusion would not bring damage and shame to themselves and others.

The philosopher does not allow that a wife be insulted by her husband:

It is insulting for him to have intercourse with other women.[264]

He blames unchastity, and yet—oh wise Aristotle, oh learned Hesiod—many men are endowed with such bad habits that I do not understand how they could possibly want a woman to learn their ways, while they themselves provide such ugly and shameful examples. I understand that you were thinking not of these men, but rather of those who are moderate, just, and endowed with noble and holy habits and who demonstrate holy modesty in their words and deeds (*sit pudor in verbis et in operis*).

If you find that you are not good and that your wife is evil, you should know that you have been an example for her. Correct your own flaws, so that the husband may not cause his wife's turpitude (*uxoris turpitudinem ne vir praebeat*). Correct your life, devote yourself to good deeds, and make virtue shine in you first, that your wife might be enlightened by your perfection and blush before committing a deed that is anything less than noble and worthy of a dignified and sublime person. Divine favors are never late. You should never blush with shame at the memory of having done something bad. The memory of noble deeds and glorious successes should make your soul and heart happy.

From these few words I want men to realize that, as the heads of their households, they must set the example and the law for women and others to lead a moral life. This applies all the more if they believe that God has given more intellect to them than to women—if, that is, we can talk in terms of quantity with regard to the intellect, which does not fall under such a category.

---

264. Marinella's Latin phrasing ("Iniuria fit si foris cum aliis feminis consuescat") is close to the concept expressed by Aristotle in *Economics* III.ii.

8. WE EXHORT PARENTS TO RAISE AND EDUCATE
THEIR CHILDREN TO EXCELLENT HABITS AND
INTELLECTUAL DISCIPLINES, SO THAT THEY
MAY BRING GLORY AND PRAISE TO THEMSELVES,
THEIR HOUSE, AND THE FATHERLAND: THIS IS
WHAT HAPPINESS IS.

We have formed the household, which Charondas calls "homosti-tios" and Parmenides calls "homocapnos"[265] and which is part of the city.[266] We have established the household as the place for virtuous life. We have expelled vices, established the man as a noble example for the woman, and made the woman the ruler of her household, that together they might raise, nourish, train, and educate their children with virtue, justice, and love. Children become loving advocates and tutors for their aging parents. They provide loving and respectful care and are the faithful and careful keepers of the household and of its honor.[267] Children inherit the glory and reputation of their parents' lineage. Many also inherit the rule of their household and the city. This important and heavy responsibility can be considered the goal of every laudable operation.

Raising children is a difficult task that requires solicitude and labor, as Plato says in *Theages*: children's upbringing is a source of anxiety.[268] This difficult job, however, is so sweet and useful that you do not feel the fatigue. The wise king, considering the difficulty and uncertainty of this mission, used to say: "snake on a rock, ship in the

265. Cf. Aristotle, *Politics*, I.i.6 (1252b13): "The family is the association established by nature for the supply of men's everyday wants, and the members of it are called by Charondas, 'companions of the cupboard,' and by Epimenides the Cretan, 'companions of the manger.'" Marinella's reference to Parmenides appears to be erroneous. Trans. Jowett, in *The Complete Works*, II.1987.

266. Here Marinella adds, somewhat redundantly: "Quae ex pluribus domibus constituuntur."

267. Cf. Aristotle, *Economics* III.ii. Here Marinella begins with a Latin quote ("Sunt senectutis pastores quasi patris, matrisque reverentes custodes, ac totius domus servatores"), followed by its Italian translation.

268. At the beginning of Plato's dialogue *Theages* (121C), Demodocus refers to the difficulty and anxiety that his son's education entails. Marinella writes: "Filiorum educatio est cum timore congiuncta" (*sic*).

sea, man in adolescence."[269] The snake coils and uncoils over a smooth rock, sliding this way and that; a ship in the ocean is ruled by the ever-changing winds. A man in his youth is almost always under the sway of the senses, and his outcome is uncertain.

Therefore, fathers and mothers must exercise great care. Their natural task is to direct their beloved offspring toward goodness, as parents love, desire, and long for their children's happiness and want them to behave in a virtuous and good manner.

As the philosopher says, mothers love their children without asking to be loved in return. All they ask is that their children bend their will toward goodness.[270] This is a sign of true and honest love. Parents rejoice in seeing their affectionate children behave in virtuous and noble ways. They love them as they love themselves, for in them they feel they are born again. Therefore, we should not be surprised that wise and sensible parents tolerate fatigue, inconvenience, and suffering to raise children who will provide an honorable model for their household, for the city government, and for the people. When people see an ill-bred child, they immediately attribute his behavior to the parents' neglect and ineptitude, which is indeed undignified and shameful. To allow children to grow up deprived of virtue and full of vice, as often results from parents' negligence and carelessness, is a sin deserving of punishment. When both parents lead good and irreproachable lives, their example greatly benefits their children who, like fruit, naturally tend to be sweet and lovable, but nevertheless can turn bland and tasteless if deprived of the sun.

The moon and the stars are dark but, following the shining sun's example, appear bright and decorate the universe. Likewise, children, even those who are not naturally good, strive to emulate the goodness and perfection of their parents and become diligent imitators of those who generated them. There are indeed some who are

---

269. "Serpes in petra, navis in mari, vir in adolescentia," Marinella says. The passage recalls the *Book of Proverbs* (usually attributed to Solomon, who could be the "wise king" to whom Marinella alludes): "There are three things that are too amazing for me, four that I do not understand: the way of an eagle in the sky, the way of a snake on a rock, the way of a ship on the high seas, and the way of a man with a maiden." (Proverbs 30:18–19).

270. Aristotle, *Nicomachean Ethics*, 1159a25–30: "Matres amant et redamari non curant, gaudent videre filios suos bene agentes." Trans. Ross, in *The Complete Works*, II.1832.

naturally averse to virtue, for personalities are different. Threats and promises from their prudent parents will turn them, like blind bats, toward the light of virtuous deeds, that they might learn to bear such light, even if with some pain and sorrow.

We agree with the Philosopher and other learned men that those who care about the health and strength of a newborn baby should make milk his special nourishment, as it is for other animals. We must believe that Nature, our universal mother who is neither wasteful nor avaricious, did not err in this matter. Therefore we prescribe milk as the baby's first and natural food.[271] Nannies should be very mature and exercise great care that the tender children's little bodies not become misshapen and distorted, as sometimes happens when nannies lack diligence, experience, or knowledge. Therefore the mother should not go away or refuse to be present when her baby is swaddled and tied in white pieces of cloth. It is best that the mothers, who are in general educated, noble, and civil, provide milk for their babies, since the wet nurses, who are born poor and have lowly manners, have similarly lowly milk that is inferior to a lady's.

It is good and laudable that children grow accustomed to the cold, which is beneficial to their health and increases their strength. By virtue of the law of contrast (*anstiparistasim*) natural warmth increases through its concentration. Some people train children to withstand cold temperatures by dipping newborns in rivers, as Numanus (also known as Remulus) attests when he speaks of his warriors' worth:

> We first bring our newborn sons to the river, and
> harden them with the water's cruel cold.[272]

---

271. Cf. Aristotle, *Politics*, VII.xv.1 (1336a5), trans. Jowett, in *The Complete Works*, II.2119. A maxim in the margins ("Natura neque deficit in necessaris nec abundat in superfluis" [Nature is never lacking in things that are necessary, nor is abundant in those which are superfluous]) refers to St. Thomas Aquinas's *Summa Theologica* (Iᵃ-IIae q. 91 a. 2 arg. 1).

272. Virgil, *Aeneid*, IX.603–4 (Loeb, 156). Here Marinella provides not only the original Latin ("Natos ad flumina primum / deferimus, saevoque gelu duramus et undis"), but also its Italian translation by Annibal Caro: "I nostri figli non son nati a pena, che si tuffan ne' fiumi" (Firenze: Ciardetti, 1827), vol. 2, 137.

The French cover their children in little and light clothing that they might learn to withstand the opposite inconveniences of cold and heat. The innate heat that is abundant at that age allows them to easily endure the elements. Therefore it is useful for their bodies to undergo some suffering. This is especially important for those who are to pursue a military career.[273]

Until they turn five, children should not be devoted to any particular activity and undergo only moderate labor so that their growth is not hindered. They should, however, be active, so as to get rid of laziness and indolence as well as the superfluous humidity that is always abundant in children.[274] Their exercise must consist of pleasant games to avoid placing undue stress on either the soul or the body. They must nevertheless practice some activities that imitate the noble deeds and laudable behavior that will bring them honor and glory at a more mature age. Plato reasons:

> As we said at first, our children's games must from the very beginning be more law-abiding, for if their games become lawless, and the children follow suit, isn't it impossible for them to grow up into good and law-abiding men?[275]

Fairy tales and words addressed to children must convey honesty and goodness, for at this age children are easily subject to both good and bad influences. They are like a white and spotless cloth that

---

273. Cf. Aristotle, *Politics* VII.xv.2 (1336a11 ff.): "To accustom children to the cold from their earliest years is also an excellent practice, which greatly conduces to health, and hardens them for military service. Hence many barbarians have a custom of plunging their children at birth into a cold stream; others, like the Celts, clothe them in a light wrapper only." Trans. Jowett, in *The Complete Works*, II.2119–20.

274. Cf. Aristotle, *Politics* VII.xv.4 (1336a24): "The next period lasts to the age of five; during this time no demand should be made upon the child for study or labor, lest its growth be impeded; and there should be sufficient motion to prevent the limbs from being inactive." Trans. Jowett, in *The Complete Works*, II.2120.

275. Plato, *Republic* IV (424E): "Statim a primis annis pueri honestis iocis assuefaciendi, nam si iocis minus decentibus assuescant, legitimi probique viri numquam evadunt." Trans. Grube, in *Complete Works*, 1057.

is easily stained and contaminated; often the stains cannot be removed without at the same time ruining the cloth.

Children must be totally protected from the conversation of male and female servants alike because both the subject matter and the language of these vile and low-class people are filled with meanness and indignity, and rarely show any goodness, modesty, good manners, and civility.[276] Parents should be wary of such practices because they are like dangerous and deadly illnesses for their children. Licentious and vulgar language is not appropriate in the presence of noble people, and even less so in the presence of children, for the frivolous utterance of shameful words leads to shameful deeds.[277] Both Aristotle and Plato prohibit outspokenness and scandalous speech, especially in houses where children live. Let decency inspire our words and deeds (*Sit pudor in verbis et in operibus*).

These philosophers also prohibit wine for the most part.[278] Many doctors uphold this prohibition, for wine perturbs the internal organs and thereby confounds the mind, which cannot be at its best because of the many fumes wine generates. Mists conceal even the sun's beautiful face.

It is laudable and honorable for parents to educate their children in the Christian faith, that they might love religion and justice and avoid fallacies and vanity. Parents must always be truthful, not only when dealing with important matters but also in matters of little or no relevance, for the enemies of truth deserve blame (*mentientes autem vituperio sunt afficiendi*) and bad habits are shameful. Older children must be entrusted to preceptors who lead laudable lives. If

---

276. A Latin gloss in the margins ("Quam minime cum servis versentur") recalls Aristotle's *Politics*, VII.xv.6 (1335a41): "The Directors of Education should have an eye to their bringing up, and in particular should take care that they are left as little as possible with slaves." Trans. Jowett, in *The Complete Works*, II.2120.

277. Marinella continues to model her argument on Aristotle's by quoting the Latin equivalent of *Politics*, VII.xv.7 (1336b7): "Ex turpiter loquendi libertate sequitur et turpiter facere." Trans. Jowett, in *The Complete Works*, II.2120.

278. Aristotle indeed discourages the drinking of wine in children in *Politics* VII. xvii.1336b20 (trans. Saunders, *The Complete Works*, II.1356). Plato is stricter: no wine at all until eighteen, and only in moderation until thirty (*Laws* II, 666a, trans. Jowett, *Complete Works*, II.2120).

instead they are left without knowledge, discipline, and the arts, they will be deprived of all goodness.

> Of all wild things, the child is the most unmanageable: an unusually powerfully spring of reason, whose waters are not yet canalized in the right direction, makes him sharp and sly, the most unruly animal there is. That's why he has to be curbed by a great many 'bridles,' so to speak.[279]

As this philosopher shows, a child without virtue and a proper education is like an animal without reason—insidious, cruel, and insolent. Therefore he must be under the tutelage of good preceptors, so that he, like metal that shines when used and rusts when left idle, may lead a just and laudable life. Education is a second nature (*educatio est altera natura*). The parents' lives and education are extremely important. It is crucial that they provide good and just examples, which perfectly educate children to perfection when they are still in the cradle. Children adopt the habits of their parents, who can shape them as they please. They are like tender shrubs that can be bent in any which way and then grow and harden in that form, from which they cannot be turned without being broken. Likewise, a child's soul receives excellent habits and good teachings, which become so engrained that it is impossible for the child to behave differently. It is a father's duty to educate his children as extensions of his own life and to establish his example as their law, as if they were parts of his own body.[280]

The father must diligently rule over his children, as if they were extensions or parts of himself. He must set an example for them. He must be adorned by true qualities, practice noble and laudable behavior, and never allow anybody to say or do something dishonest. In fact, in those first years, one learns even the smallest things, and

---

279. Plato, *Laws*, VII (808D–E). Marinella quotes it in Latin: "Est autem puer omni bestia intractabilior, nam cum prudentiae fontem nondum perfectum habeat, insidiousissimus est acerrimusque, et petulantissimus omnium bestiarium. Ideo multis quasi frenis vinciendus est." Trans. Saunders, in *Complete Works*, 1476.

280. "Patris familias officium est filios colere, ut proprie vitae propaginem, et proprio exemplo regere, tamquam membra." Unknown source.

even a little cloud ruins the clear air. Therefore parents must be flaw-less, that their children might be the same. This is why Aristotle warns parents to set good examples for their children:

> For unless parents have given their children an exam-ple of how to live, the children in their turn will be able to offer a fair and specious excuse. Such parents will risk being rejected by their offspring for their evil lives.[281]

In other words, parents must set the example for their children's lives. If they fail to do so, they cannot be excused, and should fear being likewise abandoned in their old age. Therefore, I do not believe it pos-sible for a father to be so negligent or a mother so worthless and crazy that they do not sweat, struggle, and labor to raise their children to be good and dignified among civil people and in their households and cities.

After the first years, once children have grown and been raised following their parents' honorable and appropriate ways, they will be introduced to learned preceptors, that they might cultivate virtue, knowledge, and intellectual disciplines. Children must do their best to demonstrate that they are true imitators of their parents and true dis-ciples—indeed, almost offspring—of their preceptors as far as military art, literature, fortitude, and other laudable qualities are concerned.

In the eighth book of *Politics*, the Philosopher shows that the young must learn four things: reading and writing, gymnastics, draw-ing, and music.[282] This way, they will become well versed in the most important domains.

Gymnastics includes every form of military exercise, such as throwing spears and arrows, frontal clashes of armies, leading a squad, forming and building ramparts and lodgings, ordering and forming the squads, and all of the actions, labors and dangers that war entails.

---

281. Aristotle's *Economics*, III.ii, which Marinella quotes as: "Nisi parentes exemplum vitae filiis praestent excusationis causam ergo se relinquunt, ac timendum est ne contempti a filiis, quasi non bene vixerunt, in senectute deserantur." Trans. Armstrong, *The Complete Works*, II.2148.

282. Aristotle, *Politics*, VIII.iii.3 (1337b23). Trans. Jowett, *The Complete Works*, II.2122.

In addition, gymnastics includes boxing, running, handling the iron ball,[283] and many other exercises that develop strength, speed, vigor, agility, and ease of movement. Gymnastics also includes the five kinds of strength the Philosopher describes:

> Strength is the power of moving something else at will; to do this, you must either pull, push, lift, pin, or grip it. Thus you must be strong in all of those ways or at least in some.[284]

Aristotle believes that this virtue constitutes the true beauty of a young person. He writes:

> In a young man beauty is the possession of a body fit to endure the exertion of running and of contests of strength [...]; and therefore pentathlon athletes are the most beautiful, being naturally adapted both for contests of strength and for speed also.[285]

283. The weapon described by Marinella as "pallo di ferro" was known since Medieval times and consisted of an iron ball fastened to a chain which was often attached to a shaft. See Henry Swainson Cowper, *The Art of Attack. Being a Study in the Development of Weapons and Appliances of Offence, from the Earliest Times to the Age of Gunpowder* (Ulverston: W. Holmes, Ltd., Printers, 1906), 80-1. At the beginning of the 17th century, the Venetian government sponsored four academies "for the double purpose of promoting law and order and providing trained cavalrymen in time of war." The statutes of Verona's Academia Filotima prescribed a curriculum similar to the one outlined by Marinella, including the "handling of the iron ball" ("trar il pallo di ferro"). See John Rigby Hale, "Military Academies on the Venetian Terraferma in the Early 17th Century," in *Renaissance War Studies* (London: Hambledon Press, 1983), 286-307: 295.

284. Aristotle, *Rhetoric*, I.v.1361b15: "Necesse est alterum movere, vel trahendo, vel impellendo, vel tollendo, vel deprimendo, vel collendo, robustus ille valensque; aut his omnibus, aut quibusdam eorum valebit." Trans. W. Rhys Roberts, in *The Complete Works*, II.2164.

285. Aristotle, *Rhetoric* I.v (1361b8–11): "Pulchritudo iuvenis est habere corpus aptum ad labores sustinendos, et ad cursum, et ad celeritatem. Pentathli pulcherrimi habentur, quod ad vim inferendam apti erant." Trans. Rhys Roberts, in *The Complete Works*, II.2164. The ending of Marinella's Latin quote ("apti erant") is incongruous in the copies at the Biblioteca Aprosiana and Antoniana. The pagination errors in the copy at the Bibliothèque Mazarine perhaps originated from a desire to redress this mistake. The corresponding passage in fact correctly reads "ad vim inferendam et ad celeritatem apti sunt."

I believe that Hercules possessed a similar strength when fighting Achelous for the sake of his beloved Deianira. In book VIII, Ovid says:

> Foot locked with foot, fingers with fingers clenched, brow against brow,
> with all my body's forward-leaning weight I pressed upon him.[286]

And later:

> He gave me no chance to regain my strength.[287]

As the fight continues, the poet adds:

> He fixed his vice-like grip upon my throat. I was in anguish, as if my throat were in a forceps' grip.[288]

Those who recall the entire fight will find it full of art and science. Boxing contests, which, according to Plato, are a form of gymnastics, are appropriate to generous and noble souls.[289] Everybody marveled when Entellus threw two gloves into the ring:

> He threw into the ring a pair of gloves of giant weight, wherewith valiant Eryx was wont to enter contests.[290]

286. Ovid, *Metamorphoses* IX (not VIII as Marinella states), 44–45 (Loeb, 5): "Cum pede pes iunctus, totoque ego pectore pronus et digitos digitis et frontem fronte premebam."

287. Ovid, *Metamorphoses* IX.59 (Loeb, 7): "Prohibetque resumere vires."

288. Ovid, *Metamorphoses* IX.77–78 (Loeb, 9): "summo digitorum vincula collo / inicit: angebar, ceu guttura forcipe pressus."

289. Contrary to Marinella's statement, Plato is critical of boxing, which he finds "absolutely useless in a military encounter" (*Laws* VII.796a, trans. Saunders, in *Complete Works*, 1464). She might have been misled by Plato's simile of boxers' training in *Laws* VIII.830a.

290. Virgil, *Aeneid* V.401 (Loeb, 499): "In medium geminos immani pondere caestus / proiecit, quibus acer Eryx in proelia suetus / ferre manum."

Running must also be considered, as it, too, is part of gymnastics. This skill is apparent in those who are very fast and elegant in their movements. They are the ones who are fit for running and speed (*ad cursum et ad celeritatem apti sunt*).

Gymnastics trains the body to be strong, robust, and ready to withstand the discomfort and danger of horrible battles, and it teaches us how to win any military action. This pertains to all citizens, but particularly to noblemen, who must be able to defend with arms, if necessary, their rights and their cities, provinces, and republics. These deeds are so important and notable that there is no greater or more laudable task than defending the fatherland. It is a dear and desirable thing to expose one's chest to danger for the fatherland and say, if the need arises,

> Before it touches you the sword should pass
> Through this bare throat or through this heart alone.[291]

"To die for one's country is a beautiful thing."[292] Those who help to preserve or increase the greatness of the fatherland deserve always to have their fame sung and their deeds rewarded.

> All those who have preserved, aided, or enlarged their
> fatherland have a special place prepared for them in
> the heavens, where they may enjoy an eternal life of
> happiness. For nothing of all that is done on earth
> is more pleasing to that supreme God who rules the
> whole universe [...][293]

---

291. Marinella quotes the words that Armida addresses to Rinaldo in Tasso, *Gerusalemme liberata*, XVI.50: "Per questo sen, per questo collo ignudo, / pria che giungano a te passeran l'armi." Trans. Esolen, 310.

292. "Mori pro patria pulchrum est:" in spite of a note in the margins that indicates Homer's *Iliad* as the source, the closest reference seems to be to Horace's *Odes*: "Dulce et decorum est pro patria mori" (*Odes*, III.ii.13; Loeb, 175: "'Tis sweet and glorious to die for fatherland").

293. Cicero, *De re publica*, trans. Clinton Walker Keyes (Cambridge, MA: Harvard University Press, 1970), VI.13 (Loeb, 264–65): "Omnibus, qui patriam conservaverint, adiuverint, auxerint, certum est in caelo definitum locum ubi beati aevo sempiterno fruantur; nihil est enim illi principi Deo, qui omnem mundum regit, quod quidem in terris fiat, acceptius [...]."

I do not want to extol the greatness of the fatherland or incite young hearts to such a laudable virtue any longer, for I am sure that a generous soul, without further invitation, would run to undertake any difficult deed for the fatherland. There are, as Plato says, other virtues that make people great:

> For children three subjects still remain. The first is number computation; the second is the measurement of lines, surfaces, and solids; the third is the properties of the heavenly bodies.[294]

He invites the young to learn each of these parts of geometry. One need not become an expert in all of them, but at least in some, and more or less according to one's inclinations. God did not give all the virtues to one person, but distributed them among all the people. The poet from Smyrna suggests this in his verse: "To another he granted to play the cithara."[295]

He shows that no one person possesses all knowledge. It is sufficient for each individual to possess some knowledge, that together the citizens might provide valiant knights, prudent captains, and other such brave souls for the honor and reputation of the fatherland. When the occasion and times require that peace be broken, it must be possible to find among one's citizens courageous people who can assure happy victories in the uncertain wars. Foreign help, in fact, procures no happiness, safety, or praise. On the contrary, it is shameful to place the most important affairs of republics and kingdoms under the thumb of far and perhaps unfriendly nations, as I could prove with examples of those who tried and gained little honor and even less profit. Therefore, the young must work diligently to become strong and valiant in the art of war so that, when the time comes, they may put these skills into practice and astonish and amaze their enemies,

294. "Sed liberis tres restant doctrinae. Una est computatio numerorum, altera longitudinis, latitudinis, profunditatisque mensura, tertia virtutis astrorum." Marinella is referring to the curriculum outlined by Plato in *Laws*, VII (817e).

295. "Alio dedit citera canere." Perhaps Marinella is alluding to Ulysses's proud response to Euryalus in *Odyssey* VIII.167–68: "So true is it that the gods do not give gracious gifts to all alike, not form, nor mind, nor eloquence." Trans. Murray, rev. Dimock (Loeb, 285).

bringing praise and glory to their cities and republics, as well as to themselves. Nor can a city boast a glory greater than having nurtured invincible champions, knights, princes, and leaders whose fortitude is beyond compare, like those born of Rome and now eternally glorified in arms and literature.

As our fickle nature cannot always delight in the same things, it is impossible to engage in difficult and arduous studies without getting tired. Therefore, it is necessary to engage in some honest pleasure to find relief from the difficult tasks. The philosopher allows the young to enjoy music and the sound of different instruments to relax (*gratia relaxationis*). Our nature requires that we behave laudably during periods of activity as well as of rest. By engaging in these pleasurable entertainments, the young emulate runners who, in order to gain speed, move two or three steps behind their starting point and then race toward their goal with increased speed, like flying birds; likewise, young children will be entertained by the sweetness of sound and music. Once they have refreshed and heartened their tired minds, they can return to their studies with renewed vigor. Some virtuous entertainment is certainly necessary so that tired souls may return, restored and with increased desire, to the studies they had interrupted. As music is dear and welcome to everyone, I am not surprised that a philosopher said: "The Muses, under Love's guide, found music."[296] Therefore, music is a work of love. That it is so sweet and welcome is logical if you consider that Love, the sweetest and most pleasant of the Gods, led to its discovery. No soul is too rough, no mind too vile to shun sweet harmonies and not be pleased by their charm. Many tasks and occupations often leave the mind busy and fatigued, and music is so pleasant and sweet that, like a new sun, it can dispel and consume the melancholic clouds that surround the heart. Its virtue does not seem earthly, but celestial and divine.

Therefore we should not be surprised that Plato, Pythagoras, and Macrobius, those ancient wise men, believed our music to be but a small, even minimal part of the celestial music. They believed that the skies release harmony, a wonderful and divine sound, from which our music originates. They were also sure that people enjoyed music.

---

296. "Musae musicam, amore Duce, invenerunt." The closest reference seems to be Agathon's speech in Plato's *Symposium*, 197b.

Our souls come from heaven, whose movements, as I said, produce a wonderful and pleasurable concert. Therefore, our souls enjoy and desire music because through music they remember what they once heard. These philosophers also believed that a Siren dwells in each circle of the universe,[297] and that she graciously and tirelessly sings divine praises in a harmony audible only to those with a very pure and noble intellect, like Pythagoras, who claimed he heard the sweet song of the divine Sirens, because his sublime and noble senses were indifferent to earthly beauty.

Music has the power to sweeten and mitigate the anger of souls burning with revenge and disdain. Therefore, one should not be surprised that David's harmonic lyre calmed and restrained Saul's furious soul.[298] Although music is not a useful or necessary discipline, the young should nevertheless learn it as a graceful and pleasing art that brings sweetness and pleasure. It takes the mind away from melancholic concerns; the splendor of its beauty and sweetness can make a cloudy sky serene again. It resembles a noble medicine for the boredom and hassles that work and study induce.

"All men agree that music is one of the pleasantest things."[299] Music brings the noblest satisfaction and pleasure as its own adornment and natural grace. Therefore, people of different ages, customs, and nationalities welcome and appreciate it. You cannot find a person so removed from pleasure that he finds no joy and grace in music. The ancients believed that Apollo invented both medicine and music, for music has treated many illnesses, perhaps no fewer than medicine has. Melancholy is a serious and bothersome illness, but musical harmony can nevertheless heal and dispel it. Its sweet nature can overcome many other diseases. In the *Symposium*, Plato praises this art.[300] An

297. Plato talks about the Sirens who produce celestial harmony in *Republic* X (617b).

298. Samuel 16:13: "Whenever the spirit from God seized Saul, David would take the harp and play, and Saul would be relieved and feel better, for the evil spirit would leave him." (http://www.vatican.va/archive/ENG0839/P7A.HTM)

299. Aristotle, *Politics* VIII.v (1339b19), which Marinella quotes in an abridged form ("musica ex iocundissimis") from Leonardo Bruni's translation: "Musicam vero omnes fatemur esse ex iocundissimis." Trans. Jowett, in *The Complete Works*, II.2125.

300. Marinella is probably thinking of the discussion on music that takes place in *Symposium* 187ff, where we find an analogy between medicine and music similar to the one she

art that is so delightful and dear and pleasing to all sorts of people is certainly appropriate for young people, who are by nature inclined to happiness and delight. Taken by its sweetness, noble minds rise above the stars and, forgetful of themselves, rest in eternal beatitude and enjoy the celestial harmony of the divine Sirens. They never grow tired of listening to them. We can therefore say that Venus, who in her chariot brings a man, Adonis, into the sky to contemplate the eternal powers, represents music's sweetness and beauty.[301] Children will easily learn this subject, which does not prevent noble civil actions, make the body inadequate to warfare, or render a warrior unfit. In fact, we read that Alexander the Great was both a formidable warrior and an expert lute player. Hearing the sweetness and softness that came from the noble instrument, his father declared it shameful for such a reputable captain to know so much of that art, as if he had nothing else to do. His father was afraid that music would make Alexander neglect his military glory.[302] Alexander, however, was so smart and ingenious that he neglected neither art, as the world well knows.

I believe that Aristotle also spoke against those who thought music would make men sordid and weak. He called music noble and laudable, capable of restoring strength and inspiring the mind.[303] Musaeus maintains that music is unusually sweet to mortal senses:

Song is to mortals of all things the sweetest.[304]

---

just made. However, there is no close equivalent to the Latin quote she inserts at this point: "Musica pulcherrima res est quae optimos, et eruditos delectat, maxime vero si qua unum virtute, et eruditione, excellentem."

301. The tragic love of Venus and Adonis is recounted in Ovid, *Metamorphoses* X. However, Venus is alone in riding her chariot (708).

302. Philip the Macedonian's concern about his son's passion for music is reported in Plutarch's *Life of Pericles*: "And so Philip once said to his son, who, as the wine went round, plucked the strings charmingly and skillfully, 'Art not ashamed to pluck the strings so well?' It is enough, surely, if a king have leisure to hear others pluck the strings, and he pays great deference to the Muses if he be but a spectator of such contests." (Plutarch, *Lives*, ed. Bernadotte Perrin, vol. 3, I.5 (Loeb, 5).

303. Aristotle defends the inclusion of music in the curriculum in *Politics* VIII.

304. Aristotle, *Politics*, VIII.v (1339b20): "Carmen dulcissimam rem esse mortalibus." Trans. Jowett, in *The Complete Works*, II.2125.

With its sweet ways, music built the walls of Thebes.[305]

Aristotle also distinguishes between different kinds of music. Phrygian music can awake virtue, as it takes the soul outside itself.[306] He also mentions a kind of music that is most appropriate for the young, and recommends

> any mode, such as the Lydian above all others appears to be, which is suited to children of tender age, and possesses the elements both of order and education.[307]

Therefore, we maintain that Lydian music is so powerful that it can lift our will to virtue. He also discusses another kind of music, which similarly grounds us in perfection. He says, in fact, that children should be taught Dorian music, which is the gravest and manliest of all.[308]

All of these kinds of music are therefore appropriate for the young because they point the way to goodness and virtue. This makes us realize how beautiful and useful the different kinds of music are. Phrygian music raises the soul with invisible hooks to moral and noble deeds, awakens virtue, and enraptures the spirit, leading it to the divine with something close to a sweet violence.

Dorian music is highly beneficial to young restless people, as it grounds them in moral virtues and makes their thoughts virile and mature. Music produces nothing but wonders. Lydian music fills our minds with beauty and knowledge. It is therefore very appropriate for noble children who wish to adorn themselves with great virtue.

305. Clinias acknowledges Amphion as the inventor of the lyre in Plato's *Laws* III.677d. Horace (*Ars poetica* 394–96) and Statius (*Thebaid* X.873) tell of how his music moved the stones, which arranged themselves in such a way as to build the walls of Thebes.

306. Aristotle, *Politics* VIII.v (1340b5): "Musica frigia distrahit et rapit animum, et quasi extra se ponit." Trans. Jowett, in *The Complete Works*, II.2126.

307. Aristotle, *Politics* VIII.vii (1342b30): "Praeterea, si qua est talium harmoniarum quae conveniat puerorum aetati ex eo quia possit ornatum simul doctrinamque afferre: quod Lidia maxime omnium harmoniarum habere videtur." Trans. Jowett, in *The Complete Works*, II.2129.

308. Aristotle, *Politics* VIII.vii (1342b10). Marinella quotes two passages from Bruni's translation: "Doricam praeteris decens est iuniores addiscere" and "Doricam autem constantem esse ac firmam moremque continere virilem." Trans. Jowett, in *The Complete Works*, II.2129.

It is said that when departing for the Trojan War, the great king Agamemnon was upset at leaving Clytemnestra, his beautiful and noble queen. He knew the power of music—in particular, Lydian music—and therefore left a musician with her, that the sweetness of his singing might keep her modest and chaste. When Aegisthus, who had pursued the queen in vain, realized that it was the singer who was keeping her far from lasciviousness and dishonest thoughts, he killed the sweet singer and was able to enjoy the beautiful woman.[309] How many graces are born of this pleasing science!

This beautiful art incites souls to honest living, inflames them to greatness, moves them to compassion, devotion, and weeping, and purifies the sinful from dishonest feelings. Many philosophers, after considering music's many divine effects, claim that our souls are made of numbers and harmony. Xenocrates says that the soul is a self-moving number.[310] Plato and Empedocles, like other wise men, say that the soul is harmony (*Animam esse harmoniam*).

The general term "music" includes sounds, musical instruments, verses, rhymes, and singing. Instruments, rhymes, and harmony have different qualities and produce different results. Some sounds and singing calm and cheer the unbalanced and angered soul. Others, on the contrary, rekindle and inflame peaceful souls, leading to wrath and bellicose confrontations. Some harmonies enhance our minds with moderate desire and laudable morality; some inspire maturity, wisdom, and prudence; some invite laughter, lasciviousness, and flattering vanity; some lead the mind to pity, compassion, and fear; some, with superhuman powers, move souls to generosity, honor, and supremacy; others stir sad desires, obscure and murky thoughts, and crazy cogitations and fantasies. Almost like a celestial hand, some music brings consolation by chasing away from our souls melancholic and bothersome concerns. Therefore music deserves to be praised and wondered at for the many different emotions it inspires, and one should not be surprised that Aristotle and Plato prescribed it as a dis-

---

309. Nestor of Gerenia tells Telemachus about Aegisthus's ploy in *Odyssey*, III.262–75.

310. Whether this famous definition ("Animam esse numerum se ipsum moventem"), recalled also in Aristotle's *On the Soul*, I.ii (404b29) should be attributed to Xenocrates or Plato is open to debate. See *The Dictionary of the History of Ideas*, ed. Philip P. Wiener (New York: Charles Scribner's Sons, 1973–74), vol. IV,36.

cipline for the young, not because it is necessary but because it brings relaxation.[311] It puts one at ease with pleasure, enjoyment, and praise, so that the soul may return to tiresome occupations restored, reinvigorated, and with renewed strength.

Children must be presented with poetic versions of the lives of great and virtuous men, that a generous envy might spur them to imitate, out of longing for their own praise and glory, the valor of those great men. Plato praises this habit:

> Children must read poems by great writers, so that they might imitate the deeds of great men.[312]

This is why Plutarch gives children poems written by worthy and virtuous authors. He maintains that poetry is useful for the soul's modesty and moderation. Having learned the magnanimity and greatness of other people's deeds, one can prepare the mind to tolerate any event, however unfortunate, with peace and magnanimity and without disdain or perturbation.[313] This is the sign of a great and invincible soul, firm in the face of fortune's changes.

These poems must be full of goodness and modesty so that, as I said, they can inspire young people to imitate the glorious deeds of great men. Works dealing with injustice and evil must be kept away from young people's pure hearing and sight. Like the feathers of a swan, they are easily darkened. It is therefore important to hide from them all that is not good.

311. "Sed gratia relaxationis," Marinella says, echoing Aristotle in *Politics*, VIII.v (1339b15): "for the sake of relaxation." Trans. Jowett, in *The Complete Works*, II.2124.

312. Marinella's Latin quote ("Poemata bonorum poetarum sunt legenda a pueris ut emuli imitentur facta bonorum virorum") echoes Plato's prescription in *Protagoras* 325e–326a.

313. "Poetica est utilis, primum moderationi animi famulatur, alterum virum instruit ad magnanimitatem, quae ad omnes fortunae casus ita componat animu, ut non turberis." Marinella is probably referring to the *De pueris educandis*, a Greek tract commonly attributed to Plutarch and translated into Latin by Guarino Guarini in 1411. See Sandra Sider, *Handbook to Life in Renaissance Europe* (New York: Oxford University Press, 2007), 271.

Youth should be kept strangers to all that is bad, and
especially to things that suggest vice or hate.[314]

This pertains to both words and deeds.

Aristotle also recommends that young people avoid tragedies,
comedies, and the theater until they reach an appropriate age and that
they be kept separate from people who are licentious and dishonest in
their conduct. The same philosopher prohibits paintings or sculptures
that represent immodest actions.

We should also banish indecent pictures or speech-
es. Let the rulers take care that there be no image or
picture representing unseemly actions, except in the
temples of those gods at whose festivals the law permits even ribaldry.[315]

Aristotle adds a fourth subject to these three when he exhorts
young people to learn how to draw or paint. Some, he says, recommend drawing, not in order to avoid being cheated when buying or
selling vases, but to understand and comprehend the beauty and perfection of the human body.[316]

Aristotle also recommends that children's exercises be moderate and nonviolent, so that the body does not take on an ugly,
monstrous shape, but rather becomes robust, agile, strong, and able
to tolerate discomfort in war and other inconvenience and trouble.
Gymnastics must consist mostly of military exercises, as Plato says:

We are establishing gymnasia for all physical exercises
of a military kind—archery and deployment of mis-

---

314. Aristotle, *Politics* VII.xv (1336b30): "Oportet a pueris omnia turpia removere, [et
maxime] quaecumque habent in se obscenitatem, vel improbitatem." Trans. Jowett, in *The
Complete Works*, II.2120.

315. Aristotle, *Politics* VII.xv (1336b15): "Aspicere picturas aut actus deformes prohibe-
mus. Sit igitur cura magistratibus nullam neque picturam, nec statuam taliuum reum imita-
tricem, nisi apud Deos quosdam quibus etiam lasciviam mos tribuit." Trans. Jowett, in *The
Complete Works*, II.2120.

316. See Aristotle, *Politics* VIII.iii (1337a40). Trans. Jowett, in *The Complete Works*, II.2123.

siles in general, skirmishing, heavy-armed fighting of
every variety, tactical maneuvers, marches of every sort,
pitching camp, and also the various disciplines of the
cavalryman. In all these subjects there must be public
instructors paid out of public funds; their lessons must
be attended by the boys and men of the state, and the
girls and women as well.[317]

Therefore riding a horse, jousting, wrestling, and several other arts are
subsumed under the word "gymnastics."

Plato criticizes mothers who terrify and depress a child's soul
with sad and scary tales and tearful fables or describe hellish punishments or other such stories that may instill terror in young and
inexperienced minds.[318] He also prohibits children from watching
comedies or tragedies. All these things bring either fear and dismay or
tiresomeness and little profit. When they are sad, they are depressing;
when they are happy, they are indecent and invite the mind to pleasure
and weakness. They need to be kept away from youthful eyes and ears.

Following Plato, Aristotle, and others, we have trained the
young body to withstand activity and fatigue and made it robust, agile, quick, and skilled at gymnastics, which encompasses many disciplines. It is now reasonable that we mention at least some of the
virtues young people must learn to embellish their souls.

The philosopher divides the soul into two parts: one is rational, the other irrational.

Prudence, industry, memory, and other similar things derive
from the rational part of the soul. The irrational part brings forth
those things that we call virtues and that deserve praise, such as temperance, fortitude, justice, which are laudable in themselves. People

---

317. Plato, *Laws*, VII.813d-e: "Gymnasticam omnes esercitationes bellicas appellemus. Sag-
ittandi, iaculandi, omnium armorum dimicationes, acierumque ordinationes, ductiones ex-
ercitus, castrorum positiones, quorum publicos esse magistros a civitate ductos, qui pueros
puellasque, viros et foeminas doceant." Trans. Saunders, in *Complete Works*, 1481.

318. Cf. Plato, *Republic*, II.381e: "Nor must mothers, believing bad stories about the gods
wandering at night in the shapes of strangers from foreign lands, terrify their children with
them." Trans. Grube, in *Complete Works*, 1020.

are praised not for being wise or prudent, but for being temperate, fair, and strong.[319]

> Moral excellence is an active habit that is destroyed by defect and excess and is not without pleasure and pain.[320]

Virtue is a middle ground where one can avoid excess. Someone who gets angry without a reason or more than is necessary does not deserve praise. Likewise, it is undignified and crazy not to get angry when it is reasonable to do so and to instead tolerate harm (*omnia tollerare et non irasci stultum est ac puerile*).[321] Getting angry is not reproachable when done at the right time, in the right way, and in the right measure, and in such a way as to obey the command of reason.[322]

Moral virtue sits with dignity between the extremes. It is a middle ground that avoids both excess and defect. Just as too much food makes the body sick, so, too, does too little. The same is true of exercise. While too much labor destroys strength, slowness and laziness lead to evil; the right measure saves and maintains health and strength.[323]

---

319. Cf. Aristotle, *Magna Moralia*, I.v (1185b1–10) and *Nicomachean Ethics*, I.xiii (1102a27).

320. Marinella's argument ("Virtus est habitus activus, qui corrumpitur ab excessu, et defectu, non sine voluptate, et dolore") combines two passages from Aristotle's *Magna Moralia*, 1185b10 and 1185b35.

321. Cf. Aristotle, *Nicomachean Ethics* IV.5 (1126a4).

322. "Quando oportet, quantum oportet et quo oportet," Marinella writes. The concept was crucial in the Aristotelian moral system, and it is repeated in *Nicomachean Ethics*, II.vi (1106b21) and II.9 (1109a27).

323. This is another very important concept. Aristotle writes that excellence "is a mean between two vices, that which depends on excess and that which depends on defect; and again it is a mean because the vices respectively fall short of or exceed what is right in both passions and actions, while excellence both finds and chooses that which is intermediate" (*Nicomachean Ethics*, II.vi.2 [1107a2]). Trans. Ross, in *The Complete Works*, II.1748. The examples of food and exercise can be found in *Magna Moralia*, I.v (1185b15–20): "Now, that defect and excess destroy can be seen from perceptible instances, and we must use what we can see as evidence for what we cannot see. For one can see this at once in the case of gymnastic exercises. If they are overdone the strength is destroyed, while if they are deficient the same thing happens. And the same is the case with food and drink. For if too much is taken

Few people are good, for finding a happy medium in every-thing is difficult and tiresome. For instance, it is difficult to be liberal without leaning toward either prodigality or avarice. It is easy for the archer to hit the circumference of a target, but it is difficult and tiring to strike the center.[324] Therefore, he who approaches the middle and avoids the extremes can be said to be good. Not everybody can reach the middle, but only those who are good and love virtue.

In regard to such difficulties, the Goddess Calypso recom-mended to Ulysses, who was about to set sail, that he travel far from water and smoke and instead follow a happy medium:

From this smoke and surf keep the ship well away.[325]

She exhorted him to recognize the middle route as the best way to complete his tiresome trip. Everybody loves the happy medium, which befits the nobility.

The Holy Scriptures say that when the Philistines sent the ark of the Lord to Israel, the cows went straight along the road mooing, without leaning to the left or the right. This shows how good the happy medium is.[326] Daedalus instructed his son to travel in midair:

I warn you, Icarus, to fly in a middle course, lest if you go too low, the water may weight your wings; if you go too high, the fire may burn them. Fly between the two.[327]

---

health is destroyed, and also if too little, but by the right proportion strength and health are preserved." Trans. Stock, in *The Complete Works*, II.1874.

324. "Capere medium difficile est, sed quod ambit circulum facile." Unknown source.

325. *Odyssey*, XII.219:"procul a fumo et mari longe compelle carenam". The example is in Aristotle, *Politics*, II.ix (1109a32).

326. 1 Samuel 6:12: "Ibant autem in directum vaccae per viam quae ducit Bethsames et itinere uno gradiebantur pergentes et mugientes et non declinabant neque ad dextram neque ad sinistram." http://www.vatican.va/archive/bible/nova_vulgata/documents/nova-vulgata_vt_i-samuelis_lt.html#6

327. Ovid, *Metamorphoses*, VIII.204–6: "Icare, ait 'moneo, ne, si demissior ibis, / unda gravet pennas, si celsior, ignis adurat: / inter utrumque vola!" Trans. Miller (Loeb, 421).

Likewise, the Pythagoreans say that good is singular, evil infinite.[328] On that ground, we know that good is unique and situated in the middle, whereas evil is infinite. Therefore, we must aim our actions and thoughts toward the happy medium. If the young grow accustomed to virtue, they will imitate he who redresses the branches that are bent. By fleeing excess and defect, they will adopt the laudable habit of virtue, which, as an operation of the soul, needs to be exercised (*habitus est propter usum*). Virtue is not something that is simply known, like science, but something that must be exercised, that we might not only be good, but also operate well (*ut boni simus, et bona agamus*). The goal is not to know what temperance and justice are, but to be temperate and just.

Virtue must be practiced because we cannot know how men really are, and many are the opposite of what they are believed to be. This is why we must exercise our virtue. Habits are acquired through practice, and practice is better than habit. While practice is not better than nature, it is believed to be better because it reveals a person's good qualities. This moral virtue is acquired through habit, is not something given to us by nature. If that were the case, it would be so intrinsic to us that we could not act otherwise. What is natural is always the same.[329]

A stone is naturally heavy and cannot be otherwise. It will never learn to hang in midair, no matter how often it is thrown upward. Its weight is intrinsic to it.[330] On the contrary, the moral faculty is not something given to us by nature. Man, however, can gain it with time and effort. The philosopher does not believe that any man is naturally good:

328. "Bonum unum, malum omnimode." Marinella writes. It is probably a reference to Aristotle, *Nicomachean Ethics* II.vi [1106b29]: "Evil belongs to the class of the unlimited, as the Pythagoreans conjectured, and good to that of the limited." Trans. Ross, in *The Complete Works* II.1748.

329. "Habitus est propter usum et usus est melior habitu." Marinella here tackles the issue presented in the opening lines of Plato's *Meno*, 70: "Can you tell me, Socrates, can virtue be taught? Or is it not teachable but the result of practice, or is it neither of these, but men possess it by nature or in some other way?" Trans. Grube, in *Complete Works*, 871.

330. This example can be found in Aristotle, *Nicomachean Ethics*, II.i (1103a21), and *Magna Moralia*, I.xiv (1188b1).

Now some think that we are made good by nature, others by habituation, others by teaching. Nature's part evidently does not depend on us but, as a result of some divine causes, is present in those who are truly fortunate.[331]

He believes that it is impossible for someone to be granted goodness, common sense, and knowledge from nature. These qualities do not hold the same power over everyone. It is necessary for the listener's soul to be predisposed in such a way as to love virtue and hate vice. However, a young person who lives sensually will either not listen to or not understand those who invite him to goodness:

> For he who lives as passion directs will not hear argument that dissuades him, nor understand it if he does; and how can we persuade one in such a state to change his ways? And in general passion seems to yield [...] to force.[332]

Therefore, laws will pacify the sensual souls. Unless the young are nourished with and raised under laws, it will be difficult for them to possess moral virtue.

Temperance and tolerance are not well accepted, particularly by the young.[333] Therefore it is fair to raise them under the discipline of laws. Those who live sensually cannot appreciate something that opposes their will and cannot walk the right path, which lies at an equal distance between opposite extremes. Plato agrees and says that virtue comes to us neither by nature nor by knowledge.[334]

---

331. Aristotle, *Nicomachean Ethics*, X.ix (1179b20) (Loeb, 631): "Fieri autem bonos alii natura, alii consuetudine alii doctrina exstimant. Quod a natura accidit ex divina causa est iis qui re vera fortunati sunt." Trans. Ross, in *The Complete Works*, II. 1864.

332. Aristotle, *Nicomachean Ethics*, X.ix (1179b25): "Quia ex perturbatione vivit, qui autem ita affectus est dissuadere quis potest? Sed vi cedere perturbatio videtur." Aristotle describes young people as intoxicated by passions in several passages and in particular in *Rhetoric*, II.xii (1139a-1139b10). Trans. Ross, in *The Complete Works*, II.1864.

333. Marinella continues to follow Aristotle. Cf. *Nicomachean Ethics*, X.ix (1179b30).

334. "Virtus utique nec doctrina, neque natura nobis aderit." Cf. Plato, *Meno* 99e.

Therefore, we conclude that virtue comes with practice. When laws clearly show what must be avoided, no one will find it difficult to live according to virtue. Laws will cease to be painful once they have become customary.[335]

> We shall need laws [...] to cover the whole of life; for most people obey necessity rather than argument, and punishments rather than what is noble.[336]

Those who are good are inspired by love (*virtutis amore*), while those who are bad only seem to be good because they fear punishment (*formidine pena*). When the good and the bad both seem to be good we, who cannot judge souls but only actions, will believe that those who are bad are actually good. The only difference is that good people will rejoice when they behave well while bad people will despair, as the philosopher says. People hate those who oppose their impulses, even when they are right.[337] This is why laws are necessary. The law has the power of compulsion, while proceeding at the same time from a sort of practical wisdom and intellect.[338] Youth is ruled and moved by pleasure and pain as if by a rudder.[339] A person who lives virtuously and flees vice because he fears the law cannot be said to be to good. He will not rejoice that he is forced to operate within the good, but rather will resent it with acrimony and displeasure. Therefore he will not experience the happiness that is the goal of virtue. The young abstain from evil actions not out of morality but out of fear. It is impossible to lead most of them to honesty. They are used to obeying fear, rather

---

335. Aristotle, *Nicomachean Ethics*, X.ix (1179b30): "Itaque fiet ut consuetudine tractata molesta esse desinant."

336. Aristotle, *Nicomachean Ethics*, X.ix (1180a3–5): "Et omnino ad omnem vitam opus legibus est. Plerique enim necessitati potius quam rationi, et multis [*sic*], quam honestati obediunt." Trans. Ross, in *The Complete Works*, II.1864.

337. Aristotle, *Nicomachean Ethics*, X.ix (1180a20): "Atque homines qui appetitibus adversatur, etiam si recte id faciant, plerique odio prosequuntur." Trans. Ross, in *The Complete Works*, II.1865.

338. "Lex cum prudentiam quadam ex mente profecta oratio sit, cogendi vim habet." Ibid.

339. "A voluptate et dolore iuvines tamquam a gubernaculo diriguntur." Cf. Aristotle, *Nicomachean Ethics*, X.ix (1172a20). Trans. Ross, in *The Complete Works*, II.1852.

than modesty, and avoid evil out of fear of punishment, rather than out of shame. They are defeated by force, not by honesty. They follow their instinct and flee everything that brings annoyance. They like comfort, happiness. Their desire for joy is endless.

A virtuous and good young person will suffer in gaining moral virtue but then will enjoy the pleasure that is born of good behavior. This, then, is happiness: an operation of the soul perfected by virtue, nothing more than living and acting well. This is the goal of everything good. A young person should not do anything against honesty, either by his own will or because he is forced to do so. The philosopher says:

> For such actions men are sometimes even praised,
> when they endure something base or painful in return
> for great and noble objects gained.[340]

Perhaps he values the goodness that derives from evil. This is why he says that men are sometimes praised.

Nevertheless, the pleasure man derives from virtue is beyond compare. By abstaining from opposite extremes and surpassing his own self through practice, he will gain praise for his victory.

> Stronger is he who conquers himself than he who
> breeches the strongest fortifications, nor can virtue go
> any higher.[341]

Since we are talking of the man who triumphs over himself, it is appropriate that we now discuss the virtue of courage.

Courage is the ornament of a kind and noble soul. This quality, according to Plato, must precede temperance, for it is useful to cities and republics. It is laudable and dear to everybody. Courage derives from gymnastics, as discussed above. Young people who desire glory

---

340. Aristotle, *Nicomachean Ethics*, III.i (1110a24): "Ob actiones autem eiusmodi interdum, laudantur homines, cum pro magnis et honestis rebus turpe aliquid sustinuerint." Trans. Ross, in *The Complete Works*, II.1753.

341. The proverbial Latin phrase ("Fortior est qui se, quam qui fortissima vincit moenia"), slightly altered by Marinella—who adds "nec virtus altius ire potest"—is close to Proverbs 16:32.

and want to make themselves useful must fully devote themselves to this discipline. We are not born only to ourselves, but to the fatherland, to our fathers, to the innocent who need protection, to those who suffer. Courage is intrinsic to a generous soul and must adorn all those who desire honor and glory. It is a happy medium that concerns difficult and terrible things.

> Courage is a mean with respect to things that inspire confidence or fear, in the circumstances that have been stated; and it chooses or endures things because it is noble to do so, or because it is base not to do so.[342]

Courage lies between two extremes, cowardice and audacity. The former, in particular, brings shame because it oversteps the natural fear of formidable things. Audacity, on the other hand, exceeds the limits of bravery and tends more toward fury than toward courage. Courage takes from both extremes, for it is not the absence of fear, but rather a combination of caution and confidence.

Those who are so reckless as to despise and treat carelessly their own lives are not worthy of praise. They should not be considered strong. They are led by a mad fury like unreasonable animals, not by sound reason and justice like a strong person. Anyone who does not fear lightning and other horrible things outside of man's power must rather be considered crazy than strong.[343] A strong person will fear dangerous and formidable things, but only in the right measure, as determined by sound reason. He will not do undignified and cowardly things, such as throwing away one's arms and fleeing and other actions that do not suit an invincible knight, but only befit a man of little value who is careless about his honor. However, the most famous authors have celebrated great warriors who have not avoided this in-

342. Aristotle, *Nicomachean Ethics*, III.vii (1116a10): "Fortitudo est mediocritas circa terribilia, et ea quae fiduciam afferunt in rebus maximis, atque pulcherrimis ut in maximo, atque pulcherrimo periculo et hac de causa quia honestum." Trans. Ross, in *The Complete Works*, II.1762.

343. Cf. Aristotle, *Nicomachean Ethics*, III.vii.7 (1115b24): "Of those who go to excess he who exceeds in fearlessness has no name [...], but he would be a sort of madman or insensible person if he feared nothing." Trans. Ross, in *The Complete Works*, II.1761.

dignity, as in the case of Turnus, a most esteemed warrior, who was nevertheless humiliated and stripped of his usual bravery.

> In supplication he lowered his eyes and stretched out his right hand: "I have earned it," he cried "and I ask no mercy; use your chance. If any thought of a parent's grief can touch you, I beg you—you too had such a father in Anchises—pity Daunus's old age, and give me—or, if you prefer, my lifeless body—back to my kin. You are the victor; and the Ausonians have seen me stretch forth my hands as the vanquished: Lavinia is your wife; do not press your hatred further."[344]

This formidable hero, valiant and boastful, begs for his life and in front of the armies concedes Lavinia to the enemy. In creating a character that loves his life more than his honor—which does not suit a valiant knight—the poet failed to observe decorum. Horace harshly criticizes this move in his *Ars poetica*:

> [I]f you boldly fashion a fresh character, have it to the end even as it came at the first, and have it self-consistent.[345]

Horace advises authors to maintain decorum in their compositions. He adds:

---

344. *Aeneid*, XII.930–38, trans. Faircloth, rev. Goold (Loeb, 365–67). "Ille humilis supplexque oculos dextramque precantem / pretendens 'Equidem merui, nec deprecor,' inquit: / "Utere sorte tua. Miseri te si qua parentis / tangere cura potest, oro (fuit et tibi talis / Anchises genitor), Dauni miserere senectae / et me, seu corpus spoliatum lumine mavis / redde meis. Vicisti et victum tendere palmas / Ausonii videre; tua est Lavinia coniux: / ulterius ne tende odiis."

345. Horace, *Ars Poetica*, 125–27: "Et audes / Personam formare novam; servetur ad imum / Qualis ab incepto processerit, et sibi constet." Trans. H. R. Fairclough (Cambridge, MA: Harvard University Press, rev. 1929, rpt. 1999), 461.

Let Medea be fierce and unyielding, Ino tearful, Ixion
forsworn, Io a wanderer, Orestes sorrowful.[346]

Similarly Aristotle, when considering decorum and behavior,
says that characters must be appropriate and consistent.[347] Perhaps the
author of the *Aeneid* decided to dispense with the appropriate decorum because he thought that a strong man could easily turn into a
coward. Perhaps he did it on purpose to show that our nature does not
always remain in the same state and that sometimes even brave men,
when fearful, lose their first nature and this is why we sometimes see
entire armies fleeing in shame.

I believe this can proceed only from some occult power. We
cannot explain its cause, but only consider its effects. For this reason
a poet said:

Be satisfied with *quia* unexplained, oh human race!
The first origin is hidden from us, too profound is its
rule.[348]

We can observe the same in warriors as strong and brave as
Hector when he left Troy to fight Achilles. He later regretted his actions and that he did not listen to Polydamas, who had exhorted him
to remain in the city. Overcome by fear, he reproached himself for not
having stayed in Troy. When appraising the danger, he did not trust

346. Horace, *Ars Poetica*, 123–24: "Sit Medea ferox invictaque, flebilis Ino, / Perfidus Ixion,
Io vaga, tristis Orestes." Ibid.

347. "Sicut convenientes et constantes sibi," Marinella writes, echoing Aristotle's words prescribing that characters be "consistent and the same throughout; even if inconsistency be
part of the man before one for imitation as presenting that form of character, he should
still be consistently inconsistent" (*Poetics*, 15 [1454a26]) Trans. Bywater, in *The Complete
Works*, II.2327.

348. "Humana gente state attente al quia, / che 'l propter quid ha troppo occulta sede, /
troppo profonda è la sua monarchia." The lines quoted by Marinella recall Dante, *Purgatorio*,
III.37–39: "State contenti, umana gente, al quia; /ché, se potuto aveste veder tutto, / mestier
non era parturir Maria" ("Be satisfied with *quia* unexplained, / O human race! If you knew
everything, / no need for Mary to have borne a son.") Both quotes exhort men "to accept
things as they are, without attempting to understand their causes" (Robert Hollander's commentary at http://dante.dartmouth.edu/).

his strength, but shame did not allow him to go back.[349] Therefore, he regretfully said:

> Ah, me, if I go inside the gates and the walls, Poly-
> damas will be the first to put reproach on me, since
> he told me to lead the Trojans to the city during that
> fatal night when noble Achilles rose up. But I did not
> listen—surely it would have been far better! But now,
> since I have brought the army to ruin through my
> blind folly, I feel shame before the Trojans, and the
> Trojans' wives with trailing robes, lest perhaps some
> other, baser than I am, may say [...][350]

Therefore he moved against Achilles not because he was inspired by his honor (*honestatis gratia*), but because he feared his shame. That is not real courage, but rather one of the five kinds of false courage the philosopher mentions. Many, in fact, expose themselves to danger simply because they fail to recognize it as danger, and, for that failure, they are not considered strong. At seeing Achilles approach shaking the Pelian spear, Hector was so overcome by fear that he fled. We certainly cannot consider this a fearless action. The poet writes:

> But trembling seized Hector when he caught sight of
> him, and he dared no longer remain where he was,
> but left the gates behind him, and fled in fear.[351]

He fled, racing around the city of Troy in fear of the enemy knight. This shows us that even a strong warrior can relinquish his virtue—

---

349. Aristotle discusses Hector's behavior (*Iliad*, XXII) in *Nicomachean Ethics*, III.viii (1116a21) and *Magna Moralia*, I.xx (1191a5).

350. Homer, *Iliad*, XXII.99–106: "Hei mihi, si quidem portas et muros intrabo, Polisdamas primus reprensionem faciet qui me consulabat Troianis ad civitatem ducem esse, noctem sub hanc perniciosam, in qua motus est Achilles. Sed ego non obedivi, certe multo melius fuisset. Nunc, postquam amisi populum stultitiis meis, verecundor Troianos, et Troianas trahentes longas vestes. Ne quando aliquis dicat imbecillior alius me [...]." The quote is incomplete. Trans. Murray (Loeb, 459–61).

351. Homer, *Iliad*, XXII.136–38: "Hectora, postquam cognovit, cepit timor, neque toleravit illic manere: retro autem portas liquit, ivit autem timens." Trans. Murray (Loeb, 463).

though I cannot tell whether this is the result of a natural fear or an occult power.

A strong man must face dangers out of love of goodness, rather than out of fear of shame (*honestatis gratia, non propter timorem infamiae*). It is always necessary to follow the best. Therefore, a young person must possess this virtue, which brings honor and praise and sits, like a queen, between fear and audacity. He must adorn his soul with it, often recalling the valor, victories, and glorious deeds of so many knights and famous captains remembered in history. Following in their footsteps, young people will honorably foreshadow future glory, even as they are far from danger. Their fatherland, their fathers, their families will rejoice, hoping that their generous children will perform glorious deeds. In times of war, they can hope to achieve eternal glory through them.

Having considered the dignity of this virtue, we must not neglect beautiful and charming justice. Like a precious gem, it includes in itself the excellence of all laudable qualities. It is more beautiful and desirable than Venus, either rising or setting. This virtue gives to each person his due, at the right time and in the right measure. It is, in fact, important that distributive justice consider individual merits and reward those who deserve it. It is not appropriate for a just prince to distribute and dispense to mimes, actors, and vagabonds the same honors and favors given to serious, mature, and learned men. This is not justice, because honoring the unworthy offends the worthy. Justice means giving to each according to his merits.

It is not fair to deprive a man of letters of the honor due to him in order to benefit a depraved man. And yet, this is what often happens. I cannot tell whether this is the result of ignorance or of contempt of knowledge. Some say that being placed in a position of power forces men to show their true nature and whether they love or hate virtue. Regarding this, Bias said that being in a position of power reveals a man's nature.[352]

To deprive a worthy man of his due is offensive and vicious. Vice is so ugly that the Philosopher and Plato, when considering this

---

352. Marinella is following St. Thomas Aquinas: "Secundum Biantis proverbium: principatus virum ostendit" (*De regno ad regem Cypri*, I.10. Bias is one of the seven sages mentioned by Plato in *Protagoras*, 343a.

problem, said that it is better to suffer a wrong than to commit one.[353] This sin is so deplorable that being a victim is preferable to being a perpetrator.

A just man would not offend anyone by depriving him of his life, his belongings, and especially his honor, for it is said that "honor is of greater value than life."[354] Therefore, hurting one's friends or anyone else does not befit a just man.[355]

A prince or other ruler must be careful not to commit injustice against anyone. However, I do not believe that it is possible to find such rulers, as I have heard many complain. Justice is the virtue most appropriate to an innocent and noble man; indeed, it is fair to say that justice embraces all other virtues (*amplectitur omnes virtutes*).

Plato compares the just man to a learned man and the unjust man to an evil and ignorant one (*Est itaque similis iustus sapienti, iniustus malo et inscio*).

For children to be virtuous and good, this philosopher invites parents to hire excellent and irreprehensible teachers. He repeats this in several places, for he is very interested in the goodness of the youth and wants them to learn justice. Parents should entrust their children to laudable preceptors who will teach them justice—if justice can be taught—and train them in justice—if justice can be acquired through exercise and training.[356] Note that this philosopher was not convinced that justice could be taught, given that the world is so full of vice. This is why he says "if justice can be taught."

If a man is just, he will not be able to be anything less than just in his dealings with everyone. He will know, in fact, that every time he offends someone, he reveals himself as unfair and vicious. Therefore, he will try to distribute honors and favors according to merit. When

---

353. Plato, *Gorgias*, 479E : "Melius est affici iniuria, quam afficere." Trans. Zeyl, in *Complete Works*, 825.

354. Ariosto, *Orlando furioso*, XXXVIII.4: "L'onore è di piú pregio che la vita." Trans. Waldman, 455.

355. "Non igitur iusti est in aliquo amico nocere, vel alteri cuiquam," Marinella writes, summarizing Socrates's point in Plato's *Republic*, I.334b–336a.

356. "Patres praebeant pueros preceptoribus commendatos ut doceant iustitiam si doceri potest aut exercitatione, aut consuetudine comparanda [est]." The closest reference is Plato, *Clitophon* 407b.

a deserving person realizes that he is held in contempt, he cannot but suffer, while a vicious and unjust man will rejoice and consider virtue a crime. He will hold himself in great esteem and derive glory from something that deserves reprehension. Therefore, a prince must shy away from such a mistake.

This beautiful quality suits all civil and noble youth, particularly those who are destined to administer justice in government offices, tribunals, and other places where one learns who is just and who is not, who is innocent and who is guilty. Justice subsumes all grace, all beauty, all virtue, and this is why it is considered more beautiful than both the morning star and the evening star (*admirabilior Hespero et Lucifero*).[357] But let us put it aside, for its prerogatives are infinite, and so is its praise.

Let us move on to temperance, which according to Plato is very decent and proper and shines in young people like the first light of the day. The Philosopher defines it like this:

> A temperate man is so called because he is not pained
> at the absence of what is pleasant and at his abstinence
> from it.[358]

This happy medium lies between lack of control and indifference with regard to pleasure. Lack of control concerns taste and touch and involves offenses common to all unreasonable animals. It is therefore a shameful and undignified vice.

An abstentious and temperate person rejoices in this virtue, which his temperate reason makes known to him. He abstains from the opposite extremes, content with this happy medium.

Excess is much more shameful than its opposite, which is called deficiency or lack and is not the object of much contempt because it is not contrary to reason (*non discrepat a ratione*).[359] You can

357. Aristotle, *Nicomachean Ethics*, V.i (1129b25).

358. Aristotle, *Nicomachean Ethics*, III.xi (1118b32): "Temperans est ille, qui a presentibus voluptatibus se abstinet, et absentibus non dolet." Trans. Ross, in *The Complete Works*, II.1766.

359. Having adopted a moral stance in this discussion of temperance, Marinella has strong words for those who pursue pleasure excessively, but she cannot find much to blame in those

recognize a person who is used to goodness from his pleasure or displeasure following a particular action. A good and temperate person is happy to remain far from sensual pleasure; if he is sad to be so, then he must be considered intemperate and immodest.

Temperance is a moral virtue that concerns pleasure and pain and rules over sensual pleasure. Seneca says:

Temperance controls our desires.[360]

Plato recognizes a temperate person based on his pleasure and sorrow. The Philosopher says that education should lead adolescents to enjoy or hate what they ought to. This way, they can learn to distinguish a good habit from a bad one—such as the habit that led Philoxenus to desire to have a crane's neck, that he might prolong his pleasure when drinking.[361] An intemperate person does not regret the evil he has committed. On the contrary, he does everything he can to derive pleasure from it.

A bad man, whose desire is for pleasure, is corrected
by pain like a beast of burden.[362]

This vice brings great dishonor. Lack of control and a life of luxury are attributes of bad people (*sunt ex pravis*), whereas restraint and moderation belong to good and laudable people (*ex bonis et laudabilibus*). The former must be avoided, and the latter must be followed. Abstinence brings praise. As this virtue moderates feelings, it is very appropriate for a child. This light will shine all the more in him, for those of his age are deceived and inspired by instinct and sensual desires. He will reach this goal through habit and by shunning the ex-

---

who are completely indifferent to pleasure.

360. Seneca, *Epistulae Morales*, LXXXVIII.29 (Loeb, 367): "Temperantia voluptatibus imperat."

361. "This is why a certain gourmand prayed that his throat might become longer than a crane's, implying that it was the contact that he took pleasure in." (Aristotle, *Nicomachean Ethics*, III.x [1118a32]). Trans. Ross, in *The Complete Works*, II.1765. See n228.

362. *Nicomachean Ethics*, X.ix (1180a10): "Qui turpia appetit castigandum esse non aliter quam iumentum." Trans. Ross, in *The Complete Works*, II.1865. See n237.

tremes. In this way, he will gain an incomparable, noble and laudable treasure, namely, temperance. This virtue makes men blush, which is most appropriate—and not to be blamed—in young people.

> At first Charmides blushed and looked more beautiful
> than ever, and his bashfulness was becoming at that
> age.[363]

The Philosopher also says that blushing is caused by fear of having done something bad.[364] This is most appropriate for young people, who are sometimes guilty of venial sin.

> We praise young people who are prone to this pas-
> sion, but an older person no one would praise [...]
> We think he should not do anything that causes this
> sense. For the sense of disgrace is not even character-
> istic of a good man.[365]

According to these philosophers, old men should not do anything that will make them blush. Therefore, blushing is laudable in a young person but shameful in an old person, who should have no reason to blush. Temperance tends to spread the redness of its roses on the face of a modest person.

> It seems to me that temperance induces bashful blush-
> ing and makes men modest. I therefore believe that
> temperance is actually modesty.[366]

---

363. Plato, *Charmides*, 158C: "Tunc ergo Charmidis genae rubore suffusae gratiorem spe-
ciem ostenderunt, nam pudor eam aetatem decet." Trans. Rosamond Kent Sprague, in *Complete Works*, 644.

364. Cf. Aristotle, *Nicomachaen Ethics*, IV.9 (1128b10).

365. Aristotle, *Nicomachaen Ethics*, IV.9 (1128b19): "Iuvenili convenit etati, non autem se-
nili, nihil agere debet in quo pudor consistat, nec pudor est probi viri." Trans. Ross, in *The
Complete Works*, II.1781.

366. "Videtur temperantia mihi verecundum ruborem inducere, verecundum hominem
facere, pudorem esse temperantiam arbitror." Cf. Plato, *Charmides* 160e.

Therefore, Plato considered blushing to be not simply a sign of temperance, but temperance itself, which flees the heart and rushes to the face, where it unveils the flowers of its dawn. Lack of control is so ugly that an unrestrained person cannot be considered prudent.

Of the four main virtues, prudence is the least suited to a young person.[367] Preserved by temperance, prudence is a reasonable attitude toward a laudable action in the face of changeable events.[368] Men gain prudence through experience, which is acquired through many repeated actions (*Ex multis actibus iteratis fit experientia*). Time is therefore necessary to make a man prudent, for it is length of time that grants experience (*Prudentiam temporis affert longitudo*).[369] As a young person has not seen much, he cannot have the experience that precedes prudence. Therefore, this virtue cannot exist at a young age, although one can have other virtues.

> While young men become geometricians and mathematicians and wise in matters like these, it is thought that a young man of practical wisdom cannot be found.[370]

This is because they lack the experience necessary for the development of prudence.

As prudent people have seen and considered many things, they can provide advice and recommend what is useful and honorable to themselves and to others. Those who do so, such as Pericles and others, gain this happy reputation of being prudent, which a vicious

---

367. The four virtues to which Marinella refers are the ones outlined by Plato and known in the Christian tradition as the four cardinal virtues: wisdom (or prudence), courage (or fortitude), temperance, and justice.

368. Aristotle, *Nicomachean Ethics*, VI.v (1140b5): "It remains, then, that it is a true and reasoned state of capacity to act with regard to the things that are good or bad for man." Trans. Ross, in *The Complete Works*, II.1800.

369. Aristotle, *Nicomachean Ethics*, VI.viii (1142a15). Trans. Ross, in *The Complete Works*, II.1803.

370. Aristotle, *Nicomachean Ethics*, VI.viii (1142a12) (see Loeb, 349): "Iuvines licet geometrici et matematici evadant, tamen prudentes evadere non videntur." Trans. Ross, in *The Complete Works*, II.1803.

man does not deserve.[371] Nobody can be called at the same time out of control and prudent. You cannot be said to be prudent if you are not good.[372] As Plato says, prudence is the culmination of all the other virtues (*Omnes virtutes prudentia efficiebat*).

While a young man trains and grows accustomed to the virtues discussed earlier, time marches with long steps and brings experience, which endows him with prudence. He will become rich in this and other moral virtues, and the fatherland will become adorned with strong, just, and learned princes, captains, and leaders. They will bring their feelings to a happy medium through abstinence, resilience, and tolerance, and they will strive to gain the splendor of magnificence, gratitude, pleasantness, and liberality. These virtues are necessary for civil and noble people, who will always prove to be strong and resistant to contrariety, and unfazed by the events brought by hostile fate. This way, they will neither rejoice excessively in times of prosperity nor be overwhelmed by adversity (*nec in prosperis laetantur nec in adversis obruuntur*), but will stand steadfast in the happy middle. As such, they will be able to control their passions and avoid the ugliness of vice, which causes men to hate themselves. We see how those whose wickedness brought them shame desire their own death, however contrary this is to our nature. They become like horrible monsters and turn their own hands against themselves, taking revenge for the sins that brought them shame. But virtuous young people will embellish their virtues with magnanimity and other qualities and disciplines necessary for city government, so that they may become glorious and laudable in war and peace.

Parents should spare no expense, labor, diligence, or inconvenience, in order for their children to appear illustrious and remarkable for their virtues in the eyes of the world. They should educate and teach their children and also hire learned and well-mannered preceptors to diligently train them. This is indeed laudable and meritorious work before God and the world and will bring parents, as well as their fatherland, their friends, and their children, consolation, happiness, and profit.

371. Aristotle cites Pericles as an example of prudence in *Nicomachean Ethics* VI.v (1140b7).

372. "Nemo diceret incontinentem, prudentem. Prudens dici non potest, nisi bonus sit." Unknown source.

Among those who exercise virtue joyfully, there may be a man who does not take pleasure in the company of such a beautiful lady. Such a man should consider how necessary it is for him to practice virtue, if not for his own sake, then at least for his honor and that of his fatherland. He should say with Euripides: "No subtle arts for me, but what the state requires."[373]

A young person who has gained good habits will take so much pleasure in performing virtuous actions that he will fill himself with pleasure and happiness, which are the goals of virtue. Nothing could be better (*nihil melius*). I also exhort young people to labor and struggle to be like new wonders in other people's eyes and to keep their minds far from sensuality. They should show ripe fruit when the flower is barely blooming. They should do their best to imitate the valor of the generous Gracchi, Cornelia Gracca's worthy and dear sons, who were the ornaments and gems of their mother.[374] Were young people to imitate them, they would be the apples of their parents' eyes. These parents, marveling often at the excellence of their offspring, will echo Priamus, king of Troy, when he considered how Hector surpassed his other children:

He did not seem the son of a mortal man, but of the great race of the Gods.[375]

Hector's virtue and goodness were so great that he deserved to be compared by his father to the Gods. Many in fact are called gods for the excellence of their virtue.[376]

---

373. "Non mihi speciosa, sed ea, quarum civitas indiget." These words are attributed to Euripides by Aristotle in *Politics* III.4 (1277a17). Trans. Jowett, *The Complete Works*, II.2026.

374. Cornelia Gracca's referred to her sons as her jewels ("Haec ornamenta mea") in response to a Roman matron's display of gems. This proverbial manifestation of maternal pride is reported in Valerius Maximus's *Facta et Dicta Memorabilia* 4.4 (*Memorable Doings and Sayings*, ed. and trans. D. R. Shackleton Bailey, 2 vols. [Cambridge, MA: Harvard University Press, 2000]), vol. 1, 385.

375. "Non hominis mortalis filius ille esse videbatur, sed magna ex stirpe Deorum." Cf. Homer, *Iliad*, XXIV.258.

376. "Ob excellentiam virtutis divini efficiuntur." Cf. Aristotle, *Nicomachean Ethics*, VII.i (1145a28): "Now since it is rarely that a godlike man is found—to use the epithet of the

Many children give honorable presage from the cradle and are admired from birth, as was Hercules, who strangled the snakes in his cradle with his tender baby fingers, which truly is a wonderful thing. However, when he reached a mature age, to perfect all the good he had already done, he wore the distaff on his side and, spinning thick thread, knitted the apex of his glorious greatness.[377]

There are also many men who resemble a beautiful day at sunrise. Full of light, it gives honorable signs of a happy journey. However, as soon as dark clouds envelop the sky, the day is forever perturbed and deprived of its light. There are others who in their childhood, adolescence, youth, and maturity always grow in virtue. They devote their lives to immortality and bring honor and glory to their parents and the fatherland. These, however, are few and far between. Vice is proud and cannot tolerate that a woman called Virtue, spurned by everybody, may compete with and almost dethrone him, much to his shame and dishonor.

Truly unhappy are those parents who try to make their children good, learned, and exemplary, and yet waste their time and effort because their insolent and harsh children disobey their preceptors and their parents. They belie Aristotle's claim that everyone naturally desires knowledge[378] and, on the contrary, reveal the truth of Plato's statement:

> Of all wild things, the child is the most unmanageable.[379]

Tullius considered himself most unhappy because his son was unfriendly to virtue, devoted to sensual pleasures, deaf to reproaches, and deep in the sea of dishonesty.[380] For Tullius, this was the root of

---

Spartans, who when they admire anyone highly call him a 'godlike man.'" Trans. Ross, in *The Complete Works*, II.1809.

377. Marinella relates Hercules's exploits in several passages. See notes 25 and 104.

378. Aristotle, *Metaphysics*, I.i (980b20): "All men by nature desire to know."

379. Plato, *Laws*, VII.808D: "Est puer intractabilior omni bestia." Trans. Saunders, in *Complete Works*, 1476.

380. Marinella could have found this reference to Marcus Tullius Cicero's parental sorrows in Plutarch, *Lives* (*Life of Cicero* xxiv.8): "Furthermore, there are letters from Cicero to

the ignominy and dishonor of his lineage, his fatherland, and himself. Even more unhappy and miserable are those who want to have good, abstentious, and temperate children, and yet themselves boldly walk the licentious road of youthful pleasure, leading a shameful and ugly life, bringing scandal to good people, and dishonoring their lineage. How can these intemperate and unrestrained parents, who live sensually, provide a good example to their children? If they are blind, how can they point the way? If they swim in the deep ocean of vice, how can they reproach their children? And yet there are many who have passed the age of youth and maturity and have been parents for a long time and nevertheless do not blush, and are not petrified by shame. Synderesis[381] does not cry out in them when they allow their wives and children to see how unchaste and dishonest they are and how they live like a new Sardanapalus, immersed in gambling, pleasures, and gossip.[382] How can they exhort their children to self-restraint, sobriety, and modesty, if they themselves are devoted to gluttony and indulge in the delicacy of food, banquets, lasciviousness, and pleasure? As if asleep in the lap of iniquity, they do not realize the shame they bring to themselves, their children, and their relatives. Good Lord, which words can they use to raise their children and invite them to virtue, greatness, and honor? What kind of example are they to set, what mirror are they for their young children, who in adolescence are tricked and controlled by sensual forces and by the beauty of their youth, which is predisposed to enjoy the pleasures of the world? These unhappy fathers do not realize that they serve as a mirror for their children's adornments. They want their children to live according to reason (*secundum rationem*).[383] They want to correct their children

---

Herodes, and others to his son, in which he urges them to study philosophy with Cratippus. But Gorgias the rhetorician he censured for leading the young man into pleasures and drinking parties, and banished him from his son's society." (Trans. Perrin, vol. VII, p. 143).

381. The term "synderesis" (or "synteresis") is used in scholastic philosophy to indicate men's knowledge of the principles of moral action. See St. Thomas Aquinas, *Summa Theologica*, I, q. 79, a. 12.

382. A quote in the margins ("Nam ubi senes minus pudici sunt, necesse est iuvines impudentissimos esse") refers to Plato's *Laws*, V.729C: "Where the old are shameless the young too will inevitably be disrespectful to a degree." Trans. Saunders, in *Complete Works*, 1412.

383. Here Marinella inserts a quote from Isaiah 65:20 ("Puer centum annorum") that is difficult to interpret in this context.

and deprive them of the same things that they licentiously and recklessly concede to themselves. Therefore their children, who have their parents' examples before them, forsake virtue. They do not want to be second to their fathers in vice. On the contrary, they want to surpass their fathers, so that people may say:

> O you the greater son of a great sire.[384]

Thus, honorable and wise fathers consider how their own irreproachable lives profit the well-being of their children. These imitate their fathers' actions, and follow like shadows in the footsteps of those who generated them. Those who are raised and nourished in vice do not know what good is, nor, blinded by the evil vapors of sin, do they know themselves. In vain does the Delphic oracle cry "Know thyself" (*nosce te ipsum*).[385] Just as a virtuous and temperate father brings profit and glory to his family and household, a vicious and unrestrained father brings shame and disgrace.

Fathers must love their children's virtue more than their own lives and must spare no effort to provide their children with an example of honorable qualities. The glory of the parents is a rich treasure for their children (*parentum gloria natis praeclarus thesaurus est*).[386] This is why Aeneas spared neither labor nor danger to leave worthy memories of himself to his son Ascanius. Looking at his son and desiring that he imitate him, he told Ascanius:

> Learn valor from me, my son, and true toil; [...]
> See to it, when later your years have grown to ripeness,
> That you remember, and, as you recall the example set by your kinsmen,

384. Tasso, *Gerusalemme liberata*, V.9 : "O di gran genitor maggior figliuolo." Trans. Esolen, 93.

385. See n230.

386. Cf. Plato, *Menexenus*, 247b. Trans. Paul Ryan, in Plato, *Complete Works*, ed. John M. Cooper, 962.

That your father Aeneas and your uncle Hector stir
your soul![387]

Glory does not proceed from children to parents, but from
parents to children. A valuable example is great and powerful for a
generous child.

Fame charms, invites, and incites to laudable deeds not only
the souls of children, but also those of adults. Themistocles could not
rest his soul in peaceful slumbers because Miltiades's glory kept him
awake.[388]

It is said that Julius Caesar, considering Alexander's glorious
accomplishments, would complain of having done nothing worthy of
praise.[389]

I believe it was this generous envy that touched Alexander's
own heart when he reached the tomb of Achilles, sung by Homer, and
exclaimed: "Lucky man, who had such an illustrious poet who sang so
highly of you."[390]

More than anything else, paternal glory shakes with bitter
reproach the locks of negligent and lazy children. Therefore, it is ap-

387. Virgil, *Aeneid*, XII.435, 438–39: "Disce, puer, virtutem ex me, verumque laborem / [...] Tu facito, mox cum matura adoleverit aetas / Sis memor et te animo repetentem exempla tuorum / Et pater Aeneas et avunculus excitet Hector." (Trans. Fairclough, rev. Goold, 331).

388. Cf. Plutarch, *Lives* (*Life of Themistocles* iii.3–4): "It is said, indeed, that Themistocles was so carried away by his desire for reputation, and such an ambitious lover of great deeds, that though he was still a young man when the battle with the Barbarians at Marathon [490 BCE] was fought and the generalship of Miltiades was in everybody's mouth, he was seen thereafter to be wrapped in his own thoughts for the most part, and was sleepless o' nights, and refused invitations to his customary drinking parties, and said to those who put wondering questions to him concerning his change of life that the trophy of Miltiades would not suffer him to sleep." Trans. Perrin, vol. II, p. 11.

389. "Se nihil preclarum et memorabile egisse." The episode is in Plutarch's *Lives* (*The Life of Julius Caesar* xi.2–3): "In like manner we are told again that, in Spain, when he was at leisure and was reading from the history of Alexander, he was lost in thought for a long time, and then burst into tears. His friends were astonished, and asked the reason for his tears. 'Do you not think, said he, 'it is matter for sorrow that while Alexander, at my age, was already king of so many peoples, I have as yet achieved no brilliant success?'" Trans. Perrin, vol. VII, p. 469.

390. The anecdote is in Plutarch, *Lives* (*The Life of Alexander*, xv.4). Trans. Perrin, vol. VII, p. 263.

propriate for fathers (and others) to strive to leave honorable riches of praise and integrity to those who come after them.

There are also parents who are negligent and indifferent to the idea of teaching and having their children taught, of correcting and leading them on the right path. They may expect punishment from heaven and dishonor from the world, for they are inept and coarse and their soul lowly and vile.

What can we say about crazy and disgraceful parents who teach their little children to swear, use dishonest and ugly words, and perform undignified and indecent actions? They clap and laugh at the little child, praising his intellect. The child, who does not know or understand his father's crazy love, grows to enjoy these bad habits, which will be difficult to change.

This sort of child has no hope of devoting his life to virtue. This is the crime of a father who offers his child false love. His mistake makes him wretched and deprives him of the greatest good and the greatest happiness Nature can offer him—a virtuous and temperate son. He should have cared for him more than he cared for his own eyes. Jealous of his own good, and his son's, he should have supported and directed him towards a virtuous life.[391]

In Athens, wisest of cities, there was a law. Fathers were obliged to care for, feed, and teach their children. Likewise, children were obliged to care for and feed their parents when necessary. But Theseus, the great legislator, did not like the law. With a sense of justice he changed it so that children were obliged to help and comfort their parents in poverty only if their parents had raised and taught them properly. Otherwise, they were not expected to provide help and nourishment. This is indeed a good initiative worthy of such a man. Nevertheless, it seems to me that the Philosopher does not approve of the law; on the contrary, he wants children to feed and help their parents more than themselves if need be, for their parents gave them life.

The wise legislator will introduce good laws that oblige parents to teach their children and entrust them to good preceptors. He knows that many of those children will bring honor to and govern the city, which needs judges, counselors, princes, and rulers. Others will have to

---

391. Aristotle, *Nicomachean Ethics*, VIII.xii (1162a5). Trans. Ross, in *The Complete Works*, II.1836.

master military affairs, which they will have learned in childhood. Habit is a second nature (*habitus est altera natura*). As they have become accustomed to the good in their first years, they cannot but behave virtuously. They are like the natural elements, which are impossible to remove from their sphere. Nature acquired through habit becomes, simply, nature. Those who have been raised and trained to practice justice cannot but behave well. Therefore a disciplined and learned man will enjoy the exercise of virtue. The life most appropriate for him is a life of reason, like that of a prince who with love and care rules over his subjects. A man of this sort will not imitate a tyrant, who loves only his own convenience and good and, like a wolf, devours and wastes his unfortunate subjects. He will instead imitate a perfect king, who strives for the welfare of the people and cares little for his own because he remembers that God made him father and shepherd to the people.

> I gave you a royal scepter.[392]

He is sad when he sees that his subjects are sad, and imitating David he asks the Lord:

> It is I who have sinned; it is I, the shepherd, who have done wrong. But these are sheep; what have they done?[393]

He will try anything to win the peace of his people; he will burden his subjects not excessively but modestly. He knows, in fact, that he must exercise justice more than the others. If you take away justice from kings and rulers, then they turn into destroyers of other people's welfare, corrupters of peace, and sources of unrest and sedition. No gift, no promise, no praise, no riches should be sufficient to corrupt a just and a perfect ruler, who will assure that help is provided to those in disgrace as well as punishment to those who break laws and justice. This is why Tasso says:

392. "Tibi dedi sceptrum regale," Marinella writes, alluding to the ninth station of the cross. See http://www.preces-latinae.org/thesaurus/Filius/PrecesStationum.html.

393. 2 Samuel 24:17: "Ego sum qui peccavi, ego sum qui ingiuste egi; isti, qui oves sunt, quid fecerunt?"

Their arts will be to lift the poor, and put the arrogant down.[394]

Those who disturb the peace will tremble before the perfect ruler; those who persecute the innocent and oppress widows and children will blanch before the eyes of the uncorrupted prince. They will flee the light of his perfection, like a blind bat flees the splendor of the sun.

He will put down the guilty and the vicious, although, as the wise man states, it is hard to punish and cure the perverted from their perversion:

The perverse are difficult to be corrected.[395]

Nevertheless, the punishment for crime prescribed by the law must be neither prolonged nor shortened. Laws must be executed as they are. If culprits realize that they can soften the law through prayers, friendship, gold, or promises, the law will lose its authority and will no longer command the proper respect. This would bring little honor to the legislator or to the prince, the ruler, or the governor. It is better not to impose punishments at all than to impose them and have them disregarded. If this happens, the greatness of the ruler, which must be honored with great respect, is diminished. Although the tasks of kings, monarchs, princes, and rulers have different types of dignity, they nevertheless share the same goal: to treat everybody with the same equity and justice, to reward the worthy and punish the guilty, and to drive away the many who act like warriors to oppress the innocence and goodness of those who are less fortunate.

Therefore the ruler will use white and pure justice. Remembering that the sword of Divine Justice hangs over his head, he will be placid and pious and will provide refuge to the neglected and wandering virtue, as appropriate to a just and well-costumed prince. As Tasso says in his *Goffredo*, it befits a prince

---

394. Tasso, *Gerusalemme liberata*, X.76: "Sollevar gli innocenti, e punir gli empi fian l'arti loro" (modern editions read: "Difender gli innocenti, e punir gli empi fian l'arti lor"). Trans. Esolen, 212.

395. Ecclesiastes 1:15: "Perversi difficile corriguntur."

To nourish and support the arts and sciences,
Spread seeds of peace and tranquility,
Weigh in just scales rewards and punishments,
And look ahead, providing for all events.[396]

These are works of justice and providence. Justice embraces all other virtues. The church proclaims:

Love justice, you who rule the earth.[397]

Like a prudent prince, this virtue can accomplish everything. This is why those who do not exercise this virtue are so threatened:

Judgment is harshest for those who rule.[398]

He who rules must not sin and should always be above suspicion. A sin is ugly and deformed in itself, but if a ruler commits it, then it grows even larger because many will tend to imitate him. It is not appropriate for a prince to be irascible and prone to pleasures or haughty, proud, and arrogant. He should instead be just, grave, magnanimous, liberal, benevolent, and pleasing. He should always extol and protect men of letters. Many of the prince's defects can in fact remain hidden in the works of his favorite writer. Sometimes, as Ariosto said, writers must abandon their noble art because of the ruler's ingratitude:

396. Tasso, *Gerusalemme liberata*, XVII.92: "Nudrir, e fecondar l'arti, e l'ingegni, / sparger semi di pace, e di quiete. / Partir con giusta man le pene, e i premi, / e mirar lungi, e proveder gli estremi." Marinella's quote differs from modern editions of the poem, which read: "nutrire e fecondar l'arti e gl'ingegni, / celebrar giochi illustri e pompe liete, / librar con giusta lance e pene e premi, / mirar da lunge e preveder gli estremi." Trans. Esolen, 334.

397. Wisdom 1:1: "Diligite iustitiam, qui iudicatis terra." The admonition figures prominently in Dante, *Paradiso*, XXVII.91–93.

398. Wisdom 6:5: "Quoniam durissimum iudicium eis qui praesunt."

Partly through the fault of niggardly lords who leave
the heaven-sent geniuses to beg. Suppressing good
and exalting evil, they banish the fair arts.[399]

He who governs must not soil himself with such a stain or
extol vice and oppress virtue by being insolent, unjust, and lacking in
courage and fortitude such that a new Achilles might reproach him for
his cruelty, saying:

You heavy with wine, with the face of a dog but the
heart of a deer,

And later on:

people-devouring king, since you rule over nobodies![400]

What an ugly way to speak to one's king, and how ugly it is to be able
to reproach him for his vices. This reveals both a king's shame and a
subject's great audacity. Merits and shortcomings deserve praise and
reproach, respectively. Rulers who deserve glory are like the praiseworthy House of Este sung by Tasso:

And from the wrongs of rebel and emperor
Defend the Holy Church. Their arts will be
To put the arrogant down, and lift the poor,
Punish the workers of impiety
And shield the innocent. Past the sun shall fly
The eagle of the Este family.[401]

399. Ariosto, *Orlando furioso*, XXXV.24: "Sí per gran colpa de i Signori avari / Che lascian mendicare i sacri ingegni: / Che le virtú premendo, et esaltando / I vitii, caccian le buone arti in bando." Trans. Waldman, 424.

400. Marinella quotes the words that an enraged Achilles addressed to Agamemnon: "Vino gravis, oculos caninos habens, cor vero cervi" (*Iliad*, I.225) and "Populi vorator rex, quoniam vilibus imperas" (*Iliad*, I.231). Trans. Murray, 29, 31.

401. Tasso, *Gerusalemme liberata*, X.76: "E da' Cesari ingiusti e da' rubelli / Difenderan le Mitre e i sacri Tempi / Premer gli alteri e solevar gli imbelli, / diffender gli innocenti e punir gli empi / fian l'arti loro; onde avverrà che vole / l'Aquila estense oltre le vie del sole." Trans. Esolen, 212.

These are acts of justice, which reinforce the rule of a powerful king. "By righteousness the throne endures" (*iustitia firmatur solium*).[402]

402. Proverbs 16:12.

9.   EXHORTATION TO WOMEN SO THAT THEY MAY
      KNOW THAT THERE IS NO REASON TO BOAST OR
      BE PROUD OF BEAUTY, WHICH IS A FRAGILE AND
      FLEETING THING. RATHER THAN A DIVINE RAY, AS
      SOME HAVE GATHERED, BEAUTY IS EPHEMERAL
      AND MORTAL.

It is impossible to deny that beauty is an ornament and a grace dear
to all and that it is, as some say, an image of or a ray that derives from
divine beauty. Stolen by the eyes and taken into the soul, it is admired
by the intellect, which nourishes it with celestial sweetness, sweeter
than ambrosia. With a silent voice, beauty charms us and invites us to
love its joys, as it is a lovable and desirable good.

    Leone Ebreo says that beauty is a ray, a light from the supreme
good, which emanates from a well-shaped body and shows us how to
rise to heaven to contemplate the origin and cause of perfect beauty.[403]
Marsilio Ficino, a wise commentator on Plato's works, judged beauty
to be a light, a splendor deriving from the first, eternal cause.[404] Plato
in *Phaedo* believes and proves the same.[405] Sometimes, these authors
agree that beauty is a divine light that wounds our souls, and, like a
hook, steals our freedom and leads us like prisoners. However, Ficino
later says that its splendor is human, rather than divine.[406] I agree.
Beauty is not a celestial light, but an earthly and mortal one. Were
it divine, as many philosophers maintain and as I myself stated in
my chapter on beauty in *The Nobility and Excellence of Women*, I do

---

403. Portuguese-born Yehudah Abravanel was known in Italy as Leone Ebreo. Written
around 1502, his *Dialoghi d'amore* became an influential neo-Platonic text throughout Europe. See Leone Ebreo, *Dialoghi d'amore*, ed. Delfina Giovannozzi (Rome: Laterza, 2008);
The Philosophy of Love, trans. F. Friedeberg-Seeley and Jean H. Barnes, introd. Cecil Roth
(London: The Soncino Press, 1937).

404. A note in the margins reads: "Pulchritudo autem splendor quidam est, humanum ad se
rapiens animum." Cf. Marsilio Ficino, "Commentarium in Convivium Platonis de Amore,"
Oratio Secunda, Caput IX (*Opera Omnia* II.1328).

405. Marinella could be referring to Socrates's statement that "if there is anything beautiful besides the Beautiful itself, it is beautiful for no other reason than that it shares in that
Beautiful" (*Phaedo*, 100C). Trans. Grube, in *Complete Works*, 86.

406. Unknown source.

not believe it would flee and vanish as quickly as it does.[407] It can be compared to a rose, which is lovely, beautiful, and remarkable in the morning but pale in the evening, when its fallen petals decorate the field beneath.

Likewise, this earthly beauty flees and disappears. Were it divine, it would not lose its grace so quickly. Our soul, which partakes of the divine, does not suffer as time passes; it is the suffering of the sensitive and earthly part that gives the impression that the soul suffers. This, however, is brought by circumstance and the infirmity of the senses. The divine soul does not age with the passage of time, nor feels the damage aging brings. Similarly, were beauty's graciousness to come from Heaven, it would not suffer and disappear. It would never be altered or change appearance, similar in this to our soul, which maintains its divine nature.

Therefore human beauty is not a celestial light. Its grace, which some believe to be divine, derives from the harmony of well-disposed parts. Everything can produce some kind of beauty or lovable manner that is pleasing and charming to the soul. This is true not only of humans, but of everything. The well-disposed parts of a wild horse seem to possess some kind of beauty, which cannot be said to be a divine splendor but rather is a grace that derives from the animal's well-proportioned body. A similar quality can be seen in all created things, or at least in many of them, such as dogs—indeed, there are some beautiful dogs, cats, and rabbits. Depending on the different qualities and their arrangement, you can find some degree of beauty shining in everything.

Some philosophers, such as Varro, Zeno, and Thales, say that God is in everything and that He infuses all things created with the beauty of His nature. Aristotle also says that God is in everything in the universe and that everything is in Him.[408] But if this were true, we

---

407. This passage is a new recantation of *Le nobiltà*. In the treatise, the idea of beauty's divine origin found its conceptual justification in Plato ("Pulchritudo externa est divinae pulchritudinis imago") was supported by a wealth of literary examples and provided further evidence of women's excellence: "Concluderemo adunque, che le donne essendo più belle de gli huomini, sieno altresì più nobili di quelli" (23) (we will therefore conclude that, as women are more beautiful than men, they must also be more noble).

408. "Deus est in universo, et cuncta in ipso." Unknown source.

would be unable to find anything without such beauty because the divine light would be recognizable even in creatures that we consider vile and ugly, and this is not the case. Even inanimate things such as a beautiful embroidery or a composition of many flowers possess a certain grace. These things generate beauty, a delicate and dear grace so attractive to our souls that people spare no expense to own them. Similarly, the jewels created by an ingenious mind that skillfully puts together different colored gems enchant and enslave everybody and deprive people of their freedom. Such power, such beautiful and enticing strength is born from their graceful union and desirable beauty, which forces men to take possession of such beauty and adornment. And yet, we cannot say that the origin of this grace is the divine light and splendor that emanates from the soul. We certainly cannot define beauty as a celestial thing. The combination and arrangement of colors produce that vague quality we call beauty. It is a human splendor, rather than a divine light.

Similarly, the quality that emanates from the parts, features, and colors of a shapely countenance, which we call grace, light, and other names indicative of something divine, is none other than a well-proportioned and graceful disposition, which is an ephemeral and mortal thing.[409]

Therefore, women must realize that their faces do not possess the beauty of angels, but a grace that derives from the condition of well-formed parts. Thinness, malady, and the passage of time so oppresses, beats, and strikes this harmonious constitution, which masterful Nature so ably arranged, that the colors of flowers disappear, grace fades, the eyes become dark and sad, the gold of curly locks turns silver, and the polished and well-disposed parts become tired and decrepit and must lean on a stick for support. These fleeting beauties are not divine, but drooping flowers that fall when the North Wind or Auster blow. They are like flowers that wither when the sun is weak. Once greatly desired, they are now oppressed and stepped on. Once her beauty has fled, a woman is left like the owner of a poor rose garden stripped of the roses that everyone used to admire but is now

---

409. Cf. Aristotle, *Metaphysics*, XIII.iii (1078b1): "The chief forms of beauty are order and symmetry and definiteness." Trans. Ross, in *The Complete Works*, II.1705. Cf. also *Poetics*, VII (1450b34).

surrounded only by thorns. Everyone avoids it, especially those who most used to love its roses.

Were beauty a divine ray and splendor, it could not be ruined or suffer from adversity because this cannot befall something immortal. Therefore, we maintain that beauty is a human splendor that darkens as time passes and as the colors and beauty of its parts flee, overcome by adversity.

Therefore, I do not know why those who possess this mortal and fleeting beauty are so proud and disdainful, why they do not open their eyes and shun these human splendors, these fragile privets that, like flashes of lightning, bring clarity and double the horrors. You are deluding yourself if you believe that beauty is a divine ray and an example of the angelical countenance. While you are absorbed in this thought, the years go by and, like a flowing stream, carry away those earthly lights that you love so much. Therefore one should not wonder why so many women weep at the fading of human grace, like Helen, who covered her mirror in tears:

> Helen also weeps when she sees her aged wrinkles in
> the looking-glass, and tearfully asks herself why she
> should twice have been a lover's prey.[410]

She cried over her lost beauty and could not believe that time had declared war on her, for she was once believed to be and treated as a goddess among women (*divina mulierum*). She realized, by looking in the mirror, that the light and beauty of her forehead had disappeared; she saw that her cheeks, which used to be smooth and embellished by natural roses, had wrinkled and yellowed; that her eyes, where love used to hide its bow and arrow, were now drooping, tired, and teary, and that she lacked the gracious manners she once had. Helen cried over the passage of time, which had made horribly ugly all the parts that once made her lovable. The poor woman wept as she gazed at her extinguished splendor in the mirror. This is why a poet wrote in the vernacular:

---

410. Ovid, *Metamorphoses*, XV.232: "Flet quoque, ut in speculo rugas adspexit aniles, / Tyndaris et secum, cur sit bis rapta, requirit." Trans. Miller (Loeb), 381.

The daughter of Tindarus grieves at seeing another woman in the mirror, and regrets the lies and fables that are gone for her.[411]

She realized too late that beauty is vain and that being Zeus's daughter was of no use to her, as it did not make her partake of the divine. Such thoughts were silly and deceitful, for human beauty is mortal and perishable. It falls like a light flower, as is evident in canto 19 of my *Henry*:

Contrary winds soon sweep away beauty, and the flower of the face and the age that Love painted.[412]

Therefore, my beloved women, do not put faith in something fleeting that clears the path more quickly than does a leopard or a hare or, as the poet says,

that Time so suddenly doth bear away![413]

You must not dream that your lost grace will ever return, and neither should you think about it, for a useless thought cannot give hope to impoverished hopes.

It flees; it is mortal, not divine! Do not listen to the fables of the poets, flatterers, and other untruthful writers like the above-mentioned poet, who calls Laura's beauty divine. It flees and does not return, and we can say with Tasso:

Spring may return, but these will pass away; the green will fade, and youth will lose its power.[414]

---

411. "La figliuola di Tindaro si duole, che nello specchio un'altra vede, e piange le passate per lei menzogne e fole." Unknown source.

412. Marinella, *Enrico, ovvero Bisanzio acquistato* XIX.91: "Che tosto adugge / Fiato contrario la bellezza e 'l fiore / del volto e de l'età che pinse Amore."

413. Petrarch, *Trionfo dell'eternità*, 51: "Che 'l tempo le ne porta sì repente!" Trans. Wilkins, 109.

414. Tasso, *Gerusalemme liberata*, XVI.15: "Né perché faccia indietro april ritorno, / si rinfiora ella mai, né si rinverde." Trans. Esolen, 303.

Remember that beauty disappears and cannot be regained because consonance turns into dissonance. All the things that bring beauty are harmonies and temperament. When their beauty disappears, they transform into ugly dissonances and deformities. Therefore, you should not find it difficult to despise this flattering beauty and draw ever closer to virtue. Somebody who used to be beautiful is often left uglier than another who was never beautiful. Therefore you should not trust this vanity, but listen to what Sabba, a Knight of Jerusalem, said of a very beautiful lady. He wrote that beautiful women struck by time or long disease are like a particular lady whose beauty everyone had praised before she was robbed of it. This is how he describes her:

> She used to be tall but because of age she has become bent, small and hunchbacked. Once white, she has now become pale and dull, the color of fresh wax. She is toothless, even more than I am. She drools, her nose is always runny, her eyes are droopy and teary, and her cheeks are tired and saggy. She is so wrinkled and rough that she resembles an old turtle. Her golden hair, which was used to build many snares and nets to rob men of their freedom, now resemble my old horse's mane.[415]

He describes this lady in this way to show what beautiful women become, once age and sorrows have worn them out. Loveliness turns into the horror of a thorny desert. The beauty that was once compared to that of an angel turns into the ugliness of a demon from hell, and its sweet harmony changes into ugly dissonance. Hence she remains despised and abhorred, offensive to the eyes and the soul just as all disaster is ugly and bothersome. Therefore, you must try to overcome these natural defects and flaws through virtue. You must know which virtues pertain to women: seclusion, temperance, chastity, the administration of the household, and the others I have mentioned. When

---

415. Sabba di Castiglione, *Ricordi overo ammaestramenti* (Milano: Antonio degli Antonij, 1561), 107v–108. Sabba di Castiglione (1480-1554), Knight of the Order of Rhodes, first published his *Ricordi* in 1546. The book was republished twenty-five times until 1613.

you lose the little grace nature gave to you, even those who used to love you will avoid you. That gracious consonance inspired love, but now that it has become an ugly and bothersome dissonance no ear is skilled enough to hear it.

I have heard that love is the master of consonance. This is why Plato says that love teaches music by filling all things, no matter how dissonant, with peace and harmony. Every temperament depends on the force of love from which it originated:

> For when moisture and heat unite, life is conceived,
> and from these two sources all living things spring.[416]

Although Love, according to Plato, was the offspring of discord and emerged from chaos and confusion, he nevertheless reconciled the dissonant parts of the world with friendly harmony. Love teaches music (*Amor musicam docet*). He harmonized the dissonance that can be found in different parts of the universe, such as heat and cold, humidity and dryness:

> Cold things strove with hot, and moist with dry, soft
> things with hard, things having weight with weight-
> less things.[417]

He[418] made these different natures friendly to one another, as if they were similar. He set the different elements "each in its own place and bound them fast in harmony."[419] He harmonized opposite and dissonant parts such that they cause one another no bother or damage. His reconciliation of these contrary forces bore sweet harmony and the tempering of opposite qualities, and this generated everything. Love

---

416. Ovid, *Metamorphoses*, I.430–31: "Quippe ubi temperiem sumpsere humorque calorque, / Concipiunt, et ab his oriuntur cuncta duobus." Trans. Miller (Loeb), 33.

417. Ovid, *Metamorphoses*, I.19-20: "Frigida pugnabant calidis, umentia siccis, / mollia cum duris, sine pondere, habentia pondus." Trans. Miller (Loeb), 3.

418. Marinella identifies the force that brings the opposites together with love. Ovid, however, defines it as "deus et melior natura" (God and kindlier nature) in *Metamorphoses*, I.21.

419. Ovid, *Metamorphoses*, I.25: "Dissociata locis concordi pace ligavit." Trans. Miller (Loeb), 5.

is the reason for all of that, as it is the reason for harmony and peace. This is why many believe that Love is the father of beauty and that he created the lovely harmony of features and the gracious correspondence of the different parts of the body. When this harmony and correspondence are lacking, decorum and beauty disappear, as they are nothing but the result of the grace that derives from well-disposed and harmonious parts.

Once a woman's beauty disappears, she is left like Alcina, whom Ariosto described:

> She was whey-faced, wrinkled, and hollow-cheeked;
> her hair was white and sparse; she was not four feet
> high; the last tooth had dropped out of her jaw.[420]

She was barely four feet tall. Old age causes people to shrink (*decrescunt senes*), as the philosopher says. As old age destroys beauty and is poor in spirit and strength, it brings little activity. This is why Cicero, who felt some pity for this age, said that old people should not work too hard.[421]

Therefore, my beloved women, consider how time, sickness, and worries rob you of everything good and beautiful nature has given you. Realize that only by acquiring virtue, which will be yours forever, can you alleviate the loss of your grace. Remember the man who, having been deprived of everything by the strength of the seas, urged people to be happy with the treasures that angry and hostile nature cannot damage or take away. If you try to remedy these defects with artifice, then you will be disappointed, for artifice is an ugly and reproachable thing. Listen to Guarino:

420. Ariosto, *Orlando furioso* VII.73: "Pallido, crespo e macilento avea /Alcina il viso, e il crin raro e canuto. / Sua statura a sei palmi non giungea, ogni dente di bocca era caduto." Trans. Waldman, 69.

421. Cicero, *De officiis*, I.37–38. Marinella's quote ("senibus minuendi sunt labores") abbreviates and simplifies Cicero's text, which distinguishes between physical and intellectual work ("Senibus autem labores corporis minuendi, exercitationes animi etiam augendae videntur").

O what a disgraceful and nauseating sight it is
To watch you as with a brush sometimes
You paint your cheeks and hide the flaws
Of nature and of time.[422]

Therefore, heed my exhortations and you will be praised, honored, and revered always. Ariosto, who loved honesty and purity in a woman, said:

Nor should your wife know how to paint with red and
white. Better if she is skilled with cloth and thread.[423]

END OF THE FIRST PART

---

422. Guarini, *Il pastor fido*, Act I, Sc.V, 977–79: "Oh come è indegna e stomachevol cosa / il vederti talor con un pennello / pinger le guance ed occultar le mende / di natura e del tempo."

423. Ariosto, *Satire* (in *The Satires of Ludovico Ariosto: A Renaissance Autobiography*, trans. Peter Desa Wiggins [Athens: Ohio University Press, 1976]), 137; V.230–31: "Né sappia far la tua bianco né rosso, / ma sia del filo e de la tela dotta."

Bibliography

PRIMARY SOURCES

Aesop. *The Complete Fables.* Trans. Olivia and Robert Temple. New York: Penguin, 1998.

Albertus Magnus. *Opera Omnia.* Eds. August Borgnet, et al. Paris: Vivès, 1891.

Apollodorus. *Library.* Trans. Sir James George Frazer, 2 vols. Cambridge, MA: Harvard University Press, 1921, latest reprints 1977 and 1979.

Aprosio, Angelico (Scipio Glareano). *Lo scudo di Rinaldo ovvero lo specchio del disinganno.* Venezia: Herz, 1646.

_____. (Cornelio Aspasio Antivigilmi). *Biblioteca Aprosiana.* Bologna: Manolessi, 1673.

Aristotle. *Complete Works.* Ed. Jonathan Barnes. Princeton: Princeton University Press, 1984.

_____. *Politicorum libri VIII. Latine ex versione Leonardi Aretini.* Roma: E. Silber, 1492.

Ariosto, Ludovico. *The Satires: A Renaissance Autobiography.* Trans. Peter DeSa Wiggins. Athens: Ohio University Press, 1976.

_____. *Orlando furioso.* Trans. Guido Waldman. Oxford and New York: Oxford University Press, 1974.

_____. *Orlando furioso.* Eds. Santorre Debenedetti and Cesare Segre. Bologna, Commissione per i testi di lingua, 1960.

Athenaeus of Naucratis, *Deipnosophists.* Trans. Charles Burton Gulick. Cambridge, MA: Harvard University Press, 1997.

Berni, Francesco. *Il primo libro dell'opere burlesche di m. Francesco Berni, di m. Gio. Della Casa, del Varchi, del Mauro, di m. Bino, del Molza, del Dolce, e del Fiorenzuola.* Usecht al Reno: Jacopo Broedelet, 1726.

Bibliothecae seminarii Sancti Sulpitii catalogus triplex, materiarum ordine dispositus, Bibliothèque Mazarine, Ms 4179–4183 (18th century), 5 vols.

Boccaccio, Giovanni. *Filocolo.* Ed. Enzo Quaglio. Milano: Mondadori, 1967.

_____. *Decameron.* Ed. Vittore Branca. Torino: Einaudi, 1992.

_____. *De mulieribus claris.* Ed. Vittorio Zaccaria. Milano: Mondadori, 1967.

_____. *Famous Women.* Ed. and trans. Virginia Brown. Cambridge, MA: Harvard University Press, 2001.

Boccalini, Traiano. *Ragguagli di Parnaso e scritti minori.* Ed. Luigi Firpo. Bari: Laterza, 1948.

Bonaventure, Saint. *Commentaria in Quatuor Libros Sententiarum.* Ad Claras Aquas: 1885. http://www.franciscan-archive.org/bonaventura/sent.html

Buoninsegni, Francesco, and Suor Arcangela Tarabotti. *Satira e antisatira.* Ed. Elissa Weaver. Roma: Salerno, 1998.

Camerarius, Philipp. *Operae Horarvm Svbcisivarvm, Sive Meditationes Historicae.* Frankfurt: Ioannis Saurij, impensis Petri Korpffij, 1602.

Capucci, Martino, ed. *Romanzieri del Seicento.* Torino: UTET, 1974.

Cartari, Vincenzo. *Le immagini degli dèi.* Ed. Caterina Volpi. Roma: De Luca, 1996. http://www.bibliotecaitaliana.it/xtf/view?docId=bibit000718/bibit000718.xml.

Cesarotti, Melchior. "Catalogo delle principali edizioni e versioni di Omero." In *Opere,* Vol. XVI, Appendix. Pisa: Tipografia della società letteraria, 1800.

Chastel, Guy. *Sainte Colombe de Sens.* Paris: de Gigord, 1939.

Cicero. *De officiis.* Trans. Walter Miller. Cambridge, MA: Harvard University Press, 1913.

_____. *De re publica.* Trans. Clinton Walker Keyes. Cambridge, MA: Harvard University Press, 1970.

Diogenes Laertius. *Lives of Eminent Philosophers.* Trans. R. D. Hicks. Cambridge, MA: Harvard University Press, 1972. 2 vols.

Evelyn, John. *Diary.* Ed. William Bray. Washington and London: M. Walter Dunne, 1901.

Ficino, Marsilio. *Opera Omnia.* Ed. Mario Sancipriano. Intro. P.O. Kristeller. Torino: Bottega d'Erasmo, 1959–1962.

Folengo, Teofilo. *Zanitonella sive Innamoramentum Zaninae et Tonelli.* Trans. Franco Loi. Milano: Mondadori, 1984.

Fonte, Moderata. *The Worth of Women: Wherein is Clearly Revealed Their Nobility and Their Superiority to Men.* Ed. and trans. Virginia Cox. *The Other Voice in Early Modern Europe*. Chicago: University of Chicago Press, 1997.

Foscolo, Ugo. "Intorno alla traduzione de' due primi canti dell'*Odissea* ec." *Opere*. Vol. II. Florence: Le Monnier, 1883. 203–41.

Franklin, Alfred. "Les Anciennes Biblioteques de Paris." *Histoire Générale de Paris*. Vol. 3. Paris: Imprimerie nationale, 1873.

Garzoni, Tommaso. *L'ospidale de' pazzi incurabili*. Ed. Stefano Barelli. Rome-Padua: Antenore, 2004.

Greek Bucolic Poets. Trans. J. M. Edmonds. Cambridge, MA: Harvard University Press, 1912, rev. 1928, rpt. 1996.

Guarini, Giovan Battista. *Il pastor fido*. Ed. Ettore Bonora. Milano: Mursia, 1977.

_____. *The Faithful Shepherd*. Trans. Thomas Sheridan. Eds. Robert Hogan and Edward A. Nickerson. Newark: University of Delaware Press; London and Toronto: Associated University Presses, 1989.

Hesiod. *Theogony. Works and Days. Testimonia*. Trans. Glenn W. Most. Cambridge, MA: Harvard University Press, 2006.

Homer. *Iliad*. Trans. A. T. Murray. Rev. William F. Wyatt. Cambridge, MA: Harvard University Press, 1999.

_____. *Odyssey*. Trans. A. T. Murray. Rev. George E. Dimock. Cambridge, MA: Harvard University Press, 1995.

Horace. *Satires, Epistles, Ars Poetica*. Trans. H. Rushton Fairclough. Cambridge, MA: Harvard University Press, 1929.

Lagnier, Pierre. *Ex M.T. Cicerone insignium sententiarum [...] compendium*. Lyon: Jean de Tournes and Guillaume Gazeau, 1552.

Leone Ebreo. *Dialoghi d'amore*. Ed. Delfina Giovannozzi. Introd. Eugenio Canone. Roma: Laterza, 2008.

_____. *The Philosophy of Love*. Trans. F. Friedeberg-Seeley and Jean H. Barnes. Introd. Cecil Roth. London: The Soncino Press, 1937.

Lucian. *Lucian in Eight Volumes*. Trans. K. Kilburn. Vol. VI. Cambridge, MA: Harvard University Press, 1961.

Marinella, Lucrezia. *La colomba sacra*. Venice: Ciotti, 1595.

_____. *Vita del Serafico e Glorioso San Francesco, descritta in ottava rima, con un discorso del rivolgimento amoroso verso la Somma Bellezza*. Venice: Pietro Maria Bertano e Fratelli, 1597.

_____. *Amore innamorato e impazzato*. Venice: 1598.

_____. *Le Nobiltà et Eccellenze delle Donne et i diffetti, e mancamenti degli huomini.* Venice: Ciotti, 1600; revised and enlarged as *La nobiltà et l'eccellenza delle donne co' diffetti et mancamenti de gli huomini.* Venice: Ciotti, 1601.

_____. *Argomenti e allegorie,* in Luigi Tansillo, *Le lagrime di San Pietro.* Venice: Barezzo Barezzi, 1606.

_____. *Vita di Maria Vergine, Imperatrice dell'universo, descritta in prosa e in ottava rima.* Venice: Barezzo Barezzi e compagni, 1602.

_____. *Rime sacre.* Venice: Collosini, 1603.

_____. *Arcadia Felice.* Ed. Françoise Lavocat. Firenze: Olschki, 1998.

_____. *Vita di Santa Giustina, in ottava rima.* Firenze,1606; revised as *Olocausto d'amore della vergine Santa Giustina.* Venice: Matteo Leni, 1648.

_____. *De' Gesti heroici, e della vita maravigliosa della Serafica Santa Caterina da Siena, Libri Sei.* Venice: Barezzo Barezzi, 1624.

_____. *Enrico, ovvero Bisanzio acquistato.* Venice: Antonelli, 1844.

_____. *Essortationi alle donne et a gl'altri se a loro saranno a grado.* Venice: Francesco Valvasense, 1645.

_____. *Enrico; or, Byzantium Conquered.* Ed. and trans. Maria Galli Stampino. The Other Voice in Early Modern Europe. Chicago: University of Chicago Press, 2009.

_____. *Life of the Virgin Mary, Empress of the Universe.* In *Who is Mary? Three Early Modern Women on the Idea of the Virgin Mary.* Ed. and trans. Susan Haskins. The Other Voice in Early Modern Europe. Chicago: University of Chicago Press, 2008.

_____. *The Nobility and Excellence of Women and the Defects and Vices of Men.* Ed. and trans. Anne Dunhill. The Other Voice in Early Modern Europe. Chicago: University of Chicago Press, 1999.

Marinello, Giovanni. *Gli ornamenti delle donne tratti dalle scritture d'una reina greca.* Venice: Francesco de' Franceschi, 1562.

Medicina per le donne nel Cinquecento. Testi di Giovanni Marinello e di Girolamo Mercurio. Ed. Maria Luisa Altieri Biagi et al. Torino: UTET, 1992.

Nogarola, Isotta. *Complete Writings: Letterbook, Dialogue on Adam and Eve, Orations.* Trans. Margaret L. King and Diana Robin. The Other Voice in Early Modern Europe. Chicago: University of Chicago Press, 2004.

Ovid. *Metamorphoses*. Trans. Frank Justus Miller. 2 vols. Cambridge, MA: Harvard University Press, 1971.

———. *Heroides and Amores*. Trans. Grant Showerman. Rev. G. P. Goold. Cambridge, MA: Harvard University Press, 1977.

———. *Fasti*. Trans. Sir James George Frazer. Cambridge, MA: Harvard University Press, 1974.

———. *Tristia; Ex Ponto*. Trans. Arthur Leslie Wheeler. Cambridge, MA: Harvard University Press, 1988.

Passi, Giuseppe. *I donneschi difetti*. Venice: Somascho, 1599.

Pausanias. *Description of Greece*. Trans. W. H. S. Jones. 5 vols. Cambridge, MA: Harvard University Press, 1979.

Petrarch. *Canzoniere (Rerum Vulgarium Fragmenta)*. Ed. Marco Santagata. Milano: Mondadori, 1996.

———. *Opere. Canzoniere, Trionfi, Familiarum Rerum Libri con testo a fronte*. Vol. I. Firenze: Sansoni, 1990.

———. *The Canzoniere, or Rerum Vulgarium Fragmenta*. Trans. Mark Musa and Barbara Manfredi. Bloomington: Indiana University Press, 1999.

———. *The Triumphs*. Trans. Ernest Hatch Wilkins. Chicago: University of Chicago Press, 1962.

Pizan, Christine de. *The Book of the City of Ladies*. Trans. Rosalind Brown-Grant. London: Penguin, 1999.

Plato. *Complete Works*. Eds. John M. Cooper and D. S. Hutchinson. Indianapolis and Cambridge: Hackett, 1997.

———. *Omnia divini Platonis opera*. Trans. Marsilio Ficino. Ed. Simon Grynaeus. Basil: Froben, 1546.

Pliny the Elder. *Natural History*. Trans. H. Rackman. 10 vols. Cambridge, MA: Harvard University Press, 1938–63.

Plutarch. *Bravery of Women (Mulierum virtutes)*. In *Moralia*. Vol. 3. Trans. Frank Cole Babbitt. Cambridge, MA: Harvard University Press, 1931, 1968.

———. *Plutarchi chæronensis Vitarum parallelarum delectus, græce et latine. Adduntur variantes lectiones insigniores, et doctorum virorum notæ et emendationes*. Vol. 1. Dublinii, 1761–62. 3 vols. Eighteenth Century Collections Online. Gale Group.

———. *Lives*. 10 vols. Trans. Bernadotte Perrin. Cambridge, MA: Harvard University Press, 1914–26.

Poetae minores Graeci. Cantabrigiae: Thomas Buck, 1602.

Sabba di Castiglione. *Ricordi overo ammaestramenti.* Milano: Antonio degli Antonij, 1561.

Seneca, Lucius Annaeus. *Epistulae Morales.* 3 vols. Trans. Richard M. Gummere. Cambridge, MA: Harvard University Press, 1917–25.

Settala, Ludovico. *De ratione instituendae et gubernandae familiae libri quinque.* Milano: Giovanni Battista Bidellio, 1626.

Statius. *Thebaid, Achilleid.* Trans. D. R. Shackleton Bailey. Cambridge, MA: Harvard University Press, 2003.

Stigliani, Tommaso. *Delle rime del signor Tomaso Stigliani, parte prima. Con breui dichiarationi in fronte à ciascun componimento, fatte dal signor Scipione Calcagnini.* Venetia: Ciotti, 1605.

Strabo. *Geography.* 8 vols. Cambridge, MA: Harvard University Press, 1917–33.

Tarabotti, Arcangela. *Paternal Tyranny.* Ed. and trans. Letizia Panizza. The Other Voice in Early Modern Europe. Chicago: University of Chicago Press, 2004.

_____. *La semplicità ingannata.* Edizione critica e commentata a cura di Simona Bortot. Padova: Il Poligrafo, 2007.

_____. *Che le donne siano della spezie degli uomini: Women Are No Less Rational Than Men.* Ed. Letizia Panizza. London : Institute of Romance Studies, 1994.

Tarcagnota, Giovanni. *Opuscoli morali.* Venezia: Comin da Trino, 1567.

Tasso, Torquato. *Aminta.* Trans. Charles Jernigan and Irene Marchegiani Jones. New York: Italica, 2000.

_____. *Discorso della virtù feminile e donnesca.* Ed. Maria Luisa Doglio. Palermo: Sellerio, 1997.

_____. *Discorsi dell'arte poetica e del poema eroico.* Ed. Luigi Poma. Bari: Laterza, 1964.

_____. *Gerusalemme liberata.* Ed. Fredi Chiappelli. Milano: Rusconi, 1982.

_____. *Jerusalem Delivered (Gerusalemme liberata).* Trans. Anthony M. Esolen. Baltimore, MD: Johns Hopkins University Press, 2000.

_____. *Le lettere.* 5 vols. Ed. Cesare Guasti. Napoli: Rondinella, 1857.

Thomas Aquinas, St. *Opera omnia.* http://www.corpusthomisticum.org/.

Valerius Maximus. *Memorable Doings and Sayings.* 2 vols. Ed. and trans. D. R. Shackleton Bailey. Cambridge, MA: Harvard University Press, 2000.

Valla, Lorenzo. *Discourse on the Forgery of the Alleged Donation of Constantine.* Trans. Christopher B. Coleman. New Haven: Yale University Press, 1922; rpt. Toronto: University of Toronto Press, 1993 (for the Renaissance Society of America). Hanover Historical Texts Project (http://history.hanover.edu/texts/vallatc.html).

Virgil. *Aeneid.* 2 vols. Trans. H. Rushton Fairclough. Cambridge, MA: Harvard University Press, 1999–2000.

_____. *Eneide.* Trans. Annibal Caro. 2 vols. Firenze: Ciardetti, 1827.

_____. *Eclogues.* Trans. H. Rushton Fairclough. Rev. G. P. Goold. Cambridge, MA: Harvard University Press, 1999.

Vita degli eremiti Paolo, Ilarione e Malco. Roma: Città nuova, 1996.

Vives, Juan Luis. *The Education of a Christian Woman: A Sixteenth-Century Manual.* Ed. and trans. Charles Fantazzi. The Other Voice in Early Modern Europe. Chicago: University of Chicago Press, 2000.

SECONDARY SOURCES

Allen, Prudence, and Filippo Salvatore. "Lucrezia Marinella and Woman's Identity in Late Italian Renaissance." In *Renaissance and Reformation / Renaissance et Réforme* 4 (1992), 5–39.

Arnaud, David and Tim Le Bon. "Key Concepts In Practical Philosophy Series: Practical and Theoretical Wisdom." In *Practical Philosophy* 3.1 (March 2000), 6–9.

Asor Rosa, Alberto. "Aprosio, Angelico." *Dizionario Biografico degli Italiani.* Roma: Treccani, 1961. Vol. 3: 650–53.

Benedetti, Laura. "Saintes et guerrières: l'héroïsme féminin dans l'œuvre de Lucrezia Marinella." In *Les Femmes et l'Ecriture. L'Amour Profane et l'Amour Sacré,* ed. Claude Cazalé Bérard. Paris: Presses Universitaires de Paris X, 2005, 93–109.

_____. "Virtù femminile o virtù donnesca? Torquato Tasso, Lucrezia Marinella ed una polemica rinascimentale." In *Torquato Tasso e la cultura estense,* ed. Gianni Venturi. Firenze: Olschki, 1999. 449–56.

Biral, Paola. *Puer ludens. Giochi infantili nell'iconografia dal XIV al XVI secolo.* Venezia: Editoria Universitaria, 2005.

Bolzoni, Lina. *L'universo dei poemi possibili. Studi su Francesco Patrizi da Cherso.* Roma: Bulzoni, 1980.

Bortot, Simona. "Introduzione. La penna all'ombra delle grate." Tarabotti, *La semplicità ingannata* 21–152.

Bradford, Ernile. *The Great Betrayal: Constantinople 1204.* London: Hodder and Stoughton, 1967.

Bradshaw, Leah. "Political Rule, Prudence and the 'Woman Question' in Aristotle," in *Canadian Journal of Political Science / Revue canadienne de science politique* 24:3 (1991), 557–73.

Brown, Judith C. "A Woman's Place Was in the Home: Women's Work in Renaissance Tuscany." In *Rewriting the Renaissance: The Discourses of Sexual Difference in Early Modern Europe*, eds. Margaret W. Ferguson, Maureen Quilligan, and Nancy J. Vickers. Chicago: University of Chicago Press, 1986. 206–24.

Chastel, Guy. *Sainte Colombe de Sens.* Paris: de Gigord, 1939.

Chemello, Adriana. "La donna, il modello, l'immaginario: Moderata Fonte e Lucrezia Marinella." In *Nel cerchio della luna: figure di donna in alcuni testi del XVI secolo*, ed. Marina Zancan. Venice: Marsilio, 1983. 95–170.

———. "Lucrezia Marinella." In *Le stanze ritrovate. Antologia di scrittrici venete dal Quattrocento al Novecento*, ed. Antonia Arslan, Adriana Chemello, and Gilberto Pizzamiglio. Venice: Eidos, 1991. 96–108.

Chiecchi, Giuseppe and Luciano Troisio. *Il Decamerone sequestrato: le tre edizioni censurate del Cinquecento.* Milano: Unicopli, 1984.

Collina, Beatrice. "Women in the Gutenberg Galaxy." In *Arcangela Tarabotti*, ed. Weaver, 91–105.

Conti Odorisio, Ginevra. *Donna e società nel Seicento.* Roma: Bulzoni, 1979.

Cotton, Juliana Hill. *Name-List from a Medical Register of the Italian Renaissance.* Oxford: [s.n.], 1976.

Cowper, Henry Swainson. *The Art of Attack. Being a Study in the Development of Weapons and Appliances of Offence, from the Earliest Times to the Age of Gunpowder.* Ulverston: W. Holmes, Ltd., Printers, 1906.

Cox, Virginia. *Women's Writing in Italy, 1400–1650*. Baltimore, MD: Johns Hopkins University Press, 2008.

———. "Women as Readers and Writers of Chivalric Literature." In *Sguardi sull'Italia. Miscellanea dedicata a Francesco Villari*, ed. Gino Bedani, Zygmunt Baranski, Anna Laura Lepschy, and Brian Richardson. Leeds: Society for Italian Studies, 1997. 134–45.

———. "The Single Self: Feminist Thought and the Marriage Market in Early Modern Venice." *Renaissance Quarterly* 3 (1995), 513–81.

Croce, Benedetto. *Storia dell'età barocca in Italia*. Bari: Laterza, 1957.

Della Chiesa, Francesco Agostino. *Theatro delle donne letterate con un breve discorso della preminenza e perfettione del sesso donnesco*. Mondoví: Gislandi and Rossi, 1620.

Di Renzo Vianello, Wilmen. *Proibito alle donne dalle leggi suntuarie a Venezia e in Romagna III sec. a.C–XIX sec*. Cesena: Comitato Consorti del Rotary Club, Anno Rotariano 1993–94.

Dionisotti, Carlo. *Geografia e storia della letteratura italiana*. Torino: Einaudi, 1967.

Fortis, Umberto. *Sara Copio Sullam, poetessa nel ghetto di Venezia del '600*. Torino: Zamorani, 2003.

Franklin, Alfred. "Les Anciennes Bibliothèques de Paris." In *Histoire Générale de Paris*. Paris: Imprimerie nationale, 1873.

Godfrey, John. *1204, The Unholy Crusade*. New York: Oxford University Press, 1980).

Grande dizionario della lingua italiana, ed. Salvatore Battaglia. Torino: UTET, 1961–.

Grendler, Paul F. *The Roman Inquisition and the Venetian Press, 1540–1605*. Princeton: Princeton University Press, 1977.

Hale, John Rigby. "Military Academies on the Venetian Terraferma in the Early 17th Century." In *Renaissance War Studies*. London: Hambledon Press, 1983. 286–307.

Harrán, Don, ed. and trans. *Sarra Copia Sulam, Jewish Poet and Intellectual in Seventeenth-Century Venice*. The Other Voice in Early Modern Europe. Chicago: University of Chicago Press, 2009.

Haskins, Susan. "Vexatious Litigant, or the Case of Lucrezia Marinella? New Documents Concerning Her Life (Part I)." *Nouvelles de la République des Lettres* 1 (2006), 80–128.

_____. "Vexatious Litigant, or the Case of Lucrezia Marinella? New Documents Concerning Her Life (Part II)." *Nouvelles de la République des Lettres* 1–2 (2007), 203–30.

Horace. *The Odes and Epodes.* Trans. C.E. Bennett. Cambridge, MA: Harvard University Press, 1988.

Infelise, Mario. *Books and Politics in Arcangela Tarabotti's Venice.* In Weaver, ed. *Arcangela Tarabotti.* 57–72.

Kelso, Ruth. *Doctrine for the Lady of the Renaissance.* Urbana: University of Illinois Press, 1956.

King, Margaret L. "Thwarted Ambitions: Six Learned Women of the Italian Renaissance." *Humanism, Venice, and Women. Essays on the Italian Renaissance.* Burlington, VT: Ashgate, 2005. 280–304.

King, Margaret L. and Albert Rabil, *Her Immaculate Hand: Selected Works By and About the Women Humanists of Quattrocento Italy.* Binghamton, N.Y.: Medieval and Renaissance Texts and Studies, rev. ed., 1997.

_____. "La donna del Rinascimento." In *L'uomo del Rinascimento*, ed. Eugenio Garin. Bari: Laterza,1988. 273–327.

Kolski, Stephen. "Moderata Fonte, Lucrezia Marinella, Giuseppe Passi: an Early Seventeenth-Century Feminist Controversy." *The Modern Language Review* 4 (2001), 972–89.

Lazzari, Laura. *Poesia epica e scrittura femminile nel Seicento:* L'Enrico *di Lucrezia Marinelli.* Leonforte (En): Insula, 2010.

Lesage, Claire. "Femmes de lettres à Venise aux XVIe et XVIIe siècles: Moderata Fonte, Lucrezia Marinella, Arcangela Tarabotti." *Clio. Histoire, Femmes et Sociétés* 13 (2001), 135–44.

Lugli, Vittorio. *I trattatisti della famiglia nel quattrocento.* Bologna-Modena: Formiggini, 1909.

Madden, Thomas F. *Enrico Dandolo and the Rise of Venice.* Baltimore, MD: Johns Hopkins University Press, 2003.

Malpezzi Price, Paola and Christine Ristaino. *Lucrezia Marinella and the 'Querelle des Femmes'in Seventeenth-Century Italy.* Madison, NJ: Fairleigh Dickinson University Press, 2008.

_____. Malpezzi Price, Paola. "Moderata Fonte, Lucrezia Marinella and their 'Feminist' Work." *Italian Studies* XII (1994), 201–14.

_____. "Lucrezia Marinella." In *Italian Women Writers. A Bio-Bibliographical Sourcebook.* Ed. Rinaldina Russell. Westport, Conn.: Greenwood Press, 1994. 234–42.

Marini, Quinto. *Frati barocchi. Studi su A.G. Brignole Sale, G.A. De Marini, A. Aprosio, F.F. Frugoni, P. Segneri.* Modena: Mucchi, 2000.

Maschietto, Francesco Ludovico. *Elena Lucrezia Cornaro Piscopia (1646–1684): The First Woman in the World to Earn a University Degree.* Ed. Catherine Marshall, trans. Jan Vairo and William Crochetiere. Philadelphia: Saint Joseph's University Press, 2007. 318.

Miato, Monica. *L'Accademia degli Incogniti di Giovan Francesco Loredan. Venezia (1630–1661).* Firenze: Olschki, 1998.

Migiel, Marilyn. *Gender and Genealogy in Tasso's Gerusalemme Liberata.* Lewiston, N.Y.: The Edwin Mellen Press, 1993.

Montanari, F. and S. Pittaluga, eds. *Posthomerica I. Tradizioni omeriche dall'Antichità al Rinascimento.* Genova: Dipartimento di archeologia, filologia classica e loro tradizioni, 1977.

Panizza, Letizia. "Reader Over Arcangela's Shoulders: Tarabotti at Work with Her Sources." In Weaver, ed. *Arcangela Tarabotti.* 107–28.

_____. "Introduction to the Translation." In Lucrezia Marinella, *The Nobility and Excellence of Women.* 1–34.

Pianigiani, Ottorino. *Vocabolario etimologico della lingua italiana.* Genova: I Dioscuri, 1988.

Rosenthal, Margaret F. *The Honest Courtesan: Veronica Franco Citizen and Writer in Sixteenth-Century Venice.* Chicago: University of Chicago Press, 1992.

Shemek, Deanna. *Ladies Errant: Wayward Women and Social Order in Early Modern Italy.* Durham, NC: Duke University Press, 1998.

Sider, Sandra. *Handbook to Life in Renaissance Europe.* New York: Oxford University Press, 2007.

Stampino, Maria Galli. "A Singular Venetian Epic Poem." In Lucrezia Marinella, *Enrico; or, Byzantium Conquered. The Other Voice in Early Modern Europe.* Chicago: University of Chicago Press, 2009).

Stradling, R. A. *Philip IV and the Government of Spain, 1621–1665.* Cambridge: Cambridge University Press, 2002.

Suleiman, Susan Rubin. "Writing and Motherhood." In *The (M)other Tongue. Essays in Feminist Psychoanalytic Interpretation,* ed. Shirley Nelson Garner et al. Ithaca, NY: Cornell University Press, 1985. 352–77.

Syme, Ronald, and Barbara M. Levick. "Asinius Gallus, Gaius." In *The Oxford Classical Dictionary,* eds. Simon Hornblower and Antony Spawforth. Oxford: Oxford University Press, 2003.

Tarabotti, Arcangela. *Lettere familiari e di complimento.* Ed. Meredith Kennedy Ray and Lynn Lara Westwater. Torino: Rosenberg & Sellier, 2005.

Tiraboschi, Girolamo. *Biblioteca modenese o notizie della vita e delle opere degli scrittori nati degli stati del serenissimo signor duca di Modena.* Vol. III. Modena: Società Tipografica, 1783.

Vasoli, Cesare. *Francesco Patrizi da Cherso.* Roma: Bulzoni, 1989.

Waddington, Raymond B. *Aretino's Satyr: Sexuality, Satire, and Self-Projection in Sixteenth-Century Literature and Art.* Toronto: University of Toronto Press, 2004.

Vredeveld, Harry. "Anthologia Latina 873e: Renaissance Latin from Strabo (*Geography* 14.5.9)." *Classical Philology* 93:4 (1998) 343–44.

Watson, Alaric. *Aurelian and the Third Century.* New York: Routledge, 1999.

Weaver, Elissa, ed. *Arcangela Tarabotti. A Literary Nun in Baroque Venice.* Ravenna: Longo, 2006.

_____. "Introduzione." In Francesco Buoninsegni e Arcangela Tarabotti, *Satira e antisatira.* 7–28.

Wiener, Philip P., ed. *The Dictionary of the History of Ideas.* New York: Charles Scribner's Sons, 1973–74.

Wolters, Wolfgang. *Storia e politica nei dipinti del Palazzo Ducale. Aspetti dell'autocelebrazione della Repubblica di Venezia nel Cinquecento.* Venice: Arsenale, 1987.

Zanette, Emilio. *Suor Arcangela. Monaca del Seicento veneziano.* Roma-Venezia: Istituto per la collaborazione culturale, 1960.

Index

Acerbi, Gaspare, 17
Aesop, 57n30
Alexander the Great, 25, 123, 162, 189
Alighieri, Dante, 12, 74n70, 75n74,
    125n213, 140n248, 176n348,
    193n397
Amoretti, Maria, 5
Anaxagoras, 79, 121
Apollodorus, 53n25, 81
Aprosio, Angelico, 23, 24n89, 36, 37
Aragona, Tullia di, 15n61
Ariosto, Ludovico, 12, 16, 21, 30, 58,
    59, 62, 63, 67n55, 72, 100n138–
    139, 144, 179n354, 193, 194n399,
    203, 204
Ariosto, Orazio, 74
Aristotle, 12, 16, 19n76–77, 25, 26,
    27, 28, 29, 30, 39, 50, 59, 69, 74,
    75n72, 78n82–83, 79, 92, 95n127,
    97n134, 107n167, 108n171,
    116n187, 119n195, 120, 121,
    122n203 and n205–206, 123, 124,
    126, 127, 128n219, 129, 130n225,
    131n227, 132n231, 134n235–
    236, 136, 137, 138, 140, 141,
    142n252–253, 145n258, 146, 147,
    148, 149n265 and 267, 150n270,
    151n271, 152n273–274, 153,
    155, 156, 161n299, 162, 163, 164,
    165n311, 166, 167, 168n319–323,
    169n325, 170n328 and n330,
    171n331–333, 172n335–339,
    173n340, 174n342–343,
    176, 177n349, 180n357–358,
    181n361–362, 183n364–365,
    183n368–370, 184n371, 185n376,
    186, 190, 197, 198n409
Asinius of Pozzuoli, 89
Asor Rosa, Alberto, 37n126

Augustus, Emperor, 90
Aurelian, Emperor, 9
Avicenna, 6

Bacelli, Gerolamo, 93
Bakhtin, Mikhail, 34
Barbaro, Costanza, 5
Bassi, Laura, 5n15
Batti, Giacomo, 34
beauty, 106–204
Biondi, Giovan Francesco, 14
Boccaccio, Giovanni, 11, 49n16,
    51n20, 71, 118, 125n213, 131n229
Boccalini, Traiano, 33, 41n3
Boethius, 143
Bolzoni, Lina, 52n23,
Bonaccioli, Alfonso, 49n17
Bradford, Ernile, 15n59
Bronzino, Cristoforo, 29n104
Buoninsegni, Francesco, 23, 34,
    106n162
Bruni, Leonardo, 27

Catherine, Saint, 8
Charondas, 149
Chastel, Guy, 8n31
Cicero, 187
children's education, 149–155
Christine de Pizan, 125n213
Claudian, 69
Colomba, Saint, 8, 9, 27
Colonna, Vittoria, 33
Constantine, Emperor, 71
Conti Odorisio, Ginevra, 1
Cox, Virginia, 1, 2, 3n7, 15n61, 17n71,
    18n73, 23, 24, 31n108 and n109,
    33n116, 37n128,
Croce, Benedetto, 15n62

Dandolo, Enrico, 41

Democritus, 79
Di Renzo Vianello, Wilmen, 22n84
Diocletian, Emperor, 13
Dionisotti, Carlo, 1
Doglio, Maria Luisa, 43n7
Doglioni, Giovanni Niccolò, 3

Empedocles, 164
Epimenides the Cretan, 149n265
Euripides, 185
Evelyn, John, 39

Fedele, Cassandra, 3, 5
Ficino, Marsilio, 78
Folengo, Teofilo, 94n125
Fonte, Moderata 1, 2, 3, 5n17, 11n40, 12, 15
Fortis, Umberto 3
fortune, 74
Foscarini, Ludovico, 28
Foscolo, Ugo, 93n121
Franco, Veronica 3, 5n14

Galen, 6
Galli Stampino, Maria, 15n61, 16n65,
Gambara, Veronica, 33
Garzoni, Tomaso, 63
Girard, René, 34
Godfrey, John, 15n59
Gonzaga, Cecilia, 5
Gonzaga, Caterina Medici, 10
Gonzaga, Margherita, 8
Gonzalez, Goretti, 39
Gorgias of Leontini, 53n24, 108
Grangier de Liverdes, 3
Gremonville, Anne de, 36
Grendler, Paul F., 4n11
Guarini, Giovanni Battista, 55, 59, 94, 117, 204
gymnastics, 155–158

Hannibal, 25, 123
Haskins, Susan, 2, 7n23, 8n28 and n29, 13n48, 14n54–58, 26n99, 29n104

Hesiod, 27, 40, 126, 127, 128, 129, 130, 133, 134, 135, 138, 141, 146, 147, 148
Hippocrates, 6
Homer, 30, 40, 59, 77, 82n92, 86n103, 87n106, 88, 89, 90, 92, 93, 95, 102n146–147, 104, 111n178, 112n180, 129, 136, 137, 138, 158n292, 177n350–351, 185n375, 189
Horace, 58, 175

Jed, Stephanie, 36n124
Julius Caesar, 189

Kelso, Ruth, 3n6
King, Margaret L., 4, 5, 28n102
knowledge, 75–79
Kolski, Stephen, 11n40

Labaste, Jacqueline, 38n132
Lagnier, Pierre 27, 61n40, 106n161
Latour, Patrick, 38n132
Lavocat, Françoise, 14n52
Lazzari, Laura, 15n61
Leni, Matteo, 35
Leone Ebreo, 196
Leone, Boncio, 14
Leopardi, Giacomo, 64n48
Licinius, Emperor 71
Loredan, Giovan Francesco, 35, 36
Lorena, Cristina of, 9
Lucian, 80

Macrobius, 160
Madden, Thomas F., 15n59
Magno, Celio, 58n31
Malpezzi Price, Paola, 34
Marcus Aurelius Antoninus, Emperor, 131n229
Marinella, Diamantina, 7
Marinella, Lucrezia: *La Colomba sacra* 8–9; *Vita del serafico e glorioso San Francesco* 9–10; *Amore*

innamorato e impazzato 10–11; *Le nobiltà et eccellenze delle donne* 11–12; *Vita di Maria Vergine imperatrice dell'universo* 12–13; *Rime sacre* 13; *Arcadia felice* 13–14; *L'Enrico, ovvero Bisanzio acquistato* 14–17; *Esortazioni,* 18–34
Marinello, Curzio, 7, 8, 14
Marinello, Giovanni, 6, 10
Marinello, Antonio, 7
Marini, Quinto, 37n126
Marro, Ruggero, 37n128
Maschietto, Francesco Ludovico, 3n10
Mazarin, Cardinal, 36
Mercurio, Girolamo, 6
Miato, Monica, 35n119, 36n123
Migiel, Marylin, 16n66
Miltiades, 189
Morales-Front, Alfonso, 39n1
music, 161–165

Namur, Arrigo of, 11
Naudé, Gabriel, 36
Nicholas of Tolentino, Saint, 13
Nogarola, Ginevra, 4
Nogarola, Isotta, 4, 5, 28

Olivier, Jacques, 37
Ovid, 60n38–39, 63, 77n78, 80n88, 84, 86, 90n117, 91n118–119, 92n120, 99n137, 100, 101n142–143, 110, 111n78, 112n79, 130, 146n262, 157, 162n301, 169n327, 202n416–419

Pallavicino, Ferrante, 35
Panizza, Letizia, 11n40, 13n50, 24n91, 26, 35n120
Papa, Giovanni, 8n28
Passi, Giuseppe, 11, 12,
Parmenides, 149
Patrizi, Francesco, 52n23, 129
Paul, Saint, 75

Paul the Hermit, Saint 52n22
Pausanias, 131n230
Pericles, 183
Perocco, Daria, 7n27
Petrarca, Francesco, 12, 30, 47, 64n48, 66, 67n53–54, 72, 73n67, 102, 103n150–151 and n153, 142n250, 144, 200n413
Phidias, 75
Philip the Macedonian, 163n302
Pirandello, Luigi, 34
Piscopia, Elena Lucrezia Cornaro, 3, 5
Plato, 10n38, 12, 24n89, 29, 30, 39, 44n8, 51n21, 54, 56n29, 61, 63, 65n50, 70, 71, 76n77, 77, 78, 92, 96, 97n133, 106, 107n164, 129, 131, 133, 140, 149, 152, 153, 154n279, 157, 159, 160, 161, 163, 164, 165, 166, 167, 170n329, 171, 173, 178, 179, 180, 181, 182n363 and n366, 183, 184, 186, 187n382, 188n386, 196, 197n407, 202
Pliny the Elder, 86
Plutarch, 43n7, 65n50, 88, 89, 130n225, 162n302,165, 186n380, 189n387–390
Polyclitus, 75
Pona, Francesco, 35
prudence, 120–125
Pythagoras, 160, 161

Quaglio, Enzo, 51n20
Quadrio, F.S., 29n104

Ristaino, Christine, 34
Rosenthal, Margaret F., 5n14

Sabba di Castiglione, 201
Sagrino, Angelo, 101
Salvatore, Filippo, 11
Sannazaro, Jacopo, 13
Sarrocchi, Margherita, 15n61
Scarano, Lucio, 7
Scipio 25, 103, 123

Seneca, 61, 181
Shemek, Deanna, 15, 16n63
silence, 99–103; and women, 105
Speroni, Sperone, 11
Stampa, Gaspara, 3
Statius, 53n24
Stigliani, Tommaso, 30, 58
Strabo, 49n17
Suleiman, Susan Rubin, 6
Sullam, Sara Coppio, 3
Sylvester, Pope, 71

Tagliamocchi degli Albizzi, Barbara, 15
Tansillo, Luigi, 12, 14
Tarabotti, Arcangela, 1, 2, 3, 13, 23, 24, 26, 31, 34, 35, 36, 106n162
Tassini, Giuseppe, 7
Tasso, Ercole, 11
Tasso, Torquato, 8, 9, 11, 12, 15, 16, 17, 30, 32n112, 43n7, 44, 46n10–12, 65, 74, 100, 104, 108, 109n172–173, 117, 128, 158n291, 188n384, 191, 192, 193n396, 194, 200
Thales, 197
Themistocles, 189
Theocritus, 80n87
Theognis, 132, 145
Thomas Aquinas, St., 50n19, 51n21, 59n34, 81n90–91, 88n110, 103n152, 115n186, 151n271, 178n352, 187n381
Terracina, Laura, 15, 33
Teves y Guzman, Gaspar, 39
Tiraboschi, Girolamo, 6n19, 7n22 and n25

Vacca, Girolamo, 14
Valla, Lorenzo, 71n64
Valvasense, Francesco, 34, 35, 36n123, 41n2
Varro, 86, 99n137, 197
Vasoli, Cesare, 52n23

Virgil, 30, 47, 50, 95, 151, 157n290, 189n387
Virgin Mary, 7, 13
virtue, 168–173
Vives, Juan Luis, 33

Waddington, Raymond B., 51n21
Watson, Alan, 9
Weaver, Elissa, 106n162
Westwater, Lynn Lara, 36n122
Wolters, Wolfgang, 15
women: writers, 2–6; seclusion of, 43–49; and learning, 54–58; virtues 61; luxury 113–116

Xenocrates, 101, 164
Xenophon, 107

Zanette, Emilio, 35n120, 36n125, 37n127
Zeno, 197